Forests of the Northern United States

Stephen R. Shifley, Francisco X. Aguilar, Nianfu Song, Susan I. Stewart, David J. Nowak,
Dale D. Gormanson, W. Keith Moser, Sherri Wormstead, and Eric J. Greenfield

STEPHEN R. SHIFLEY, RESEARCH FORESTER

Northern Research Station, U.S. Forest Service

202 Anheuser-Busch Natural Resources Building

University of Missouri, Columbia, MO 65211-7260

573-875-5341 (Extension 232)

sshifley@fs.fed.us

Corresponding author

FRANCISCO X. AGUILAR, ASST. PROFESSOR OF FOREST ECONOMICS

Department of Forestry, The School of Natural Resources

203L Anheuser-Busch Natural Resources Building

University of Missouri, Columbia, MO 65211

573-882-6304

aguilarf@missouri.edu

NIANFU SONG, POSTDOCTORAL FELLOW, FOREST ECONOMICS

Department of Forestry, The School of Natural Resources

203 Anheuser-Busch Natural Resources Building

University of Missouri, Columbia, MO 65211

573-875-5341 (Extension 230)

songn@missouri.edu

SUSAN I. STEWART, RESEARCH SOCIAL SCIENTIST

Northern Research Station, U.S. Forest Service

1033 University Place, Suite 360

Evanston, IL 60201-3172

847-866-9311 (Extension 13)

sistewart@fs.fed.us

DAVID J. NOWAK, PROJECT LEADER, RESEARCH FORESTER

Northern Research Station, U.S. Forest Service

c/o SUNY ESF, 5 Moon Library

Syracuse, NY 13210

315-448-3212

dnowak@fs.fed.us

DALE D. GORMANSON, SUPERVISORY FORESTER

Northern Research Station, U.S. Forest Service

1992 Folwell Avenue

St. Paul, MN 55108

651-649-5126

dgormanson@fs.fed.us

W. KEITH MOSER, RESEARCH FORESTER

Northern Research Station, U.S. Forest Service

1992 Folwell Avenue

St. Paul, MN 55108

651-649-5155

wkmoser@fs.fed.us

SHERRI WORMSTEAD, SUSTAINABILITY AND PLANNING COORDINATOR

Northeastern Area, State and Private Forestry

U.S. Forest Service

271 Mast Road, Durham, NH 03824

603-868-7737

swormstead@fs.fed.us

ERIC J. GREENFIELD, FORESTER

Northern Research Station, U.S. Forest Service

c/o SUNY ESF, 5 Moon Library

Syracuse, NY 13210

315-448-3203

egreenfield@fs.fed.us

CONTENTS

List of Tables

Forests of the Northern United States

PREFACE

This publication is part of the Northern Forest Futures Project, through which the Northern Research Station of the U.S. Forest Service examines the issues, trends, threats, and opportunities facing the forests of the northern United States. This report provides a broad overview of current conditions affecting forests in the 20-state region including Connecticut, Delaware, Illinois, Indiana, Iowa, Maine, Maryland, Massachusetts, Michigan, Minnesota, Missouri, New Hampshire, New Jersey, New York, Ohio, Pennsylvania, Rhode Island, Vermont, West Virginia, and Wisconsin. It draws on information from numerous sources to provide (1) an understanding of the characteristics of northern forests relative to the rest of the United States, (2) a comparative framework for understanding differences among States and how they individually and collectively contribute to the region's forest resources, and (3) a context for interpreting projections of future forest conditions in the region. Subsequent products from the Northern Forest Futures Project will examine selected aspects of the region's forests in greater depth and will analyze changes in forest conditions expected to occur over the next 50 years from alternative management and climate scenarios.

This publication is intended for natural resource managers and planners, policy makers, State natural resource agencies, politicians, students, and those who want to know more about northern forests. It complements the 2010 State forest resource assessments, part of the State forest action plans that examine individual State forest resource conditions and issues in detail (National Association of State Foresters 2010), as well as national scale documents that provide forest statistics and information (Smith et al. 2009, USDA FS 2011e). Much of the information included is organized around the Montréal Process Criteria and Indicators framework (Montréal Process Working Group 2010). Other important sections of the document summarize forest-related concerns that are unique to the northern United States and discuss characteristics associated with forest sustainability in the region.

Introduction

1

THE TWENTY STATES that make up the U.S. North are bounded by Maine, Maryland, Missouri, and Minnesota (Fig. 1). Compared to the rest of the country, the North has a higher population density, relatively little public forest land, and many private forest owners with small forest tracts. Fifty-five percent of northern forest land belongs to nearly 5 million family forest owners. Management intensity for these forests is relatively low—only 16 percent of family forest land is covered by a written management plan (Butler 2008, Smith et al. 2009, USDA FS 2009b, USDA FS 2010d).

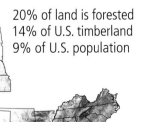

NORTH

42% of land is forested
32% of U.S. timberland
41% of U.S. population

■ Forest
□ Nonforest

Alaska

PACIFIC COAST

37% of land is forested
14% of U.S. timberland
16% of U.S. population

Hawaii

INTERIOR WEST

20% of land is forested
14% of U.S. timberland
9% of U.S. population

SOUTH

Puerto Rico

40% of land is forested
40% of U.S. timberland
34% of U.S. population

FIGURE 1

Distribution of forests and people in the United States (Homer et al. 2004, Smith et al. 2009, and U.S. Census Bureau 2010).

The Northern States

Connecticut	Missouri
Delaware	New Hampshire
Illinois	New Jersey
Indiana	New York
Iowa	Ohio
Maine	Pennsylvania
Maryland	Rhode Island
Massachusetts	Vermont
Michigan	West Virginia
Minnesota	Wisconsin

Washington, D.C. is included in calculation of urban and community forest statistics

Forest management and policies intended to meet current and future needs of people in the North require good baseline information about current conditions and trends. The information in this assessment helps put the capabilities and limitations of northern forests in perspective with the rest of the Nation. For example:

- The North is the most heavily forested region of the United States—42 percent of the landbase is forested (Table 1, Fig. 1). It is more heavily forested than the South (40 percent), the Interior West (20 percent), the Pacific Coast (37 percent), or the overall U.S. (33 percent).

- With only 18 percent of total land area, the North supports 32 percent of the Nation's timberland (forest land that is sufficiently productive and sufficiently accessible to produce commercial crops of wood and that is not otherwise restricted from timber harvest by policy or legislation such as designated wilderness or parks).

- In the last century, northern forest land increased from 134 to 172 million acres (Fig. 2) while total U.S. forest land remained essentially unchanged. This trend is attributable to a historical pattern

Table 1—Selected characteristics associated with northern forests, compared to forests in the entire United States (Smith et al. 2009; U.S. Census Bureau 2007, 2009).

Characteristic	U.S. total	Northern States (with percent of U.S. total when applicable)
Population (million)	304	124 (41)
Number of private forest owners (million)	11	5 (44)
Employment in forestry and logging, wood products, and pulp and paper industries (thousand workers)	1,097	441 (40)
Total land area (million acres)	2,264	414 (18)
Forest land area (million acres)	751	172 (23)
Timberland area (million acres)	514	164 (32)
Percent forest land (percent of total land)	33	42
Percent timberland (percent of total land)	22	40
Percent urban land (percent of total land)	3.1	6.0
Forest land per person (acres)	2.5	1.4
Volume of timber (billion cubic feet)	1,013	268 (26)
Annual growing stock growth (billion cubic feet)	26.7	6.7 (25)
Annual growing stock removals (billion cubic feet)	15.5	3.6 (18)
Annual growing stock mortality (billion cubic feet)	7.8	2.4 (31)
Ratio of annual growth to removals	1.7	1.9

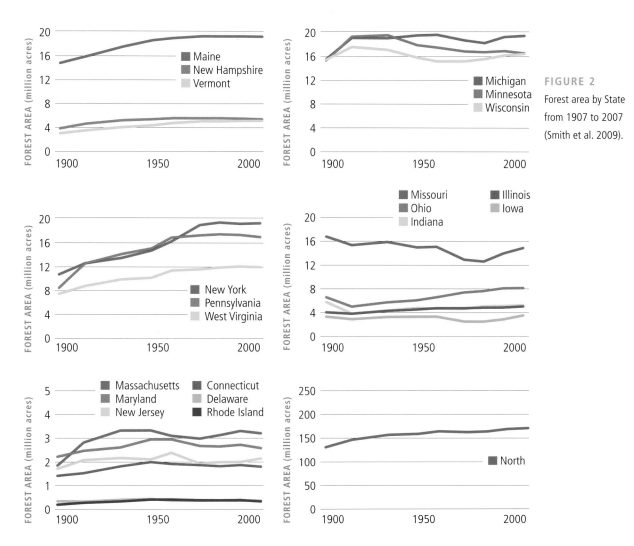

FIGURE 2

Forest area by State from 1907 to 2007 (Smith et al. 2009).

of forest harvest, land clearing, farming, farm abandonment, and urbanization that continues to exert influence today.

- The North hosts 41 percent of the Nation's population; 80 percent of the North's population lives in urban areas.

- Over the last century, population increased from 52 to 124 million people in the North. The number of forested acres per person decreased from 2.6 acres in 1907 to 1.4 acres in 2007, although total northern forest area increased. The national average is 2.5 acres of forest per person.

- The North has large areas of wildland-urban interface (WUI) compared to the rest of the United States (Fig. 3).

- Urban areas in the North cover 6 percent of the land base (compared to 3 percent nationally). Northern urban areas are expanding by about 4 million acres per decade, and 37 percent of that expansion (1.5 million acres) is into forest cover.

- Current statewide tree mortality rates are 1 to 2 percent of total volume per year, but native and invasive insects and diseases can cause severe, localized damage or mortality.

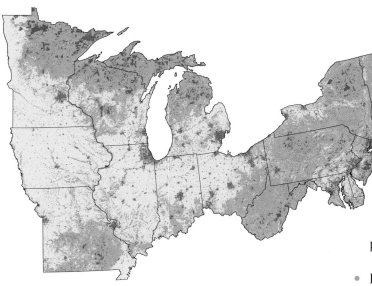

WILDLAND-URBAN INTERFACE (WUI)

WUI

▨ Intermix and interface

NON-WUI VEGETATED

▨ Very low density housing
■ No housing

NONVEGETATED OR AGRICULTURE

■ High and medium density housing
▢ Low and very low density housing
▨ Water

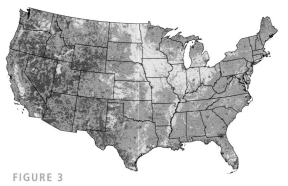

Introduction of new invasive species is an ongoing threat to forest health in the North and in the rest of the United States.

- Across the North, 48 percent of the water supply (280 billion cubic meters per year) originates on forest lands, compared to 53 percent nationally.

- In the North, one acre of forest land in six (16%) is afforded some form of protected status. That is nearly identical to the national proportion, but in the North those forests are concentrated in protected categories with fewer restrictions.

- From 1953 to 2007, the volume of standing timber in the North increased by about 140 percent (from 104 to 248 billion cubic feet), compared to about 50 percent (from 616 to 923 billion cubic feet) nationally.

- Annual volume growth of northern forests was about 6.6 billion cubic feet for State inventory cycles completed through 2008. Annual volume growth is 1.9 times greater than the rate of harvesting and other removals, compared to 1.7 times nationally.

- People in the North consume the equivalent of 8.8 billion cubic feet of wood products each year or about 71 cubic feet per person, most of which is harvested and processed elsewhere.

- The region currently employs 441,000 in the forestry, logging, wood products, and pulp and paper industries—about 40 percent of all U.S. jobs for these sectors.

The Wood You Consume

Forests provide people with wood products they use daily as well as many other ecosystem services. Major categories of wood products include sawn wood (lumber), wood panels (such as plywood, particle board, and oriented strand board), engineered wood products (such as laminated veneer lumber, wood composites, and I-joists), paper, and paperboard. Wood is also used as a source of energy to heat buildings and generate electricity. Wood may soon be used to create liquid fuels.

Annual per capita consumption of wood and wood products amounts to roughly:

- 410 pounds of paper
- 330 pounds of boxes, packaging, and other pulp products
- 75 square feet of plywood
- 25 square feet of particleboard and fiberboard
- 235 board feet of lumber
- 2 shipping pallets

Although it is convenient to split the Nation into four quadrants to facilitate regional comparisons (Fig. 1), there is also substantial diversity in forest conditions among Northern States. For example, Maine and Iowa both have comparatively low population density with more than 12 acres of total land area per capita. But Maine is 89 percent forest covered, compared to only 8 percent in Iowa (Fig. 4). Forest area per person ranges from a high of 13.4 acres in Maine (only exceeded by Alaska, Montana, Wyoming, and Idaho) to a low of 0.2 acres in New Jersey (the least of any State nationwide) (Fig. 5).

Beyond variations in forest resources, Northern States also differ in climate, geology, and native vegetation. These differences are reflected in the 11 ecological provinces (Fig. 6) that define areas with similar ecological characteristics (Bailey 1997, McNabb and Avers 1994). For example, there are large ecological differences from the central Appalachian broadleaf and coniferous forests that span across the mid-Atlantic to the Laurentian mixed forests that cover the Northern Great Lakes States. Variations also exist within individual States.

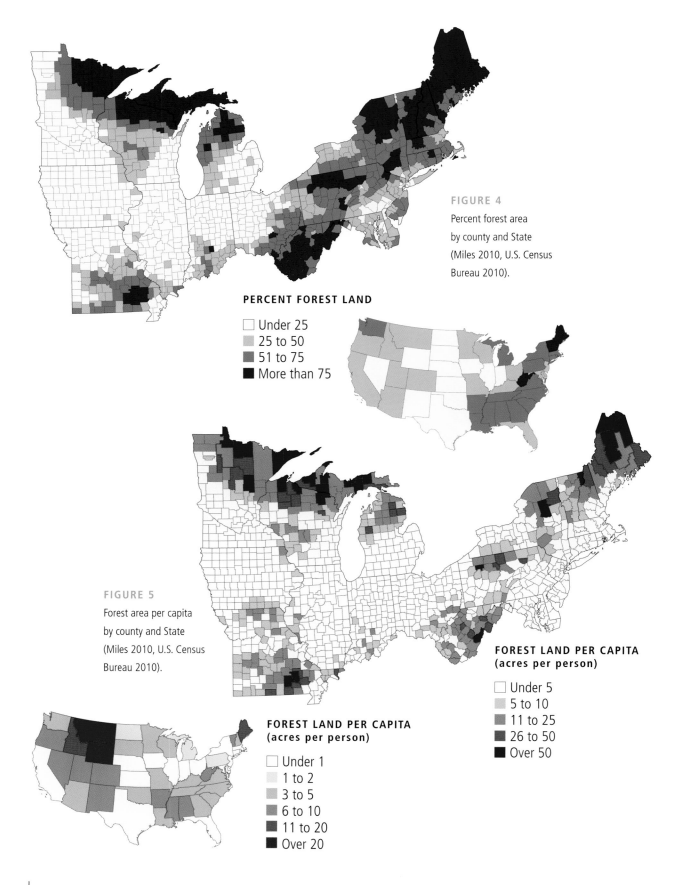

PERCENT FOREST LAND

☐ Under 25
◼ 25 to 50
◼ 51 to 75
◼ More than 75

FIGURE 4

Percent forest area
by county and State
(Miles 2010, U.S. Census
Bureau 2010).

FIGURE 5

Forest area per capita
by county and State
(Miles 2010, U.S. Census
Bureau 2010).

FOREST LAND PER CAPITA
(acres per person)

☐ Under 5
◼ 5 to 10
◼ 11 to 25
◼ 26 to 50
◼ Over 50

FOREST LAND PER CAPITA
(acres per person)

☐ Under 1
◼ 1 to 2
◼ 3 to 5
◼ 6 to 10
◼ 11 to 20
◼ Over 20

Four of the 10 largest metropolitan areas in the Nation occur in the North—New York, Chicago, Philadelphia, and Boston. In total, 80 percent of the region's population lives in urban areas. They, as well as everyone else, depend on the region's forests for wood and wildlife; for vital ecosystem services such as the provision of clean air, clean water, climate control, and biodiversity; and for recreation. Because of their close proximity to people, trees and forests within urban areas demonstrably enhance quality of life for urban residents.

Understanding forests requires a long-term perspective. Forest management practices implemented decades ago in northern forests have an impact on forests today.

Similarly, decisions made now about how, when, and where to manage northern forests will have impacts on forest resources and communities for decades to come. Understanding forests also requires the ability to see forests at multiple spatial scales. These scales include the local forest stand or management area, landscapes comprised of many forest stands covering thousands of acres, and ecoregions comprised of thousands of landscapes covering millions of acres. Political scales include local governments affecting local land-use planning, individual States that make policies governing forests within their borders, and groups of States whose shared interests in forest issues extend beyond their borders.

FIGURE 6

Northern ecoregion provinces, based on similarities in climate, topography, geology, and native vegetation (Bailey 1977, McNabb and Avers 1994); ecoregions can be split into smaller units or combined into larger units. Because of the relative uniformity of conditions within an ecoregion, it often makes sense to discuss large-scale management and policy issues by ecoregions as well as by States or other political boundaries.

ECOREGION PROVINCE NUMBER AND NAME

- 211 Northeastern mixed forest
- 212 Laurentian mixed forest
- 221 Eastern broadleaf forest
- 222 Midwest broadleaf forest
- 223 Central interior broadleaf forest
- 231 Southeastern mixed forest
- 232 Outer coastal plain mixed forest
- 234 Lower Mississippi riverine forest
- 251 Prairie parkland (temperature)
- M211 Adirondack-New England mixed forest-coniferous forest-alpine meadow
- M221 Central Appalachian broadleaf forest-coniferous forest-meadow

All forest management decisions, including the decision to do nothing, are implemented at the local scale—usually within a forest stand comprised of a few dozen acres. However, those acres are part of the larger forest landscape, and collectively management decisions have broad and cumulative impacts in the region and beyond. The combined effects of thousands or millions of individual decisions that are perfectly logical at the local scale may prove undesirable when accumulated across landscapes, ecoregions, States, the region, the Nation, and ultimately the World. Examples might include management practices that facilitate the replacement of native species by nonnative plants or animals, allow the spread of destructive insects or diseases, increase the risk of wildfire, reduce opportunities for urban residents to enjoy forests, or reduce economic opportunities in rural communities.

Northern forests are constantly changing. Many of those changes are the result of natural processes such as forest aging, species succession, and weather-related disturbances, but some processes may be perceived as threats. These include insect and disease outbreaks, conversion of forest land to other uses, and global climate change. Other processes such as the increasing volume of wood may be perceived as opportunities.

Still others can be a complex mix of opportunity and threat. For example, demand for renewable energy could lead to integrated forest management practices designed to supply renewable woody bioenergy feedstock while simultaneously improving forest health and wildlife habitat, or short-term excessive wood removal for energy could create undesirable consequences for long-term forest sustainability.

Despite some notably positive trends in northern forests, concerns and issues are numerous. Many regional issues of concern are summarized in Chapter 2, followed by definitions of sustainable forestry (Chapter 3), characteristics of sustainable forests (Chapter 4), and analyses of conditions and trends based on indicators of forest sustainability for the region (Chapter 5). Chapter 6 discusses some complex, overarching issues in the region and the potential contributions of various stakeholders in addressing them.

The way in which northern forests change in the future will affect their ability to provide products, amenities, and ecological services. Insights expected from the projections and analyses associated with the Northern Forest Futures Project should be useful in guiding policies and management practices toward a desirable future for northern forests. Forest resources and ecosystem services can improve the quality of life for people and communities without diminishing the capacity to provide similar benefits to future generations—the principle that is at the heart of forest sustainability.

PEOPLE IN THE North are concerned about forests, especially the forests near to them. Concerns reflect their diverse connections to forests and the many ways that rural and urban forests affect their quality of life.

A recent analysis by Dietzman et al. (2011) summarized more than 700 comments about issues facing northern forests. The comments came from 74 print and online sources including Federal and State government planning and resource publications; scientific papers; and issue statements from nonprofit organizations, industry, professional associations, and universities. More than 90 percent of the sources were published between 2004 and 2009. The Dietzman et al. (2011) analysis identified 55 issues that were cited multiple times. Subsequent sections in this chapter address each of the 12 most frequently cited issues in more detail.

Comparison of the issues summarized by Dietzman et al. (2011) with those presented in the 2010 State forest action plans across the North (USDA FS and NAASF 2011) shows strong alignment. State Forest Action Plans for the North identify four additional widespread issues that also are found in the second tier of issues identified by Dietzman et al. (2011): urban and community forest health and sustainability; climate change; wildfire threats to forests, public safety, and property; and state and private capacity for forestry. These are addressed elsewhere in this report.

Issues of Concern Identified with Northern Forests

- Insects and diseases
- Invasive species
- Management standards and practices
- Forest area, species composition, and size structure
- Stewardship and forest management
- Wildlife habitat and biodiversity
- Forest fragmentation and parcelization
- Water
- Wood products
- Environmental literacy
- Recreation
- Biomass and bioenergy

INSECTS AND DISEASES, INCLUDING INVASIVES

Problematic insects and diseases in the North include native as well as nonnative, invasive species. Two invasive insects of great concern are the emerald ash borer (*Agrilus planipennis*), which is spreading rapidly and has the potential to kill billions of ash trees (*Fraxinus spp.*); and gypsy moth (*Lymantria dispar*), which is already established on millions of acres of northern forest but now spreading more slowly due to some effective control measures. Other invasive insects of concern include the Asian longhorned beetle (*Anoplophora glabripennis*), fire ant (*Solenopsis invicta*), beech scale insect (*Cryptococcus fagisuga*), and the hemlock wooly adelgid (*Adelges tsugae*). Spruce budworm (*Choristoneura fumiferana*) is a native insect of particular concern.

Native diseases and decline complexes of concern include tubakia leaf spot (*Tubakia dryina*), bacterial leaf scorch (*Xylella fastidiosa*), oak decline, hickory decline, oak tatters, and oak wilt. Invasive diseases of trees include chestnut blight (*Endothia parasitica*), Dutch elm disease (*Ophiostoma ulmi* (syn. *Ceratocystis ulmi*)), and dogwood anthracnose (*Discula spp.*). Butternut canker is caused by a fungus (*Sirococcus clavigignenti-juglandacearum*) of undetermined origin. Thousand cankers disease of black walnut was recently discovered in the North; it is caused by the walnut twig beetle (*Pityophthorus juglandis*) in association with two types of fungi.

These insects, diseases, and decline complexes affect forest health, economic value, fuel load, wildfire risk, biodiversity, and future species composition. The economic losses associated with insects and diseases can be amplified in populated areas where dead or dying street and shade trees must be removed and replaced at high cost.

Introduced invasive species such as the emerald ash borer cause widespread mortality to susceptible tree species. This alters the species diversity and succession in rural forests and may result in loss of forest productivity. When urban or community trees are affected, there are large expenses associated with mitigation, tree removal, and replanting.

INVASIVE PLANTS

Through aggressive establishment, rapid growth, and efficient dispersal, invasive plant species can displace native forest plants. This can reduce forest health, degrade habitat quality, and/or impart economic losses to the recreation, timber, wood products, and nursery industries. Invasive plants of concern in the North include spotted knapweed (*Centaurea biebersteinii*), tree-of-heaven (*Ailanthus altissima*), Russian olive (*Elaeagnus angustifolia*), multiflora rose (*Rosa multiflora*), garlic mustard (*Alliaria petiolata*), and bush honeysuckle (several *Lonicera* spp.). These and other invasive plant species of concern vary geographically in their impact. Where invasive plants occur in abundance, their management often diverts time and money from other issues. Management options for invasive species can include barring entry, removing new outbreaks, and slowing or stopping propagation across the landscape.

MANAGEMENT STANDARDS AND PRACTICES

Management practices and standards include voluntary or mandatory regulations or policies intended to improve forest operations on the ground. They can cover a wide range of topics including silvicultural prescriptions, prescribed burning, soil protection, operations in riparian zones, water crossings, roads or trails, and use of herbicides. Some standards are formalized as best management practices or through a formal forest certification process.

Written management plans are usually necessary to guide the implementation of the standards and practices for individual forest tracts. Relevant, timely information for development and monitoring of standards and practices is necessary to ensure their effectiveness.

FOREST AREA, SPECIES COMPOSITION, AND SIZE STRUCTURE

Total forest area in the North has been stable, and wood volume has been increasing for decades. Although these trends are seen as positive, they are not uniform across all States. Forest acreage near cities is being lost, but forest area is being gained elsewhere, often due to natural reforestation of former agricultural lands. Maturation of northern forests has resulted in losses of early successional tree species—aspen (*Populus grandidentata* and *Populus tremuloides*), paper birch (*Betula papyrifera*), jack pine (*Pinus banksiana*), balsam fir (*Abies baslsamea*), and others—with corresponding increases in shade tolerant species. Other tree species have fallen below their historical abundance of a century ago, including oaks (*Quercus* spp.), yellow birch (*Betula alleghaniensis*), cottonwood (*Populus detltoides*), red pine (*Pinus resinosa*), white pine (*Pinus strobus*), shortleaf pine (*Pinus echninata*), and loblolly pine (*Pinus taeda*). These changes are closely linked to past forest management practices including harvest methods, harvest intensity, and wildfire management.

Wildlife management is a related concern, because in many areas, excessive deer browsing has become a barrier to regenerating desirable tree species. Concerns have also been raised about declining tree quality for timber and about scarcity of old-growth, woodland, and savanna habitats. All these changes are also related to sustaining biodiversity.

STEWARDSHIP AND FOREST MANAGEMENT

Forest stewardship—resource management and administration that maintain forests in a healthy condition for future generations—is a challenging process that is further complicated by forest ownership patterns in the North. Most of the nearly 5 million family forest owners in the region lack forest management plans, and providing so many private owners with timely information and assistance is difficult. Continuing fragmentation, parcelization, and urbanization can be barriers to stewardship if they result in forest tracts that are too small or too isolated for effective management. Public forests typically have detailed management plans. However those plans often have been the subject of conflict among interest groups that disagree about appropriate mixes of products and ecosystem services from public lands.

WILDLIFE HABITAT AND BIODIVERSITY

The complex issue of biodiversity encompasses virtually all forest-associated plants and animals at genetic, species, community, and landscape scales. Individual threatened and endangered species are often the focus of special attention, but the objective of biodiversity conservation is to maintain viable native animal and plant populations of all kinds. Losses of early-successional forests, old forests, oak forests, savannas, woodlands, and prairies are landscape-scale issues of particular concern. Management to maintain diverse habitats and connectivity among habitats is complicated by the general scarcity of public land, forest fragmentation, and the diverse objectives among the millions of private owners who control most of the region's forest land. Issues of habitat diversity are closely linked to concerns about forest fragmentation and to invasive species that may contribute to the loss of native species diversity.

FOREST FRAGMENTATION AND PARCELIZATION

Forests become fragmented through conversion to other uses, such as agriculture or residential development. Fragmentation typically results in smaller tracts of forest land scattered across the landscape or in more nonforest openings within predominantly forested landscapes. Either situation results in more forest edge habitat, less forest interior habitat, and fewer forested corridors connecting large forested parcels. Thus, movement of plants, animals, and water across the landscape is altered. Increased forest edge affects habitat suitability for plant and animal species, almost always to the detriment of species that depend on forest-interior habitat. Forest-associated plant and animal populations that become isolated within in a fragmented landscape can lose genetic diversity. The specific causes and effects of fragmentation vary from the heavily forested areas of Maine and the Lake States to agricultural areas in Iowa or Illinois and to suburban and exurban zones in proximity to cities.

Parcelization, the subdivision of tracts into smaller and smaller ownerships, does not necessarily fragment the forest physically; rather, it spreads forest management decisions to more owners who have smaller properties. This complicates the pursuit of landscape-scale management objectives, such as controlling invasive species or improving habitat for wide-ranging animals, as well as increasing the cost and complexity of providing information and assistance to a growing number of private forest owners.

WATER

Forests play a crucial role in maintaining water quality and quantity. They protect large portions of the region's watersheds, including crucial headwaters and floodplain areas. Because the quality of water from forested areas is typically higher than from agricultural or developed areas, many municipal water supplies are directly or indirectly dependent on forests. At the landscape scale, forest land provides an increasing proportion of the water supply for northern communities. Consequently practices that eliminate forests or impair their ability to protect watersheds are of great concern.

WOOD PRODUCTS HARVESTING, PROCESSING, CONSUMPTION, AND TRADE

The forest products industry is important to the economy in many northern communities. Increasingly, the industry is affected by global issues including demand and prices for imported and exported wood and the relative cost and quality of domestic versus foreign manufactured wood products. Emerging wood-based bioenergy markets have the potential to compete with other industries for wood resources.

In some situations forest products harvesting can be joined with other complementary conservation goals. For example, harvesting forest products can offset costs associated with restoring habitat, increasing biodiversity, limiting damage from insects or diseases, and responding to damage from severe weather.

Balancing the size of the forest products industry with other complementary and competing interests remains a concern in the North. Despite decades of increasing wood volume in northern and U.S. forests, the Nation is a net importer of wood and wood products. A growing population continues to increase consumption pressure and, through imports, push the consequences, good and bad, of timber harvesting to other nations. This is a wood products issue, an environmental literacy issue, and a forest sustainability issue.

ENVIRONMENTAL LITERACY

A well informed public is considered essential for developing and supporting sound practices and policies to manage northern forests and sustain them for future generations. Environmental literacy encompasses efforts to increase public awareness of forests and forestry practices.

An increasingly urban society can become increasingly disassociated from the products and ecosystem services supplied by forests, but improved environmental literacy is important for all demographic groups. Progress in improving environmental literacy may require changes in the way natural resource professionals and other educators interact with the public.

OUTDOOR RECREATION

Demand for recreation opportunities in forests is growing, especially in forests that are close to residential areas. However, there are concerns about how to provide the full spectrum of outdoor recreation opportunities while minimizing damage to the resources caused from heavy recreational uses. Demand for recreational uses includes developed, semi-primitive, and wilderness areas; on water; and using motorized and nonmotorized transportation. Off-road vehicle recreation, in particular, affects soil, vegetation, water resources, and competing recreational activities; common concerns include keeping riders within designated areas and managing roads and trails. Increasing the economic returns from recreation and tourism industries is generally considered beneficial if doing so maintains a desirable mix of recreational opportunities. The relative scarcity of public lands in the North exerts great recreational pressure on public forests and associated facilities. Building and maintaining public recreational facilities is becoming more expensive as demand for those facilities is increasing. The preponderance of private forest land in the North makes effective management of these lands crucial to maintaining the scenic quality of landscapes. Although privately owned forests provide recreation opportunities for the millions of private forest landowners and their associates, public access to private forest land has, historically, been limited.

The interaction of people and forests in the North creates resource conflicts as well as opportunities to improve people's lives

BIOMASS AND BIOENERGY

Increased use of woody biomass for energy has the potential to greatly alter the type and quantity of wood that is utilized from northern forests, but great uncertainty exists about the future of biomass and bioenergy in the region. Some concerns are associated with trying to ensure that local bioenergy markets develop. If markets develop, other concerns are associated with maintaining existing relationships among wood suppliers and users; ensuring appropriate harvest levels; and sustaining water quality, biodiversity, and other ecosystem services.

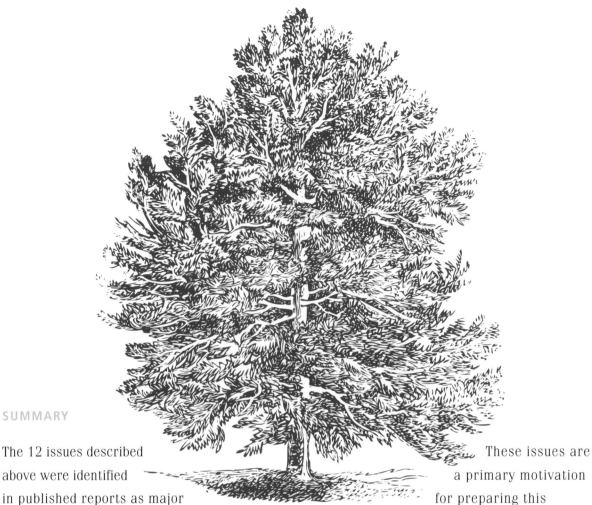

SUMMARY

The 12 issues described above were identified in published reports as major concerns about northern forests (Dietzman et al. 2011). Some are longstanding. They are all complex issues, and many are integrally linked to broader societal concerns about the economy, renewable energy, and climate change. Some issues are inherently threatening, such as invasive plants, insects, and diseases. Others are multifaceted and include both threats and opportunities, such as the interaction of wood products and wood energy production with biodiversity, fragmentation, and carbon sequestration. These issues are a primary motivation for preparing this assessment of northern forest conditions. The following chapters provide necessary background information for discussing these issues in more detail, putting the region in context with the rest of the United States, understanding how forest conditions vary regionally and over time, considering resource interactions, and exploring opportunities associated with future courses of action or inaction.

Characteristics of Sustainable Forest Management

3

FORESTS CAN PROVIDE numerous benefits to society today, tomorrow, and far into the future. Many in society seek sustainable forest management to ensure that future generations enjoy those benefits. The foundation of professional forest management is "the use of the natural resources for the greatest good of the greatest number for the longest time" (Gifford Pinchot 1947). Adherents to these concepts recognize that although it may never be possible to claim that sustainable forestry has been fully achieved, constantly striving for it in the face of changing conditions is a worthwhile pursuit.

Sustainable forest management has been defined in various ways. Despite widespread support for the concept of sustainable forest management, disagreements can arise about the specifics of how to achieve it. Forest management or forest use that seems reasonable to one person or group may not appear so to another. We are people with widely divergent interests and concerns. Therefore, conflicts over planned or ongoing forest management are inevitable, and people who share concern about forest resources sometimes disagree about priorities for those resources. The many different ways that forests and people interact tend to exacerbate some of these conflicts. However, unlike some other natural resources, forests can be managed for several purposes simultaneously, and, thus, jointly meet the interests and priorities of multiple groups.

Forests constantly change over time. These changes, whether natural or human-caused, result in species that gain resources or increase in number and species that lose resources, fitness, or habitat. Simply stated, forest change creates winners and losers among the flora and fauna (including humans) that depend on forests. Such tradeoffs are inevitable, and so is forest change. Sustainable forest management requires that we understand and manage those tradeoffs while pursuing multiple objectives for present and future generations.

Defining Sustainable Forestry

Although definitions of sustainable forestry have been offered by a variety of sources and are difficult to quantify, the following are the most widely used.

WORLD COMMISSION ON ENVIRONMENT AND DEVELOPMENT (1987), MOST COMMONLY KNOWN AS THE BRUNDTLAND COMMISSION—Development that meets the needs of the present without compromising the ability of future generations to meet their own needs; embodying two key elements:

- The concept of "needs," in particular the essential needs of the World's poor, to which overriding priority should be given
- The idea of limitations imposed by the state of technology and social organization on the environment's ability to meet present and future needs

As applied to forestry, the enhancement of human well-being by using, developing, and protecting resources at a rate and in a manner that enables people to meet their current needs while also providing future generations with the means to meet their needs as well, while simultaneously meeting environmental, economic, and community aspirations. Additional sources: USDA FS (2004), Floyd et al. (2001)

EXECUTIVE ORDER 13514, FEDERAL LEADERSHIP IN ENVIRONMENTAL, ENERGY, AND ECONOMIC PERFORMANCE (FEDERAL REGISTER 2009)—To create and maintain conditions, under which humans and nature can exist in productive harmony, that permit fulfilling the social, economic, and other requirements of present and future generations.

HELMS (1998)—An evolving concept that has several definitions:

- The practice of meeting the forest resource needs and values of the present without compromising the similar capability of future generations; note that sustainable forest management involves practicing a land stewardship ethic that integrates the reforestation, managing, growing, nurturing, and harvesting of trees for useful products with the conservation of soil, air and water quality, wildlife and fish habitat, and aesthetics.
- The stewardship and use of forests and forest lands in a way, and a rate, that maintains their biodiversity, productivity, regeneration capacity, vitality, and potential to fulfill, now and in the future, relevant ecological, economic, and social functions at local, national, and global levels, and that does not cause damage to other ecosystems; note that criteria for sustainable forestry include (1) conservation of biological diversity, (2) maintenance of productive capacity of forest ecosystems, (3) maintenance of forest ecosystem health and vitality, (4) conservation and maintenance of soil and water resources, (5) maintenance of forest contributions to global carbon cycles, (6) maintenance and enhancement of long-term multiple socioeconomic benefits to meet the needs of societies, and (7) a legal, institutional, and economic framework for forest conservation and sustainable management

Scale is a complicating factor in sustainable forest management. Forest management (or lack thereof) that appears reasonable at one spatial scale may look unreasonable when viewed across a range of spatial scales and vice versa. Management practices that appear innocuous at the local scale do not necessarily result in forest conditions that are desirable at landscape, ecoregion, State, national, or global scales. This issue of scale can be especially problematic when considering the wide array of products, amenities, and ecosystem services that forests provide and the inherent tradeoffs associated with alternative management objectives. Consequently, it is essential to examine forest conditions in a hierarchical, spatial context that includes landscapes and ecoregions (Fig. 6).

Likewise, because many forest policies are established by legislative bodies, it is informative to examine forest conditions at several political scales: local governments, States, multi-State regions, and the Nation. Issues of scale are important in both upward and downward directions. Understanding the cumulative effects of management practices or policy alternatives may require us to scale up to the ecoregion, State, or national perspective. Conversely, implementing a policy usually requires us to scale down and resolve the application logistics acre-by-acre on the ground.

It is important to emphasize that forest sustainability is a human concept. What is considered sustainable and desirable is filtered through human value sets. For as long as people have lived on the North American continent, they have relied on forests to sustain and improve the quality of their lives. Native Americans used fire extensively to shape forests and woodlands. During periods of rapid European settlement, much of the focus was on timber extraction and land clearing for agriculture. Recent decades have seen a gradual change in focus toward sustaining the ecosystem services that forests provide: clean air, clean water, repositories of biological diversity, climate stabilization, and emotional and spiritual well-being. This shift in emphasis has been accompanied by efforts to attach quantitative values to ecosystem services, which are ultimately evaluated from a human perspective. Even objectives such as maintaining forest health and biodiversity are human centered. Many people who value healthy, diverse forests do so because they believe those attributes will better sustain forests for the benefit of present and future generations.

Strategies for Sustainable Forest Management

4

SUSTAINABLE FORESTRY IS widely discussed and almost universally desired, but tangible standards, goals, targets, or thresholds to evaluate sustainability are often defined vaguely. Identifying such standards is complicated by the diversity of forests, the diversity of objectives among forest decisionmakers (both public and private), the diversity of values among people who depend on forests, and the diversity of spatial and temporal scales that must be considered. The complexity of determining what is deemed to be sustainable, and by whom, leads to challenges in implementing and monitoring forest management. As a way of framing discussions about sustainability, we offer the following strategies which we believe are important considerations for sustainable forest management for ecoregions, States, and the Nation:

- Maintain a stable forest land base. This concept embraces strong sustainability and stresses the fact that goods and services provided by forests are irreplaceable. Thus, human-created capital is no substitute for forest land. Likewise loss of northern forests cannot be fully compensated by offsetting gains in forest area in other parts of the United States or the World.

- Maintain or increase forest biodiversity. This includes sustaining diverse populations of native plants and animals, diversity of forest ecosystems and habitats across the landscape, and genetic diversity of forest-associated plants and animals. Special emphasis is given to restoring species and habitats that are threatened with extinction, and controlling invasive species.

- Maintain diverse forest size structure and species composition on the landscape. Forests constantly change, but their trajectory of change is periodically altered by fire, insects, diseases, harvesting, weather, invasive plants, and other disturbances. Healthy, diverse forests can better cope with such disturbances and continue to function as forests.

- Maintain or increase the quality and quantity of water from forest ecosystems.

- Maintain or increase soil productivity and minimize soil erosion and contamination.

- Maintain or increase the capacity for sustained yield of timber and nontimber forest products and associated economic development.

- Maintain or increase forest-based employment and community stability. Commercial forest operations may be the most economical means of altering forest structure and composition in ways that are essential to achieving other goals such as habitat restoration, hazardous fuel reduction, or invasive species mitigation.

- Maintain or enhance the quantity and quality of forest recreation and other opportunities for people to experience forests.

- Maintain a system of institutions, policies, regulations, and incentives that support forest sustainability at multiple spatial scales.

- Increase environmental literacy and engage a wide range of stakeholders in sustainable forest management

Many readers will note that these strategies cannot all be pursued equally, and pursuing some will require sacrificing the extent to which others can be pursued. Tradeoffs and compromises are inevitable in striving for sustainable forests. Sustainable forest management requires careful thought about the full range of benefits and consequences associated with management actions or inaction.

Sustainable forest management is complicated by the multiple benefits and the large temporal and spatial scales that must be considered. For example, short-term decisions about forest sector employment and harvest practices can have long-term effects on biodiversity. Similar tradeoffs can arise across large spatial scales; one State's effort to increase the area of forest reserved for wildlife habitat diversity could transfer timber harvesting to other States or to other nations and alter habitat diversity or sustained timber yield there. Urban and rural forests provide many of the same ecosystem services, but differ in the type and number of interactions with people.

Strong and Weak Sustainability

Sustainability can be further classified into weak and strong sustainability (Pearce et al. 1994), with capital existing in three forms: natural, human, and human-made.

WEAK SUSTAINABILITY— Only concerned about the total capital value (natural + human + human-made) allowing for substitution among the three forms. Human-made or manufactured capital of equal value can take the place of natural capital lost as a result of development. As long as future generations are endowed with an amount of total capital that is not less than that of the current generation, the conditions of weak sustainable development are satisfied.

STRONG SUSTAINABILITY— Not merely concerned about keeping the aggregate stocks of capital constant, but also requiring maintenance and enhancement of natural capital levels (ecological assets and environmental quality) because the functions performed cannot be duplicated by manufactured capital.

One of the most significant contributions an assessment such as this can make is to provide the context and data needed to facilitate discussions about sustainable forest management. This assessment provides information at different spatial and temporal scales to support discussion of forest policy and management options available. Choosing among options, making tradeoffs among desirable outcomes, finding the most effective or most equitable solution, or maximizing a single outcome knowing it comes at the expense of other potential achievements: this is the work of society. These issues will be resolved through discourse, legislation, changes to policies, purchases made and forgone, opinions expressed, and investments made. Our hope with this assessment, and the other products developed as part of the Northern Forest Futures Project, is that society does so from a rich understanding of the current state of northern forests and their possible futures.

Forest conditions today are influenced by events that took place many decades ago. Likewise, management decisions we make now will have long-term consequences for future generations.

Forest Conditions and Trends in the Northern United States

5

THIS SECTION DESCRIBES current conditions and trends for the 20 Northern States by focusing on selected characteristics associated with forest sustainability. Its format is based upon a set of 64 indicators within 7 broad criteria that the United States and 11 other countries have adopted under the auspices of the Montréal Process Working Group on Criteria and Indicators for the Conservation and Sustainable Management of Temperate and Boreal Forests (Montréal Process Working Group 2010).

To these, we have added an eighth criterion focused on the urban and community forests in the northern United States.

The indicators are qualitative or quantitative variables intended to relay complex ecological information in a simple and useful manner (Kurtz et al. 2001). To be effective, these variables must be indicative of a larger ecological process, easy to measure, cost-effective, and repeatable (Burger and Kelting 1999). Indicators can identify trends, but they cannot fully explain the causes for observed changes or predict future conditions. Rather, indicator data must be evaluated in association with other monitoring data and verified by rigorous and targeted research to assess potential impacts on ecosystem function (O'Neill et al. 2005).

The Montréal Process was the framework for reporting forest conditions at the national scale in 2003 (USDA FS 2004) and 2010

(USDA FS 2011e). In a collaborative effort, the U.S. Forest Service and Northeastern Area Association of State Foresters collectively measure and monitor a subset of the indicators across the region and report findings in print (Carpenter 2007) and online (USDA FS 2010d). Individual State forestry agencies have used the Montréal Process criteria and indicator framework for forest resource assessments, as have organizations assessing local forest conditions at finer spatial scales (Baltimore County Maryland Department of Environmental Protection and Resource Management 2007). This chapter draws from these sources, from the Forest Service Forest Inventory and Analysis program (Miles et al. 2010, Smith 2009), and from numerous other sources to present an overview of current conditions and recent trends in the North.

Criteria and Indicators for Sustainable Forests

The United States and 11 other nations have agreed to follow a consistent set of guidelines for summarizing information that describes the characteristics of a nation's forests, including information considered important to understanding forest sustainability. These are often called the Montréal Process Criteria and Indicators because they originated at a meeting in Montréal (Montréal Process Working Group 2010). Each of the following seven criteria is described by a number of indicators (in parentheses). An eighth criterion was added for this assessment to reflect the importance of urban and community forests in the Northern United States.

1. Conservation of biological diversity (9)
2. Maintenance of productive capacity of forest ecosystems (5)
3. Maintenance of ecosystem health and vitality (2)
4. Conservation and maintenance of soil and water resources (5)
5. Maintenance of forest contribution to global carbon cycles (3)
6. Maintenance and enhancement of long-term multiple socioeconomic benefits to meet the needs of societies (20)
7. Legal, institutional, and economic framework for forest conservation and sustainable management (20)
8. Urban and community forests

Examples of individual indicators that are particularly relevant to northern forests include:

- Area and percent of forest by forest ecosystem type, successional stage, age class, and forest ownership or tenure
- Fragmentation of forests
- Number and status of native forest associated species at risk, as determined by legislation or scientific assessment
- Annual harvest of wood products by volume and as a percentage of net growth or sustained yield
- Area and percent of forest affected by abiotic agents (such as fires, storms, and land clearance) beyond reference conditions
- Proportion of forest management activities that meet best management practices, legislation, or other relevant efforts to protect soil resources
- Total forest ecosystem carbon pools and fluxes
- Value and volume of wood and wood products production, including primary and secondary processing
- Revenue from forest-based environmental services
- Exports as a share of wood and wood products production, and imports as a share of wood and wood products consumption
- Employment in the forest sector
- Methodologies to measure and integrate environmental and social costs and benefits into markets and public policies, and to reflect forest-related resource depletion or replenishment in national accounting systems
- New technologies and the capacity to assess the socioeconomic consequences associated with their introduction

Some indicators can be evaluated using readily available data sources, but others cannot. Findings for some indicators are easier to interpret than others. Nevertheless many nations, States, and even some counties choose to follow this framework for reporting forest sustainability information, making it a relevant way to understand forest conditions in context and across multiple spatial scales.

Although other formats could be used to present this information, the Montréal Process is well developed, widely used, and especially well suited to making comparisons with forest conditions elsewhere. In addition to the usual statistics for forest area, volume, utilization, and economic output, the broad criteria of the Montréal Process emphasize other important forest characteristics that typically receive less attention or that have a shorter monitoring history: biodiversity, forest fragmentation, forest soils, water quality and quantity, carbon cycling, social benefits, and institutional frameworks. Understanding the Montréal Process is not a precondition for interpreting or understanding this chapter. However, knowledge of the Montréal Process will be helpful for those who wish to contrast the conditions of northern forests with those of the entire United States or other participating nations. Ultimately the purpose of the criteria and indicators is to provide information relevant to understanding and interpreting forest sustainability.

The following eight subsections address the eight broad sustainability criteria identified for northern forests and include information about many of the individual indicators associated with each criterion. Montréal Process indicators that lack suitable data for northern forests are omitted.

Criterion 1:
CONSERVATION OF BIOLOGICAL DIVERSITY

Montréal Process Criterion 1 (Montréal Process Working Group 2010); Northern Area Forest Sustainability Indicators 1.1-1.5, 2.1-2.3, 3.1-3.5, 4.1–4.4, 15.3–15.6 (USDA FS 2010d)[1]

The importance of conserving biological diversity

Biological diversity, or biodiversity, is the variety of life. It encompasses the variability among living organisms and includes diversity within species, among species, and among ecosystems. High biodiversity enables a forest ecosystem to respond to external influences, absorb and recover from disturbances, and still maintain essential ecosystem processes such as regeneration, nutrient cycling, support of wildlife, and purification of air and water.

The Convention on Biological Diversity (2010) defines forest biological diversity as encompassing the multitude of plants, animals, and micro-organisms that inhabit forest areas and their associated genetic diversity. Both human activities and natural processes can reduce biological diversity by altering and fragmenting habitats, introducing invasive species, or reducing a species' population size or range. Sustaining biodiversity is among the top concerns commonly expressed about northern forests (Chapter 2).

---

[1] *This and similar information at the beginning of subsequent sections cross-reference information for Northern forests with the Montréal Process Criteria and Indicator system and with information in the Northern Area Forest Sustainability Indicators System.*

Although measuring biological diversity in forests is not simple, it is important because forests are a major source of biodiversity in the North and are relatively undisturbed compared to the agricultural or developed lands that dominate in some areas. Biodiversity is often reported at three scales: (1) diversity of ecosystems on the landscape; (2) species diversity including the total number of species and their relative frequency; and (3) genetic diversity, which is difficult to measure directly and often inferred from population size.

In general, forest ecosystems that have greater diversity are considered more resilient. Northern forests are long-lived and widespread so they are inevitably afflicted by catastrophic weather, wildfires, insects, diseases, invasive species, atmospheric pollution, and climate change. Forests with diversity at landscape, species, and genetic scales are more likely to remain fully functioning forest ecosystems over the long run.

Indicators of biodiversity for northern forests

Forest area

Forests cover 42 percent of the northern land base (Table 1), a greater percentage than the three other large regions of the country and far greater than the entire U.S. coverage of 33 percent (Fig. 1, Table 1, Appendix). Over the past century, forest cover in the North has increased by 28 percent, from 134 to 172 million acres (Fig. 2), mostly the result of natural succession after the abandonment of marginal farmlands that earlier replaced native forest. Simultaneously, as urban populations have increased, adjacent forests have been converted to nonforest land uses. From 1990 to 2000 the total area of urban land in the North increased by 4 million acres of which 1.5 million acres were forest (see Criterion 8).

Key Findings for Criterion 1

- Forests cover 172 million acres in the Northern States or 42 percent of the land area.
- Forest area in the region increased by 28 percent over the last 100 years.
- The region's forests are 74 percent privately owned.
- There are 5 million private forest owners
- Oak-hickory and maple-beech-birch are the most common forest types; together they account for 64 percent of the forest area.

- Young forests and old forests are relatively rare; 70 percent of the forest area is between 40 and 100 years old.
- About 1 percent of the region's forest-associated species are presumed extinct; populations of 85 percent of forest-associated species appear to be secure. Populations of the remaining forest-associated species are at some degree of risk.
- The number of extirpated forest-associated species is greater in the Northern States than elsewhere in the United States.

Although most Northern States have seen a net increase in forest land over the past century, many have experienced periods of decrease as well as periods of increase over that time (Fig. 2). The increases in forest area for the North appear to be leveling off (Drummond and Loveland 2010); over the past 20 years about half the States increased in forest area and the other half decreased. Although total forest area is expected to remain relatively stable in the near term, forest locations will shift as some areas are cleared for development or agriculture, and others are returned to forest cover.

Most northern forest land (128 million acres, 74 percent) is privately owned (Fig. 7, Table 2). Families are the largest owner group, representing 4.7 million of the 5 million private owners. The other 300,000 private owners include forest products companies, corporations, trusts, nongovernmental organizations, and investment companies.

Most private ownerships are small; the average size is about 26 acres, and 3 million private owners have fewer than 10 acres of forest land. Conversely, the 10 percent of private owners with the most forest land collectively own more than half of all private forest acreage in the North (Butler 2008, Smith et al. 2009).

The other 44 million acres of northern forest land are publicly owned. Public forest land usually occurs in larger blocks and is managed for different purposes than private land. Compared to the U.S. average (44 percent), the North has relatively little public forest land (26 percent); the only region with less is the South (13 percent). Overall, the East trails far behind the Western States in public ownership of forests: 67 percent for the Pacific Coast and 75 percent for the Interior West. The amount of public forest land varies considerably among Northern States, ranging from 6 percent in Maine to 57 percent in Minnesota (Table 2).

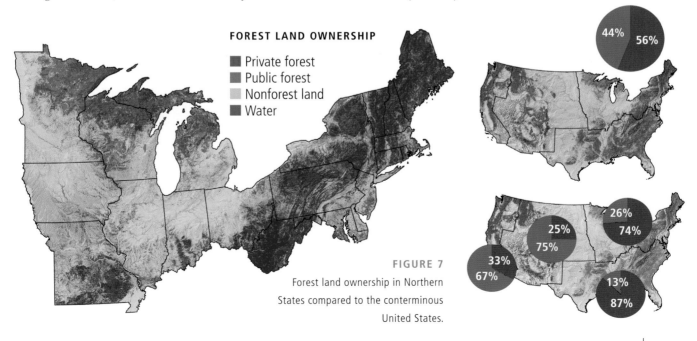

FOREST LAND OWNERSHIP

■ Private forest
■ Public forest
■ Nonforest land
■ Water

FIGURE 7

Forest land ownership in Northern States compared to the conterminous United States.

Table 2—Forest characteristics of the Northern States, 2007, ordered from most to least forest land (Smith et al. 2009). Note that data are standardized to an inventory year of 2007 and that newer State-specific data for some attributes are available from online sources (Miles 2010, USDA FS 2009b).

State	Land area	Forest land	Forest land	Reserved forest area	Reserved forest area	Public forest land	Private forest land	No. of private forest owners
	(1,000 acres)	(1,000 acres)	(percent of all land)	(1,000 acres)	(percent of forest land)	(percent of forest land)	(percent of forest land)	(1,000)
Michigan	36,275	19,545	54	325	1.7	38	62	498
New York	30,217	18,669	62	2,501	13.4	23	77	687
Maine	19,752	17,673	89	318	1.8	6	94	252
Pennsylvania	28,683	16,577	58	458	2.8	29	71	497
Minnesota	51,024	16,391	32	820	5.0	57	43	202
Wisconsin	34,791	16,275	47	107	0.7	32	68	362
Missouri	44,093	15,078	34	241	1.6	18	82	359
West Virginia	15,415	12,007	78	174	1.4	13	87	251
Ohio	26,207	7,894	30	228	2.9	12	88	345
New Hampshire	5,740	4,850	85	128	2.6	25	75	128
Indiana	22,980	4,656	20	123	2.6	16	84	225
Vermont	5,920	4,618	78	114	2.5	16	84	88
Illinois	35,608	4,525	13	162	3.6	18	82	184
Massachusetts	5,018	3,171	63	131	4.1	31	69	293
Iowa	35,842	2,879	8	15	0.5	11	89	150
Maryland	6,256	2,566	41	180	7.0	24	76	157
New Jersey	4,748	2,132	45	160	7.5	38	62	122
Connecticut	3,101	1,794	58	31	1.7	23	77	108
Delaware	1,251	383	31	0	0	8	92	55
Rhode Island	669	356	53	0	0	15	85	38
North total	413,586	172,039	42	6,216	3.6	26	74	5,002
U.S. total	2,263,870	751,228	33	74,664	9.9	44	56	11,322

Protected forests

Protected forest areas occur in a variety of forms including designated wilderness, parks, natural areas, conservation partnerships on private lands, and areas protected by nongovernmental organizations. Collectively protected areas comprise approximately 16 percent of northern forest land (see also Criterion 7). Protected forests can be categorized by their level of protection. Some have almost no human management intervention. Others allow active management to maintain biodiversity (using prescribed fire for example) but exclude timber harvesting.

Other areas—such as national forests, State forests, and some private forests—may be actively managed for multiple resources with an emphasis on sustaining biodiversity.

Reserved forest land is a category of protected forest (such as State and Federal parks and wildernesses), mostly in public ownership, that has been permanently excluded from timber harvesting, either by law or by administrative order. Six million acres (3.6 percent) of all northern forest land is in reserved forests (Table 2), a relatively small amount compared to western forests (Fig. 8).

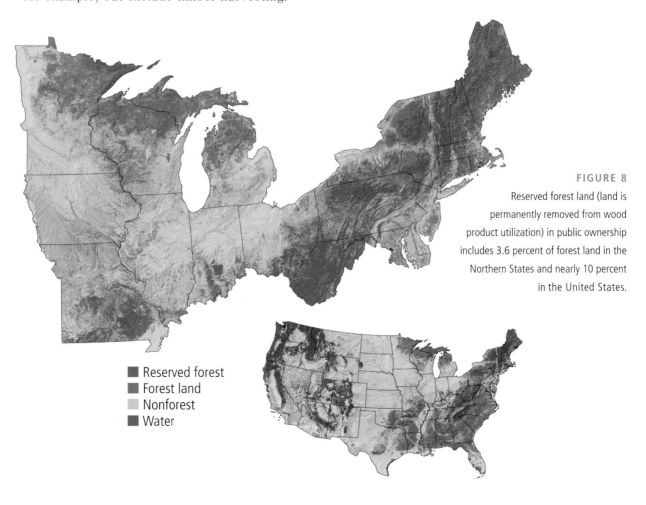

- Reserved forest
- Forest land
- Nonforest
- Water

FIGURE 8

Reserved forest land (land is permanently removed from wood product utilization) in public ownership includes 3.6 percent of forest land in the Northern States and nearly 10 percent in the United States.

Forest land preservation agreements, trusts, and other voluntary land protection agreements have increased the area of protected private forest acreage in recent years. Developing a full inventory of private forests with conservation partnerships and other forms of protection is a work in progress. State and Federal conservation agreements on private forest land cover nearly 6 million acres of northern forests (3.5 percent of all forest land). Seventeen percent (28 million acres) of private northern forest land is voluntarily enrolled in State tax reduction programs that establish forest management guidelines and land use restrictions. Approximately 24 million acres of public and private forest land (14 percent of northern forest land) are enrolled in the Forest Stewardship Council third-party forest certification program. These categories of protection are not mutually exclusive; rather they represent a range of alternative methods to maintain forest cover and sustain forest values (USDA FS 2010e, 2010f).

Forest cover types and age classes

Although nine broad forest type groups—each named for its dominant tree cover—can be found in northern landscapes (Table 3, Fig. 9), the most common are the oak-hickory and the maple-beech-birch forest-type groups occupying 35 percent and 29 percent of the forest area, respectively.

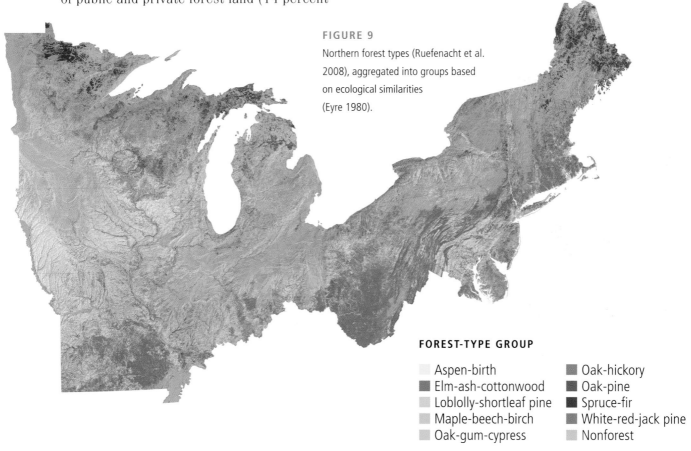

FIGURE 9
Northern forest types (Ruefenacht et al. 2008), aggregated into groups based on ecological similarities (Eyre 1980).

FOREST-TYPE GROUP

Aspen-birth   Oak-hickory
Elm-ash-cottonwood   Oak-pine
Loblolly-shortleaf pine   Spruce-fir
Maple-beech-birch   White-red-jack pine
Oak-gum-cypress   Nonforest

Table 3—Forest area for the Northern States by forest-type group, 2007, with States ordered from most to least timberland area and forest-type groups ordered from most to least proportion of area for the region (Miles 2010, Smith et al. 2009). Note that data have been standardized to an inventory year of 2007 and that newer State-specific data for some attributes are available from online sources (Miles 2010).

State and region	Forest land	Proportion of all Northern forest land	Oak hickory	Maple beech birch	Aspen birch	Spruce fir	Elm ash cotton-wood	White red jack pine	Oak pine	Loblolly short-leaf pine	Oak gum cypress	Non-stocked	Other types
	(1,000 acres)	(percent)	-----------	-----------	-----------	(percent of forest-type group area by state or region)	-----------	-----------	-----------	-----------	-----------	-----------	-----------
Michigan	19,545	11.4	16	32	16	13	7	10	3	0	0	1	1
New York	18,669	10.9	21	54	4	3	4	7	3	0	0	1	2
Maine	17,673	10.3	2	40	13	33	2	8	2	0	0	0	0
Pennsylvania	16,577	9.6	51	39	2	0	2	3	2	1	0	1	1
Minnesota	16,391	9.5	9	10	40	23	9	6	2	0	0	2	0
Wisconsin	16,275	9.5	23	26	20	9	9	9	4	0	0	1	0
Missouri	15,078	8.8	80	2	0	0	7	0	7	1	0	0	3
West Virginia	12,007	7.0	67	26	0	0	2	1	3	1	0	0	0
Ohio	7,894	4.6	62	23	1	0	8	1	2	1	0	1	1
New Hampshire	4,850	2.8	8	54	7	8	2	14	7	0	0	0	0
Indiana	4,656	2.7	62	19	0	0	11	1	3	1	1	0	1
Vermont	4,618	2.7	4	68	6	7	2	11	2	0	0	0	1
Illinois	4,525	2.6	67	5	0	0	22	1	1	1	1	1	1
Massachusetts	3,171	1.8	30	27	1	0	6	15	14	2	2	1	0
Iowa	2,879	1.7	57	11	0	0	24	0	3	0	0	3	1
Maryland	2,566	1.5	64	5	0	0	2	0	10	11	4	1	1
New Jersey	2,132	1.2	46	11	0	0	2	0	8	22	8	1	2
Connecticut	1,794	1.0	71	11	0	0	6	6	3	0	2	1	0
Delaware	383	0.2	72	0	0	0	4	0	6	10	7	1	0
Rhode Island	356	0.2	56	16	1	0	5	6	8	4	3	1	1
North total	172,039	100.0	35	29	10	9	6	6	3	1	0	1	1

Northern forests are aging. Most of the primary (old-growth) forests were cut more than a century ago, and cutover areas that were not converted to agricultural or residential use typically regenerated naturally to second-growth forest. For about the last 40 years disturbances that regenerate new forests (such as timber harvesting or intense wildfires) have been relatively infrequent. Thus, about 70 percent of northern forest land is between 40 and 100 years old, creating a distinctly bell-shaped forest age distribution (Fig. 10). Young forests and very old forests are relatively rare, so there is relatively little habitat for species that depend on these forest age classes. This reduces forest diversity compared to landscapes that have a more balanced age structure with a similar proportion of forest area in each age class. If current rates of forest disturbance and regeneration continue, the average forest age will increase over time.

Fragmentation and parcelization

Forest fragmentation occurs when patches of nonforest land are created within a forest, patches of forest land are reduced in area, and/or forested corridors connecting forest patches are broken. This reduces forest area and increases the amount of edge habitat between forest and nonforest land. As fragmentation continues, forest patches can become disconnected from one another within a mosaic of other land uses. Fragmentation alters habitat suitability for forest-dwelling species.

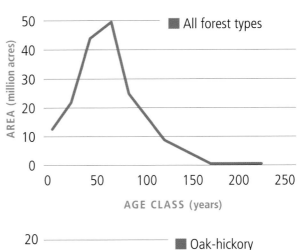

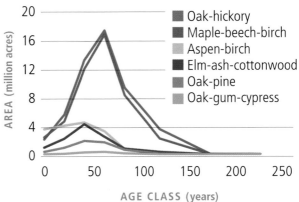

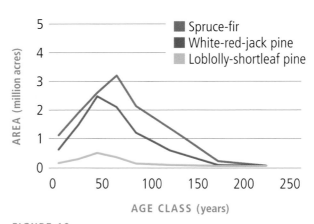

FIGURE 10

Forest age class distribution by forest-type group, Northern States, 2007 (Smith et al. 2009).

Fragmentation can reduce connectivity among forest patches, potentially restricting species movement and limiting genetic diversity within isolated plant and animal populations. Edge habitats favor different species than do the increasingly rare interior habitats of northern forests. Generally, retaining large forest patches is desirable because (1) large contiguous forest patches are relatively rare compared to small forest patches, and (2) over time human and natural disturbances tend to increase fragmentation, reduce forest patch size, and reduce the amount of forest interior habitat.

The degree of forest fragmentation cannot be distilled into a single number, because fragmentation statistics are affected by the spatial scale of analysis. For example, a relevant patch size opening in forest cover could be one-tenth of an acre, 1 acre, or 10 acres, depending on which forest-associated species are of interest. Likewise different forest-associated species (e.g., salamanders versus migrant birds versus humans) differ in the spatial scales at which they perceive and respond to fragmentation effects. In addition to patch size, the total area of forest land, density of forest land within a particular locale, the shape and pattern of forest patches, and rates of conversion of land to or from forest all play a role in fragmentation computations. Figures 7, 11, and 12 illustrate forest fragmentation in different ways and/or at different spatial scales.

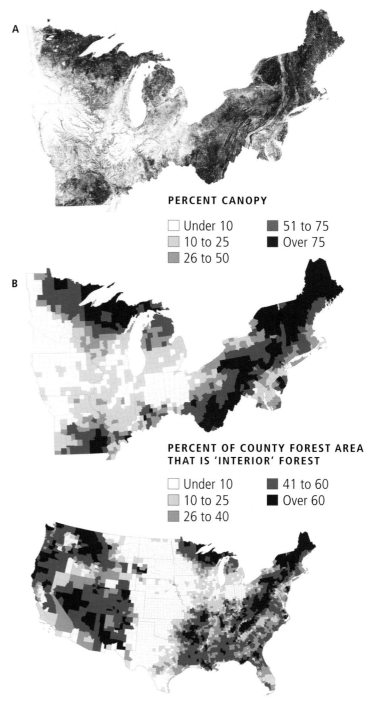

PERCENT CANOPY

- ☐ Under 10
- ☐ 10 to 25
- ◼ 26 to 50
- ◼ 51 to 75
- ■ Over 75

PERCENT OF COUNTY FOREST AREA THAT IS 'INTERIOR' FOREST

- ☐ Under 10
- ☐ 10 to 25
- ◼ 26 to 40
- ◼ 41 to 60
- ■ Over 60

FIGURE 11

Forest area and fragmentation showing (A) forest density for the Northern States (Homer et al. 2004), and (B) fragmentation for the Northern States and the conterminous United States, with percent of interior forest measured as the percent of 40-acre blocks for each county that have at least 90 percent forest cover (source: Kurt Riitters, U.S. Forest Service; USDA FS 2011e).

A

B

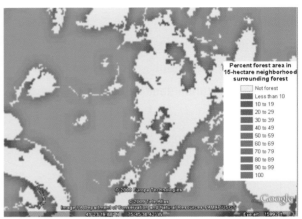

C

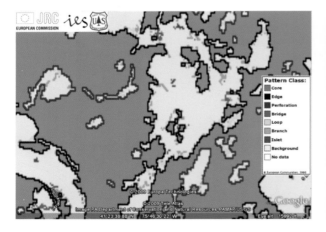

D

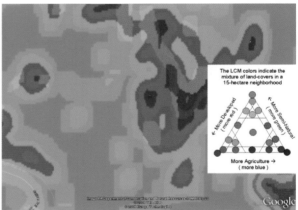

FIGURE 12

Fine scale fragmentation images from a landscape west of Scranton, PA: (A) aerial photograph of the area, (B) forest density, (C) forest fragmentation, and (D) land cover; these map layers are available for the conterminous United States and can be viewed or analyzed at large and small spatial scales [sources: Pennsylvania Department of Conservation and Natural Resources-PAMAP/USGS with additional processing by Europa Technologies©2009 and Tele Atlas©2009; Kurt Riitters; Multi-resolution Land Characteristics Consortium 2011; USGS 2010; MRLC 2011; European Commission Joint Research Centre Institute for Environment and Sustainability 2011; image processing by Peter Vogt, Institute for Environment and Sustainability; image processing by Kurt Riitters, U.S. Forest Service, using methodology by Pierre Soille, Institute for Environment and Sustainability; layer production by Kurt Riitters using methodologies of Wickham and Norton (1994) and Riitters et al. (2008)].

Parcelization occurs when forest ownerships are divided into smaller tracts. The number of private forest owners in the North increased to 5 million in 2006 from 4 million in 1993, and the average ownership size decreased from 33 to 26 acres (Fig. 13). Owners of small tracts may have different objectives and employ different management practices than those who own large tracts (Butler 2008, Gobster and Rickenbach 2004). Parcelization does not necessarily result in physical separation of forested areas, but it often results in disparate owner objectives and management practices among adjacent ownerships. This can be a barrier to building the spatial continuity in management practices needed to address broad, landscape-scale issues.

FIGURE 13

Number of private forest owners in the North by size of forest ownership, 1993 and 2006 (Birch 1996, Butler 2008).

■ Year 1993
■ Year 2006

Mean ownership size in 1993 was 33 acres
Mean ownership size in 2006 was 26 acres

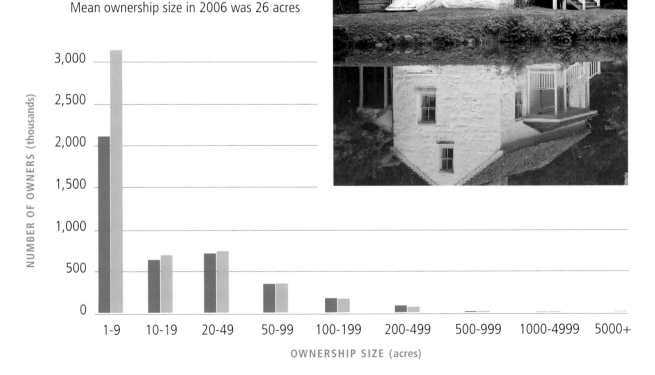

Number and status of native forest-associated species

The number of forest-associated species is an important indicator of forest biodiversity, as is the proportion of those species that may face extinction. Natural variation in forest ecosystems across the United States creates differences in the number of forest-associated species among regions (Fig. 14). Also, the amount of available information varies from one species group to the next—much is known about the number and status of forest associated birds, mammals, and vascular plants compared insects, fungi, and microorganisms.

Northern forests support 780 known animal species (USDA FS 2010f): 85 percent have populations that are apparently secure, 13 percent are at some level of risk of future extinction, 0.8 percent are presumed extinct, and 1.2 percent are classified as "unknown status" (Fig. 15). For individual States, the proportion of species that are at risk ranges from 3 to 9 percent, and less than 1 percent of species are classified as extinct. With more research, the number of known forest-associated species will increase and the proportion of extinct or at-risk species could increase or decrease although the likelihood of extinctions appears to be smaller than the likelihood of discovering additional forest-associated species in taxonomic groups such as insects or fungi.

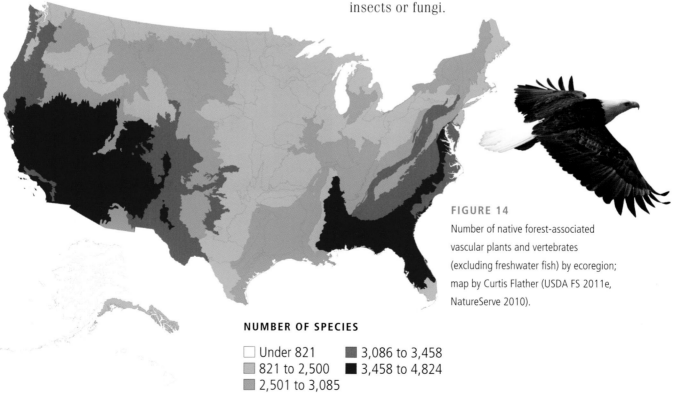

FIGURE 14

Number of native forest-associated vascular plants and vertebrates (excluding freshwater fish) by ecoregion; map by Curtis Flather (USDA FS 2011e, NatureServe 2010).

NUMBER OF SPECIES

☐ Under 821   ■ 3,086 to 3,458
■ 821 to 2,500   ■ 3,458 to 4,824
■ 2,501 to 3,085

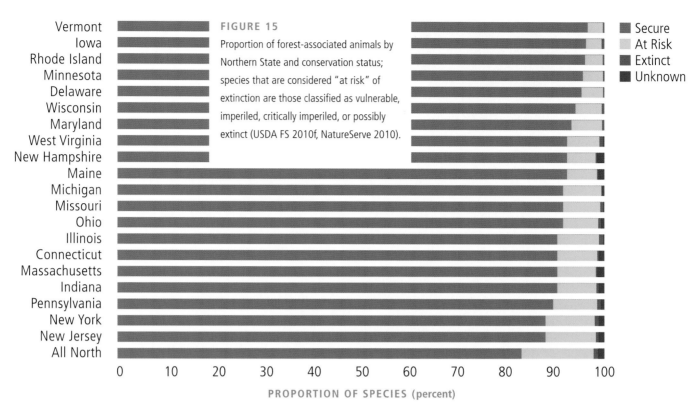

FIGURE 15

Proportion of forest-associated animals by Northern State and conservation status; species that are considered "at risk" of extinction are those classified as vulnerable, imperiled, critically imperiled, or possibly extinct (USDA FS 2010f, NatureServe 2010).

Legend:
- Secure
- At Risk
- Extinct
- Unknown

States (top to bottom): Vermont, Iowa, Rhode Island, Minnesota, Delaware, Wisconsin, Maryland, West Virginia, New Hampshire, Maine, Michigan, Missouri, Ohio, Illinois, Connecticut, Massachusetts, Indiana, Pennsylvania, New York, New Jersey, All North

PROPORTION OF SPECIES (percent)

Species that are considered "at risk" are classified as vulnerable, imperiled, critically imperiled, or possibly extinct (NatureServe 2010). However, species that are not globally extinct or even at risk may still lose ground at a more local scale. Reductions in species' ranges are one way to quantify this effect. Compared with the rest of the Nation, Northern States have large numbers of extirpated (eliminated) species (Fig. 16).

FIGURE 16

The number of forest-associated species—vascular plants, vertebrates (excluding freshwater fish), and select invertebrates—that have been extirpated within each State; map by Curtis Flather (USDA FS 2011e, NatureServe 2010.

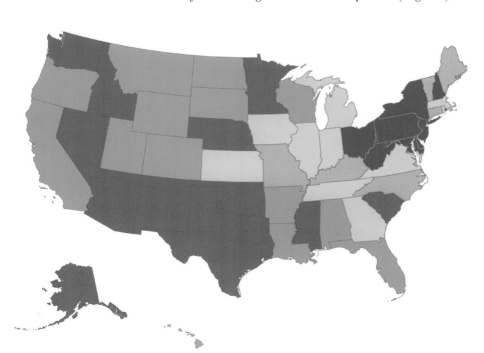

NUMBER OF SPECIES EXTIRPATED

- Under 25
- 25 to 50
- 51 to 75
- 76 to 100
- Over 100

Criterion 2:

MAINTENANCE OF PRODUCTIVE CAPACITY OF FOREST ECOSYSTEMS

Montréal Process Criterion 2 (Montréal Process Working Group 2010); Northern Area Forest Sustainability Indicators 5.1, 6.1, 6.2 (USDA FS 2010d)

The importance of the productive capacity of forest ecosystems

People rely on forests, directly and indirectly, for a wide range of goods and services. Measures of forest productive capacity are indicators of the ability of forests to sustainably supply goods and services over time. An ongoing

Key Findings for Criterion 2

- The North has 172 million acres of forest land of which 95 percent is suitable for timber production.
- The region's timberland is 77 percent privately owned, but private ownership ranges from 46 percent in Minnesota to 96 percent in Maine.
- Regional wood growth has exceeded removals for at least five decades.
- Since 1953, standing volume has increased substantially in all 20 States.

- Only 3.5 percent (6 million acres) of northern forests are plantations.
- Pennsylvania, Michigan, New York, West Virginia, and Maine have the greatest total volume of timber among States in the North,—more than 20 billion cubic feet each.
- Massachusetts, Maryland, New Hampshire, Vermont, Connecticut, and West Virginia, have the highest average volume per acre of timberland—more than 1,900 cubic feet per acre, each.

emphasis on maintaining productive capacity of forests can help ensure that utilization of forest resources does not impair long term forest productivity, even though the goods and services expected from forests may change over time due to social, economic, or technological trends.

Changes in the productive capacity of forests can arise from natural causes such as forest aging and species succession or from disturbances by weather, insects, diseases, wildfires, or invasive plants. Human interventions such as forest management and land use changes also affect the productive capacity of forests. Changes in productive capacity may signal the need or the opportunity to modify policies, management practices, or products to ensure a sustainable flow of desired goods and services.

This criterion is focused primarily on the capacity to produce wood products. However, information on harvesting nontimber forest products is reported to the extent that it is available (see also Criterion 6)

Indicators of the productive capacity of northern forests

Forest land and timberland

Timberland is the subset of forest land that is suitable for wood production. Timberland excludes forest in parks, wilderness, and other protected areas where harvesting is prohibited by policy or legislation. It also excludes forest areas unsuitable for commercial wood production because they are unproductive or physically

Table 4—Timberland area and proportion by owner group for the Northern States, 2007, sorted from most to least forest land. Note that data have been standardized to an inventory year of 2007 and that newer State-specific data for some attributes are available from online sources (Miles 2010, Smith et al. 2009, USDA FS 2009b).

State and region	Forest land	Timberland	Timberland proportion of forest land	Private ownership	Public ownership	National Forest ownership[a]
	(1,000 acres)	(1,000 acres)	(percent)	(percent of timberland)	(percent of timberland)	(percent of timberland)
Michigan	19,545	19,023	97	63	37	13
New York	18,669	16,015	86	89	11	0
Maine	17,673	17,163	97	96	4	0
Pennsylvania	16,577	16,019	97	73	27	3
Minnesota	16,391	15,112	92	46	54	12
Wisconsin	16,275	16,042	99	69	31	9
Missouri	15,078	14,674	97	83	17	10
West Virginia	12,007	11,797	98	88	12	8
Ohio	7,894	7,645	97	91	9	3
New Hampshire	4,850	4,674	96	77	23	13
Indiana	4,656	4,533	97	86	14	4
Vermont	4,618	4,482	97	86	14	6
Illinois	4,525	4,363	96	85	15	6
Massachusetts	3,171	2,946	93	72	28	0
Iowa	2,879	2,824	98	89	11	0
Maryland	2,566	2,372	92	82	18	0
New Jersey	2,132	1,877	88	69	31	0
Connecticut	1,794	1,732	97	77	23	0
Delaware	383	376	98	93	7	0
Rhode Island	356	351	99	85	15	0
North total	172,039	164,018	95	77	23	6
U.S. total	751,228	514,213	68	69	31	19

[a]*National forest timberland is a subset of public timberland.*

inaccessible. Of the 172 million acres of northern forest land, 95 percent (164 million acres) is classified as timberland, far larger than the U.S. average of 68 percent (Table 4). Most timberland in the North is physically accessible and productive with relatively few tracts devoted to parks, wilderness, or other areas where harvesting is prohibited.

Overall, 77 percent of northern timberland is privately owned (Table 4), ranging from a low of 46 percent for Minnesota to a high of 96 percent for Maine (Fig. 17). Most private forest ownerships are small (Fig. 13), and most private owners do not consider wood production as their primary objective (Butler 2008).

Wood volume

The volume of standing wood on northern timberland exceeds 268 billion cubic feet (Table 5). Approximately 92 percent (248 billion cubic feet) of that total volume is classified as growing stock—comprised of species and tree characteristics (form, size, and number of defects) that are acceptable for commercial wood products. Growing stock volume in the North averages 1,500 cubic feet per acre compared to the U.S. average

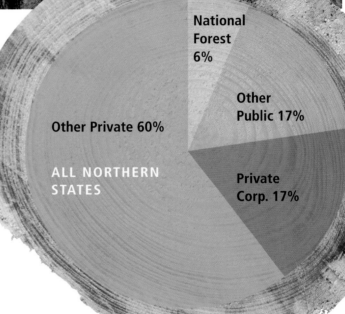

National Forest 6%

Other Public 17%

Other Private 60%

ALL NORTHERN STATES

Private Corp. 17%

FIGURE 17

Proportion of timber land by owner group for all Northern States (this page) and by individual states (opposite page) ordered from lowest to highest proportion of all private timberland (Smith et al. 2009). Colors indicate the same owner category throughout all charts.

of 1,800 cubic feet. Among Northern States, growing-stock volume ranges from a low of 988 cubic feet per acre in Minnesota to slightly more than 2,200 cubic feet in Massachusetts.

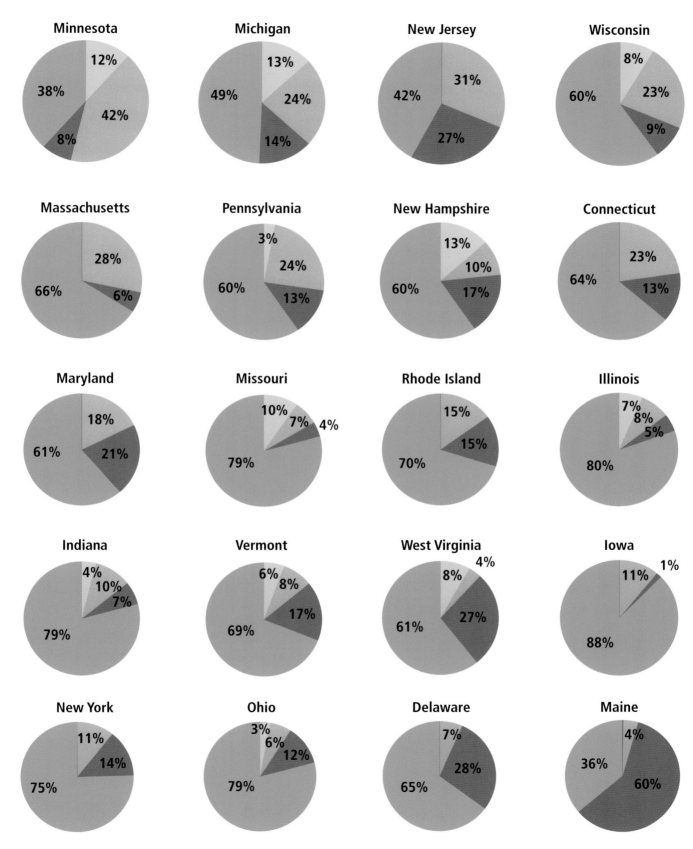

Minnesota
12%
38%
42%
8%

Michigan
13%
49%
24%
14%

New Jersey
31%
42%
27%

Wisconsin
8%
60%
23%
9%

Massachusetts
28%
66%
6%

Pennsylvania
3%
24%
60%
13%

New Hampshire
13%
10%
60%
17%

Connecticut
23%
64%
13%

Maryland
18%
61%
21%

Missouri
10%
7%
4%
79%

Rhode Island
15%
15%
70%

Illinois
7%
8%
5%
80%

Indiana
4%
10%
7%
79%

Vermont
6%
8%
17%
69%

West Virginia
4%
8%
27%
61%

Iowa
1%
11%
88%

New York
11%
14%
75%

Ohio
3%
6%
12%
79%

Delaware
7%
28%
65%

Maine
4%
36%
60%

Table 5—Area of timberland and timber volume (2007) and growth and removals of growing stock (2007 or 2008) from timberland in the Northern States ordered from the largest to smallest ratio of growing stock growth to removals—a relative indicator of utilization pressure (Miles 2010, Smith et al. 2009).

State and Region	Total timber-land area	Total volume	Cull or sound dead	Total growing-stock timber volume		Annual growth of growing stock		Annual removals of growing stock	Growth to removals ratio
			Proportion of total volume						
	(1,000 acres)	(million cubic feet)	(percent)	(million cubic feet)	(cubic feet per acre)	(million cubic feet)	(percent increase)	(million cubic feet)	
Delaware	376	737	6	695	1,851	31	4.5	7	4.5
Rhode Island	351	663	4	637	1,814	19	3.0	4	4.4
Illinois	4,363	7,642	10	6,875	1,576	231	3.4	58	4.0
Indiana	4,533	9,098	9	8,281	1,827	318	3.8	80	4.0
New Jersey	1,877	2,968	5	2,819	1,503	95	3.4	29	3.3
Missouri	14,674	18,886	12	16,596	1,131	518	3.1	175	3.0
Maryland	2,372	5,254	3	5,092	2,147	178	3.5	67	2.6
Iowa	2,824	4,046	23	3,114	1,103	105	3.4	46	2.3
Massachusetts	2,946	6,978	6	6,530	2,216	144	2.2	62	2.3
Connecticut	1,732	3,501	5	3,312	1,913	89	2.7	41	2.2
Ohio	7,645	13,311	7	12,324	1,612	410	3.3	189	2.2
Michigan	19,023	30,418	8	28,029	1,473	703	2.5	339	2.1
New York	16,015	27,761	7	25,862	1,615	600	2.3	288	2.1
West Virginia	11,797	23,539	4	22,524	1,909	611	2.7	323	1.9
Pennsylvania	16,019	31,265	4	29,859	1,864	743	2.5	414	1.8
Wisconsin	16,042	22,268	9	20,271	1,264	598	3.0	327	1.8
Vermont	4,482	9,493	8	8,696	1,940	180	2.1	109	1.7
Minnesota	15,113	16,657	10	14,931	988	417	2.8	294	1.4
New Hampshire	4,674	9,880	7	9,156	1,959	164	1.8	150	1.1
Maine	17,163	23,935	6	22,402	1,305	573	2.6	562	1.0
North total	164,018	268,303	8	248,005	1,512	6,726	2.7	3,564	1.9
U.S. total	514,213	1,013,407	8	932,089	1,813	26,744	2.6	15,533	1.7

From 1953 to 2007 the volume of growing stock on timberland in the North more than doubled from 104 to 248 billion cubic feet (Fig. 18).

FIGURE 18

Growing-stock volume on timberland by Northern State, 1953 to 2007 (Smith et al. 2009).

All 20 states in the region showed substantial increases in volume over this period. Volume in Maine increased by 40 percent, the least proportion of any state; Rhode Island increased by 400 percent, and most states more than doubled standing volume (see Appendix Table A8).

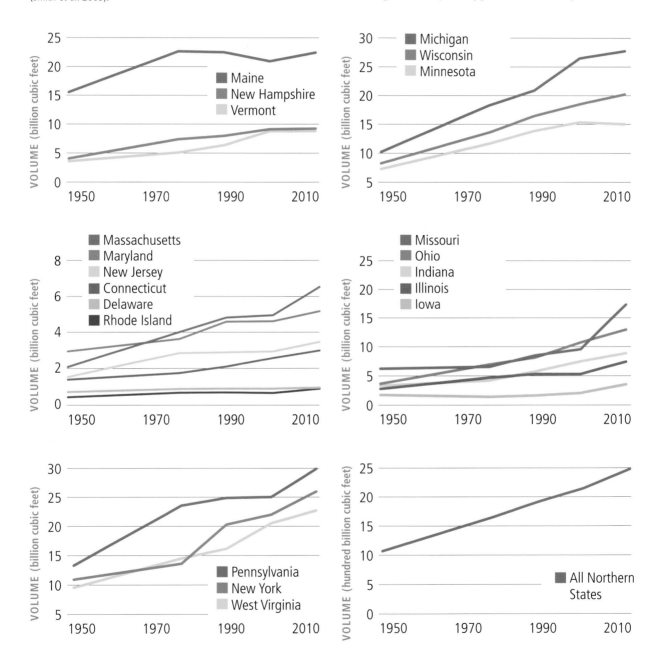

The spatial distribution of total wood volume by county (Fig. 19A) mirrors the spatial distribution of forest cover (Fig. 1). However, wood volume per acre of timberland (Fig. 19B) gives a different perspective of the region's timber resources by emphasizing counties that have high mean volume per acre of timberland, regardless of how many total timberland acres are in the county. Forests that are mature, healthy, and growing on productive sites have relatively high volume per acre.

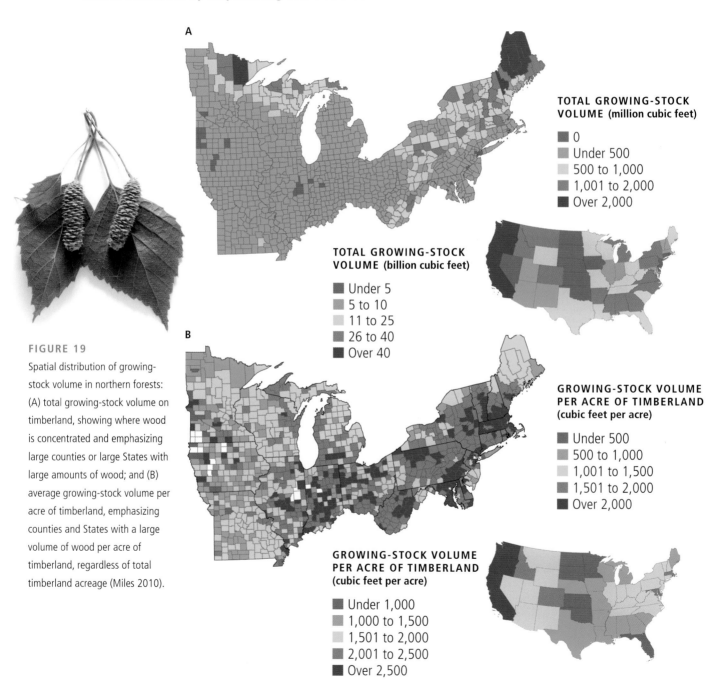

A

TOTAL GROWING-STOCK VOLUME (million cubic feet)
- 0
- Under 500
- 500 to 1,000
- 1,001 to 2,000
- Over 2,000

TOTAL GROWING-STOCK VOLUME (billion cubic feet)
- Under 5
- 5 to 10
- 11 to 25
- 26 to 40
- Over 40

B

GROWING-STOCK VOLUME PER ACRE OF TIMBERLAND (cubic feet per acre)
- Under 500
- 500 to 1,000
- 1,001 to 1,500
- 1,501 to 2,000
- Over 2,000

GROWING-STOCK VOLUME PER ACRE OF TIMBERLAND (cubic feet per acre)
- Under 1,000
- 1,000 to 1,500
- 1,501 to 2,000
- 2,001 to 2,500
- Over 2,500

FIGURE 19

Spatial distribution of growing-stock volume in northern forests: (A) total growing-stock volume on timberland, showing where wood is concentrated and emphasizing large counties or large States with large amounts of wood; and (B) average growing-stock volume per acre of timberland, emphasizing counties and States with a large volume of wood per acre of timberland, regardless of total timberland acreage (Miles 2010).

Wood growth and removals

The annual volume growth rate of growing stock trees on northern timberland is 41 cubic feet per acre, well below the U.S. average of 52 cubic feet. Nevertheless, the annual growth of wood (growing stock) in the North exceeds removals by about 3.2 billion cubic feet (Table 5). The long-term trend of annual growth in excess of removals is the cause of the substantial volume increases in northern forest since the 1950s (Fig. 18).

The ratio of annual growth to removals is an indicator of the intensity of wood utilization. Removals estimates include wood removed during silvicultural operations as well as land clearing, with total removals including trees that were cut but unused as well as those used in products. A growth-to-removals ratio of 1.0 would indicate that wood is being removed as fast as it is growing. A ratio of less than 1.0 would indicate levels of harvesting and/ or land conversion that are unsustainable over the long term because mean annual removals exceed mean annual growth. Across the North the current ratio of growth to removals is 1.9—each year growth is 1.9 times greater than removals (Table 5)—compared to a U.S. ratio of 1.7. Most Northern States have growth-to-removal ratios higher than 2; ratios are higher than 3 for Delaware, Rhode Island, Illinois, Indiana, and New Jersey. In States where management intensity and product utilization are relatively high—Maine, New Hampshire, and Minnesota—growth-to-removal ratios are lower than 1.5. Compared to Maine and Minnesota, New Hampshire has experience more conversion of forest land to urban land (see Criterion 8: Urban and Community Forests).

Planted forests

Under the proper conditions, forest plantations can grow more wood per acre over a given period than naturally regenerated forests. Attention to site and species selection, planting stock quality, competition control, fertilization, thinning, and efficient utilization often contribute to high productivity per acre from planted forests. Although plantations usually have lower species diversity than native forests, they provide increased productivity per acre that can (at least theoretically) offset timber harvesting elsewhere. And when converting sites to forest from agricultural, mining, or other land uses, planting trees is often faster than natural succession for establishing a new, closed canopy forest.

Only 3.5 percent (6 million acres) of northern forests are plantations, compared to 21 percent in the South and 8 percent (63 million acres) for the entire United States. From 1993 to 2003, planting averaged about 142,000 acres per year in the North, equivalent to 6 percent of the total planted area per year in the United States (Smith et al. 2009).

Criterion 3:

MAINTENANCE OF FOREST ECOSYSTEM HEALTH AND VITALITY

Montréal Process Criterion 3 (Montréal Process Working Group 2010); Northern Area Forest Sustainability Indicators 7.1-7.4 (USDA FS 2010d)

The importance of maintaining forest ecosystem health and vitality

Forest ecosystem health depends on stable forest composition and structure and on sustainable ecosystem processes. Forest disturbances that push an ecosystem beyond the range of conditions considered normal can upset the balance among processes, exacerbate forest health problems, and increase mortality beyond historical norms. Sometimes forest ecosystems respond to disturbances by returning to the normal range of conditions. At other times, however, the ecosystem is so altered that it follows a new trajectory—occasionally without historical precedent or known capability for resiliency—producing uncharacteristic changes in forest health and associated processes that may threaten the human, plant, or animal populations that depend on forests. The following sections describe forest health in northern landscapes using indicators based on overall mortality trends and on potential impacts of specific insects and diseases.

Indicators of forest ecosystem health and vitality for northern forests

Mortality

Mortality is a natural process in a forest ecosystem. Dead trees serve valuable ecosystem functions as wildlife habitat, substrate for young

Key Findings for Criterion 3

- Mortality rates are one indicator of forest health. Current statewide mortality rates are 1 to 2 percent of total volume per year.
- The forest-type groups with the greatest percent annual mortality on a volume basis are noncommercial hardwoods, other eastern soft hardwoods, cottonwood and aspen, and other yellow pines.
- The most frequent types of tree defects are advanced decay, cracks or seams in tree boles, cankers, galls, and dead terminal branches.

- Locations where basal area mortality is expected to increase by at least 25 percent over the next 15 years are located throughout the North but are concentrated in the Northeastern States.
- Gypsy moth and emerald ash borer are entrenched invasive species causing widespread mortality.
- Other invasive insect species that have the potential to cause extensive mortality if they become established include the Asian longhorned beetle, Sirex wood wasp, and European spruce bark beetle.

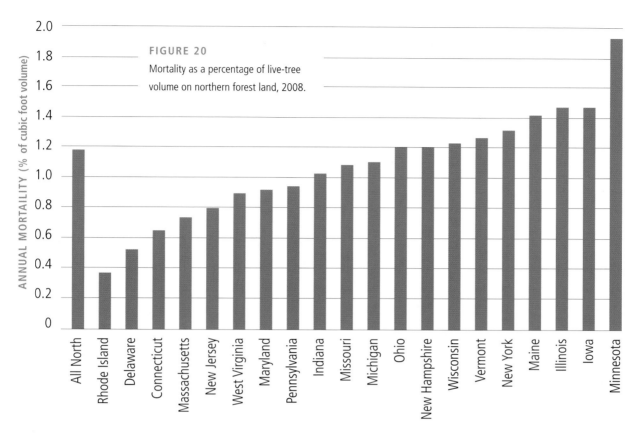

FIGURE 20

Mortality as a percentage of live-tree volume on northern forest land, 2008.

plants, and sources of nutrients for the forest floor. Patterns and trends in mortality give a sense of overall forest health. Uncharacteristic increases in mortality can indicate fundamental forest health issues that may be associated with forest age, climate, insects, diseases, weather events, or other disturbance agents.

In northern forests, statewide mortality as a percentage of current live-tree volume ranged from about 0.4 to 1.5 percent annually (Miles 2010), with the exception of Minnesota at 1.9 percent (Fig. 20). These mortality rates are within the range of the values reported from prior State surveys. A lack of historical data based on consistent sampling methods limits our ability to analyze mortality trends over time.

Mortality percentages by species group for each State provide additional insight into variation across the region (Table 6). Seven species groups—other yellow pines (*Pinus* spp.), American beech (*Fagus grandifolia*), eastern noncommercial hardwoods, spruce (*Picea* spp.) and balsam fir, other eastern soft hardwoods, jack pine, and cottonwood and aspen (*Populus* spp.)—had annual mortality rates in excess of 2 percent. Because the cottonwood and aspen group is dominated by short-lived species, relatively high mortality rates are expected. High mortality rates for many of the other species groups are partly associated with insect and disease agents.

Table 6—Annual mortality of species group as a percent of volume by Northern State, 2008. To reduce uncertainties associated with small sample sizes, mortality for a species group is reported only if the group comprises at least 3 percent of a State's volume of growing stock, but the mortality totals for individual States and for the region as a whole include all species groups. States are ordered from least to greatest mortality percent for all species groups, and species groups are ordered from least to greatest mortality percent for the combined Northern States.

State and Region	All species groups	Yellow-poplar	Tupelo and blackgum	Sweetgum	Loblolly and shortleaf pine	Eastern white and red pine	Hard maple	Select white oaks	Select red oaks	Black walnut	Eastern hemlock	Other eastern softwoods	Soft maple	Hickory
Rhode Island	0.36					0.25		0.02	0.08				0.70	
Delaware	0.51	0.15	0.10	0.55	0.57			0.03					0.66	
Connecticut	0.63					1.00	0.23	0.09	0.22		1.24		0.60	0.04
Massachusetts	0.71					0.38	0.44		0.36		0.16		1.11	
New Jersey	0.77	0.26		0.67				0.22	0.37			0.93	1.33	
West Virginia	0.87	0.44					0.36	0.71	0.71				0.44	1.06
Maryland	0.90	0.43		0.22	0.40			0.61	1.02				1.00	0.61
Pennsylvania	0.92	0.28				1.19	0.94	0.44	0.39		0.91		0.67	
Indiana	1.00	0.55					0.41	0.29	0.93				1.13	0.89
Missouri	1.06			0.35				0.52	1.81	0.60		0.17		0.58
Michigan	1.08					0.32	0.37		0.42			0.61	0.46	
Ohio	1.17	0.47					0.70	0.93	0.16				0.96	0.71
New Hampshire	1.18					0.47	0.61		0.77		0.42		0.85	
Wisconsin	1.20					0.32	0.30	0.65	0.84			0.67	0.54	
Vermont	1.23					0.67	0.68		0.53		0.45		1.13	
New York	1.29					0.81	0.57		0.46		1.11		0.68	
Maine	1.38					0.58	0.79		0.07		0.23	0.80	0.77	
Illinois	1.43						0.18	0.80	2.00	1.01			0.83	0.31
Iowa	1.43							0.65	1.16	0.15			0.91	1.36
Minnesota	1.88					0.51	1.00	0.42	0.91			1.06	0.96	
Northern States	1.15	0.41	0.47	0.47	0.49	0.56	0.58	0.59	0.65	0.69	0.70	0.73	0.73	0.74

Table 6 continued

State and Region	Basswood	Other white oaks	Ash	Other red oaks	Yellow birch	Other eastern hard hardwoods	Other yellow pines	Beech	Eastern noncommercial hardwoods	Spruce and balsam fir	Other eastern soft hardwoods	Jack pine	Cottonwood and aspen
Rhode Island				0.40									
Delaware				0.88							0.77		
Connecticut			1.27	0.65		0.63							
Massachusetts			0.98	0.60		0.43					2.01		
New Jersey	0.32		1.52	1.62		0.61	0.33				2.14		
West Virginia	0.87			0.80		1.57		2.06			1.12		
Maryland	0.44			1.49							1.09		
Pennsylvania	0.77		0.87	0.40		1.51		2.11			1.31		
Indiana			1.07	0.82							2.09		2.23
Missouri	0.63			1.80							1.92		
Michigan			1.47	0.58						2.67	3.08		2.55
Ohio			1.48	0.46				1.03			2.78		1.19
New Hampshire			0.95		1.55			1.75		2.72	3.70		
Wisconsin	0.57		0.65	1.65						3.02	3.41		2.74
Vermont			0.35	0.75				3.12		2.48	2.75		
New York			1.03	1.50				2.58		2.10	2.81		3.42
Maine					0.94			4.34		2.23	2.54		2.35
Illinois			1.66	1.66		1.56					3.55		1.23
Iowa	0.88		1.12	1.09		0.59					4.25		0.80
Minnesota	0.89		0.85							3.02	3.08		3.12
Northern States	0.77	0.77	1.05	1.15	1.26	1.40	2.11	2.35	2.43	2.44	2.45	2.59	2.66

Damage on standing timber

Tree damage is sometimes an indicator of the potential for future mortality. Although not all types of tree damage (e.g., cracks or cankers) result in tree mortality, such factors can weaken a tree and predispose it toward mortality from other causes.

Statewide forest inventories conducted by the U.S. Forest Service have recorded damage on thousands of sampled trees. The bulk of trees in the North are undamaged, but some States have evidence of certain types of damage on up to 5 percent of all trees (Fig. 21). The most prominent damage types were various forms of decay, broken trees, and brooms or cracks.

Insect and disease incidence and risk

Many different insect, disease, invasive plant, and abiotic processes can impact forest ecosystems; sometimes multiple agents act

FIGURE 21

Percent of total volume on northern forest land by category of forest damage.

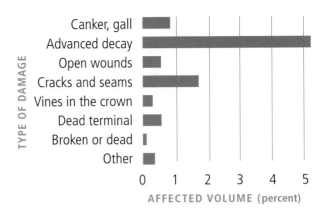

simultaneously on the same forest area. Large cumulative risks can result in forest areas where insect or disease outbreaks appear imminent. Forests at risk span the entire North, but seem particularly concentrated in portions of West Virginia and Pennsylvania (Fig. 22). These are areas where one or more "biotic processes are

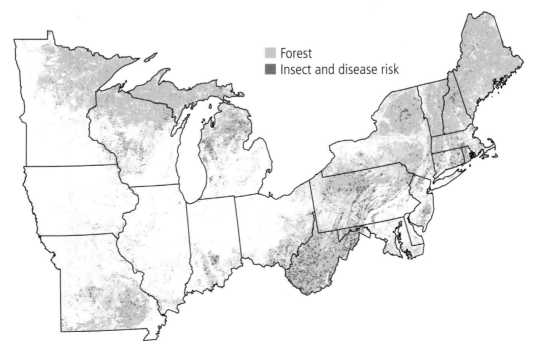

FIGURE 22

Insect and disease risk for northern forests with forest areas in red where 25 percent or more mortality (by basal area) is expected over the next 15 years. Forests at risk span the entire region, but appear particularly concentrated in portions of West Virginia and Pennsylvania. (USDA FS 2011c).

significantly out of range" (USDA Forest Service 2011e). Subsequent paragraphs examine several insect and disease agents in detail.

The Asian longhorned beetle (Fig. 23) is a vigorous, nonnative pest of maples (*Acer* spp.), birches (*Betula* spp.), elms (*Ulmus* spp.), and willows (*Salix* spp.); and it occasionally attacks ashes and poplars (*Populus* spp.). Given the prevalence of these tree species in northern forests and the many potential ports of entry through which the insect could be introduced via imported wooden pallets or shipping containers, the risk from Asian longhorned beetle is widespread (Bancroft and Smith 2001) (Fig. 23), especially for fragmented and stressed forests. Unrestrained infestation has the potential to dramatically alter forest composition, structure, and ecosystem function. The effectiveness of current Asian longhorned beetle quarantine efforts is still being evaluated.

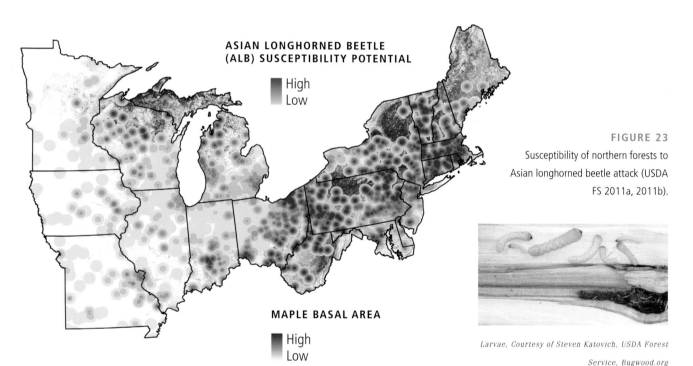

ASIAN LONGHORNED BEETLE (ALB) SUSCEPTIBILITY POTENTIAL

High
Low

MAPLE BASAL AREA

High
Low

FIGURE 23

Susceptibility of northern forests to Asian longhorned beetle attack (USDA FS 2011a, 2011b).

Larvae, Courtesy of Steven Katovich, USDA Forest Service, Bugwood.org

Susceptibility potential relates to introduction and establishment where:

Introduction potential relates to:

1. Commodities associated with ALB interceptions. Associated commodities include bricks, stones, metal, and glass materials shipped (with wood packing/pallets) from countries where ALB exists.

2. Polygon ZIP code centroids that represent businesses and personnel that import and handle the commodities of interest.

Establishment potential relates to:

Mean basal area for all maple (Acer spp.), the host species for ALB, assigned to ZIP code centroids created in the introduction component as well as 30 km buffers to include the cumulative distances that ALB could possibly disperse over a 15-year period at 2 km per year (Bancroft and Smith 2001).

Adult, Courtesy of Dennis Haugen, USDA Forest Service, Bugwood.org

The emerald ash borer is a nonnative bark-boring beetle that was discovered in southeastern Michigan in 2002 and has since killed tens of millions of ash trees in forests and along streets throughout the Northern States. Figure 24 shows the spatial distribution of the northern ash resource (USDA FS 2010b) and the risk of introduction and establishment (susceptibility) when defined as a geographic function of preferred host range, urban ash trees, proximity of urban ash trees to natural forests, and past rates of phloem insect interceptions at U.S. ports of entry.

With an estimated 15 billion cubic feet of ash volume, ash species represent 5 percent of the volume of all trees in northern forests,

Above Clockwise: 1) Second, third, and fourth stage larvae. 2) Purplish red abdomen on adult emerald ash borer. Photos courtesy of David Cappaert, Michigan State University, Bugwood.org

and all ashes are susceptible to EAB attack. Due to their relative abundance of ash trees, Minnesota, Ohio, and Pennsylvania face the potential for heavy mortality from emerald ash borers. The economic impact of losing ash species is significant. For example, Treiman et al. (2008) estimated that if emerald ash borers become established statewide, Missouri's economy would lose more than $6.7 million annually. The economic impact of losing ash

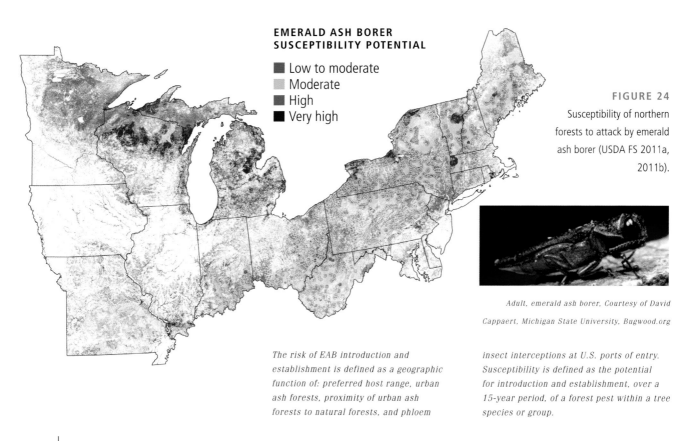

**EMERALD ASH BORER
SUSCEPTIBILITY POTENTIAL**

■ Low to moderate
■ Moderate
■ High
■ Very high

FIGURE 24

Susceptibility of northern forests to attack by emerald ash borer (USDA FS 2011a, 2011b).

Adult, emerald ash borer. Courtesy of David Cappaert, Michigan State University, Bugwood.org

The risk of EAB introduction and establishment is defined as a geographic function of: preferred host range, urban ash forests, proximity of urban ash forests to natural forests, and phloem

insect interceptions at U.S. ports of entry. Susceptibility is defined as the potential for introduction and establishment, over a 15-year period, of a forest pest within a tree species or group.

street trees is harder to estimate because the losses would include aesthetic values as well as the cost of removal and replacement, loss of property values, and impact on cooling costs. Again using Missouri as an example, Treiman et al. (2008) calculated a statewide cost of $20.3 million for street tree replacement.

In 2004, the Sirex woodwasp (*Sirex noctilio*) was discovered in a New York forest. It is an invasive insect that vigorously attacks weakened and dead pine trees. It has killed up to 80 percent of the plantations trees that it has attacked in the southern hemisphere, and

it threatens considerable forest land in the North where estimated susceptibility is based on forest species composition, density, and proximity to potential ports of entry (Fig. 25). Areas of forest along the eastern seaboard are particularly at risk (Haugen and Hoebeke 2005).

FIGURE 25

Susceptibility of northern forests to Sirex woodwasp. (USDA FS 2011a, 2011b).

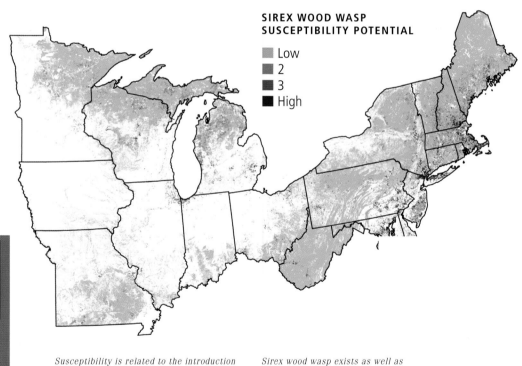

SIREX WOOD WASP SUSCEPTIBILITY POTENTIAL

- Low
- 2
- 3
- High

Susceptibility is related to the introduction and establishment potential where introduction potential is determined by the locations of the ports that handle commodities with solid wood packing materials shipped from countries where *Sirex wood wasp exists as well as distribution centers and markets. Establishment potential is determined by: pine basal area, presence of susceptible host, soil moisture index, and plant hardiness.*

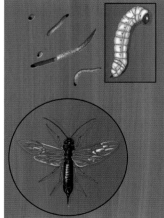

Adult, larva, and characteristic damage.
Courtesy of Robert Dzwonkow, Bugwood.org

The European gypsy moth (*Lymantria dispar*) continues to devastate North American forests. Introduced in 1868, the species has spread from Boston westward to Wisconsin and southward to Virginia (Figs. 26 and 27). Although gypsy moth larvae prefer hardwoods, they may feed on several hundred different species of trees and shrubs (McManus et al. 1989). In northern forests, larvae prefer oaks, apple (*Malus spp.*), sweetgum (*Liquidambar styraciflua*), alder (*Alnus* spp.), basswood (*Tilia* spp.), birches, poplar, willow, eastern larch (*Larix laricina*), and hawthorn (*Crataegus* spp.).

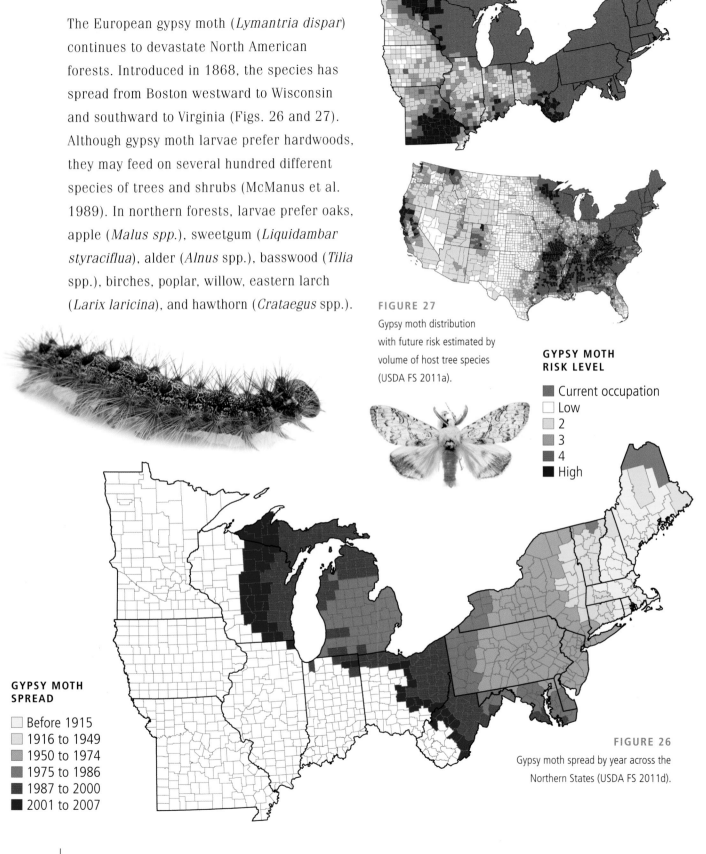

FIGURE 27

Gypsy moth distribution with future risk estimated by volume of host tree species (USDA FS 2011a).

GYPSY MOTH RISK LEVEL

◼ Current occupation
◻ Low
▨ 2
▨ 3
▨ 4
◼ High

GYPSY MOTH SPREAD

◻ Before 1915
◻ 1916 to 1949
▨ 1950 to 1974
▨ 1975 to 1986
◼ 1987 to 2000
◼ 2001 to 2007

FIGURE 26

Gypsy moth spread by year across the Northern States (USDA FS 2011d).

The list of hosts will likely expand as the insect spreads south and west. Although the invasion "front" experiences the most radical change in stand composition and tree mortality, outbreaks also recur in areas behind the front (Fig. 28). Intensive efforts to "slow the spread" through targeted treatment protocols have significantly reduced, but not stopped, the advance of this insect.

The hemlock wooly adelgid is a small aphid-like insect that feeds on the needles of eastern hemlocks (*Tsuga canadensis*) and Carolina hemlocks (*T. caroliniana*). Comprising 4 percent of all forest volume in northern forests, hemlocks fulfill critical roles within specific ecological niches (Godman and Lancaster 1990) such as provision of winter shelter and bedding for eastern white tailed deer (*Odocoileus virginianus*).

First discovered in Richmond, Virginia, the hemlock wooly adelgid has spread throughout the eastern United States since 1951 (Fig. 29), infesting anywhere from 25 percent (Morin et al. 2005) to 50 percent (USDA FS 2005) of the hemlock range. Young hemlock wooly adelgid nymphs (crawlers) can be spread by wind, on the feet of birds, or in the fur of small mammals (McClure 1990). Once settled, crawlers feed on stored starches in the twigs at the base of hemlock needles, quickly developing through the four nymph life stages and maturing in June. Hemlock decline and mortality typically occur within 4 to 10 years of infestation in the insect's northern range (3 to 6 years in its southern range). Hemlocks that are stressed by drought, poor site conditions, or attacks by other insects and diseases can decline and die more rapidly (USDA FS 2005).

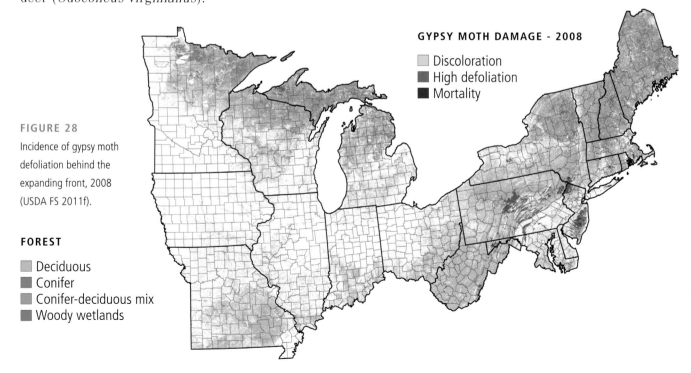

GYPSY MOTH DAMAGE - 2008

☐ Discoloration
■ High defoliation
■ Mortality

FIGURE 28
Incidence of gypsy moth defoliation behind the expanding front, 2008 (USDA FS 2011f).

FOREST

☐ Deciduous
■ Conifer
☐ Conifer-deciduous mix
■ Woody wetlands

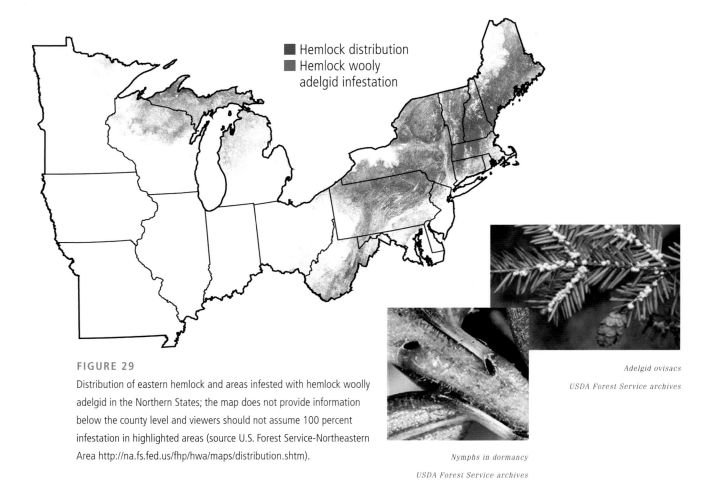

Hemlock distribution
Hemlock wooly adelgid infestation

FIGURE 29

Distribution of eastern hemlock and areas infested with hemlock woolly adelgid in the Northern States; the map does not provide information below the county level and viewers should not assume 100 percent infestation in highlighted areas (source U.S. Forest Service-Northeastern Area http://na.fs.fed.us/fhp/hwa/maps/distribution.shtm).

Adelgid ovisacs
USDA Forest Service archives

Nymphs in dormancy
USDA Forest Service archives

European spruce bark beetle (*Ips typographus*), a devastating killer of spruces, is probably capable of successfully invading any of the spruces indigenous to North America. Similar to indigenous bark beetle species, the spruce bark beetle would be extremely difficult to eradicate if it became established in North America. An outbreak in Germany after World War II resulted in a loss of more than 1 billion cubic feet of spruce. Subsequent attacks have devastated spruce forests in Norway, Sweden, Germany (again), and the Czech Republic. In addition to spruces, some species of fir, pine, and larch are known to be susceptible to spruce bark beetle

attacks. From 1985 to 2000, spruce bark beetles were intercepted 286 times in packing materials entering U.S. ports (Haack 2001) including Erie, PA (1993), Camden, NJ (1994) and Burns Harbor, IN (1995). This insect has a relatively high reproductive potential; because it breeds under the bark of host trees and is similar to several indigenous bark beetle species, infestations could go undetected for several years.

Substantial acreages of northern boreal forest are potentially susceptible to the European spruce bark beetle. Maine and Minnesota have a large spruce component, which could provide a large volume of suitable host material that would allow rapid spread in forests (Fig. 30) as well as yard and street tree plantings. Although not yet established in the United States, the European spruce bark beetle is considered a high-risk invasive species because of abundant host trees, host trees in proximity to ports of entry, and difficulty in controlling established populations. It has the potential to greatly exacerbate insect mortality in spruce-fir forests, which are already afflicted by periodic outbreaks of spruce budworm (*Choristoneura fumiferana*), that result in millions of cubic feet of lost timber with associated ecological and economic consequences.

Numerous other insects and diseases undermine the health, value, and diversity of northern forests. Some are well entrenched invasives: beech scale insect, chestnut blight, Dutch elm disease, and dogwood anthracnose. Thousand cankers disease of black walnut recently was found in Tennessee. Sudden oak death (*Phytophthora ramorum*) is a worrisome future possibility. Oak decline, hickory decline, oak tatters, tubakia leaf spot, and bacterial leaf scorch are other disease complexes of concern in northern forests.

FIGURE 30

Susceptibility of northern forests to European spruce bark beetle. The diagram shows an adult beetle, larvae, and the characteristic tree gallery (USDA FS 2011a, 2011f).

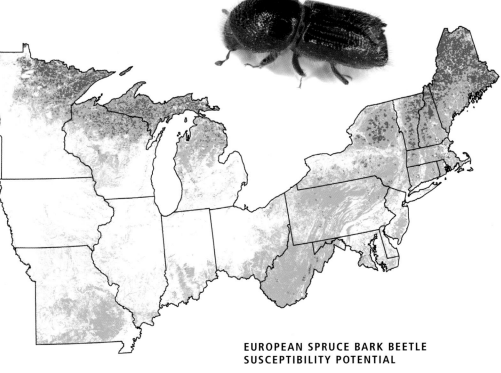

Courtesy of Robert Dzwonkow, Bugwood.org

Susceptibility potential relates to:
1. Establishment
2. Introduction

Establishment potential relates to:
1. Host species for European spruce bark beetle,
2. Disturbance factors (i.e., fires, lightening, winds tornadoes, avalanches, and hurricanes)
3. Urban forest

EUROPEAN SPRUCE BARK BEETLE SUSCEPTIBILITY POTENTIAL

Low to moderate
High

Introduction potential relates to: Ports that handle commodities and solid wood packing materials shipped from countries where European spruce bark beetle exists, distribution centers, and potential markets.

Criterion 4:

CONSERVATION AND MAINTENANCE OF SOIL AND WATER RESOURCES

Montréal Process Criterion 4 (Montréal Process Working Group 2010); Northern Area Forest Sustainability Indicators 8.1-8.5, 9.1-9.2 (USDA FS 2010d)

The importance of conservation and maintenance of soil and water resources

Soils

Soils are the fundamental resource enabling land to provide a wide array of benefits. Both humans and wildlife rely on soils for the production of life-sustaining nourishment and shelter. Soil is important to society because it supports plants that supply food, fibers, drugs, and other essentials and because it filters water and recycles wastes.

Broadly defined, soil is the natural medium for the growth of land plants, regardless of their size structure or species composition. Narrowly defined, soil is a natural body comprised of solids (minerals and organic matter), liquids, and gases that occurs on the land surface, occupies space, and has at least one of the following characteristics: (1) horizons (or

Key Findings for Criterion 4

- A potentially serious soils-related forest health threat is increasing soil acidity and associated decreasing soil calcium reserves along with increasing potentially toxic levels of exchangeable aluminum. This soil condition is strongly related to atmospheric acid deposition.
- Forests protect the soil both directly and indirectly from wind and water erosion. Wind erosion is rare in wooded areas, because they are protected by forest canopy, strong soil tree root anchor support, and forest floor mulch (tree litter).
- Soil compaction is not a widespread problem on forested lands and is largely confined to trails (walking, biking, hiking, equestrian, and motorized) and forest harvest operations.

- Across the North, 48 percent of the water supply originates on the forest lands that cover 42 percent of the region. About 94 percent of the water that originates from forests comes from State and private forest lands.
- Forests in the North have the capacity to supply about 280 billion m³ (226 million acre-feet) of water annually.
- The ability of a watershed to produce clean water increases with increasing proportion of forest cover.
- Many northern watersheds have water quality problems, especially near major metropolitan areas. Locations of concern include New Jersey, Delaware, and Ohio; and southern Illinois, Indiana, Michigan, Minnesota, and New Hampshire.

layers) that are distinguishable from the initial material and form a multiphase matrix resulting from additions, losses, transfers, and transformations of energy and matter; (2) the ability to support rooted plants in a natural environment (USDA NRCS 2010). The relative proportions of minerals, organic matter, water, and air largely determines the ability of the soil to support plant life (O'Neill et al. 2005).

Soil classification is based on soil properties observed in the field, inferred from field observations, or measured in a laboratory (USDA NRCS 2006). The general soil association units that occur in repeatable patterns on the landscape are mapped from broad-based soil inventories (USDA NRCS 2010). Figure 31 shows the distribution of the principal soil kinds in the North and the contiguous United States as classified and developed by the National Cooperative Soil Survey.

FIGURE 31

General soil map for the Northern States and the conterminous United States (USDA NRCS 2011).

Soil quality refers to the capacity of a soil to sustain biological productivity, maintain environmental quality, and promote plant and animal health (Doran and Parkin 1994). Concise definitions for soil quality include "fitness for use" and "the capacity of a soil to function." Combining these, soil quality is the ability of a soil to perform the functions necessary for its intended use. Soil functions include sustaining biological diversity, activity, and productivity; regulating water and solute flow; filtering, buffering, and degrading organic and inorganic materials; storing and cycling nutrients and carbon; and providing physical stability and support (Kuykendall 2008). Soil quality and land management both have a direct influence on water and atmospheric quality and, by extension, human and animal health (Doran and Parkin 1994, Kennedy and Papendick 1995).

Soil quality information helps answer several key questions about: (1) the productivity and sustainability of forest systems, (2) the conservation of soil and water resources, (3) the accumulation of persistent toxic substances, and (4) the contribution of forested systems to the global carbon cycle (O'Neill et al. 2005). For forestry as well as agriculture, maintenance of site productivity is vital to sustainable management.

Water

The factors that affect water quality and supply in forest ecosystems include climate and hydrology, catchment geology, natural disturbances, land management, and actual land-use activities. Water quality in undisturbed forested catchments can provide important baseline references for monitoring physical, chemical, or biological trends in catchments that have varying levels of land use, and can identify management activities that need to be altered to preserve water quality (USDA FS 2009a). The quality and quantity of runoff have long been a focus of forest management, which can have beneficial as well as detrimental effects, depending on the objectives, timing, techniques, and size of operations.

Much of the North's highest quality water supplies originate in forests (Brown and Binkley 1994). Forested watersheds provide

water purification, mitigation of floods and droughts, soil retention, and habitat maintenance. Surface water runoff in forest environments is rare with most rainfall and snowmelt moving into streams through subsurface flows, accelerating nutrient uptake, cycling, and contaminant absorption processes. The quality and abundance of fresh water in lakes, wetlands, streams, and rivers determine aquatic and terrestrial species biodiversity.

Forests are crucial to the protection of drinking water (Barnes et al. 2009). Managing forests for clean water production will grow in importance as the northern populations and water demand both increase. The water resource is also one of the many attractions for swimming, boating, canoeing, fishing, and other water-based activities. The enjoyment of these activities depends directly on the quality of the water resource. In addition, aquatic as well as terrestrial wildlife species depend on the water resource.

The North is characterized by a cool-moist-temperate climate, associated with the Lake States and higher elevations of the eastern Continental Divide. Although seasonally variable, these conditions produce large volumes of fresh water that support production of forest vegetation, provide water-based recreation opportunities, and supply the region's drinking water. Northern landscapes support the headwaters of most major eastern rivers, including the Mississippi. In the lower 48 States, although highlands and mountains constitute a relatively small land area proportion, they serve as "water towers" with water supplies originating at the tops of watersheds.

Water supplies and their uses are affected by population growth, economic trends, legal decisions, and climatic extremes such as droughts. Water is in effect a finite resource because few approaches for dramatically augmenting current water supplies are ecologically or economically viable (Barnes et al. 2009). While water shortages and restrictions are regular news in the West, they also occur in the North, particularly in urban areas. In addition to drought, the primary threat to water supplies in the North is loss of forest to development, agriculture, or other land uses.

As private lands continue to be developed, public and other protected forest lands will become more important as sources of high quality water.

Indicators of soil and water resource conservation for northern forests

Soil quality

Some disturbances and management practices can degrade forest ecosystem health and productivity by changing soil chemical or physical properties. As part of its Forest Inventory and Analysis plot network the Forest Service implements a national forest-soil monitoring program to address specific questions about the long-term sustainability of the Nation's forest soil resources (USDA FS 2011g). Although many soil and water metrics are available to gauge forest health (O'Neill et al. 2005), the focus here for northern forests is on chemical changes, compaction, and erosion.

Figure 32 shows the spatial distribution of calcium to aluminum (Ca:Al) molar ratios in northern forests. The map serves as a coarse filter for anticipating soils-related threats to forest health, one of which is increasing acidity in association with a decreasing Ca:Al ratio (indicating smaller calcium reserves and potentially toxic levels of exchangeable aluminum). This soil condition is strongly related to atmospheric acid deposition. Nutrient-poor and acidic forest soil conditions are found throughout the United States, but highly acidic soils with low calcium and high aluminum levels are concentrated in the Northeastern States and southward along the Appalachian Mountains. A continued decrease in the Ca:Al ratio could put calcium-sensitive tree species at risk of decline and die-off, with other site-specific factors influencing the outcome at any given location. Forests on soils with a low Ca:Al ratio may be

CALCIUM : ALUMINUM RATIO

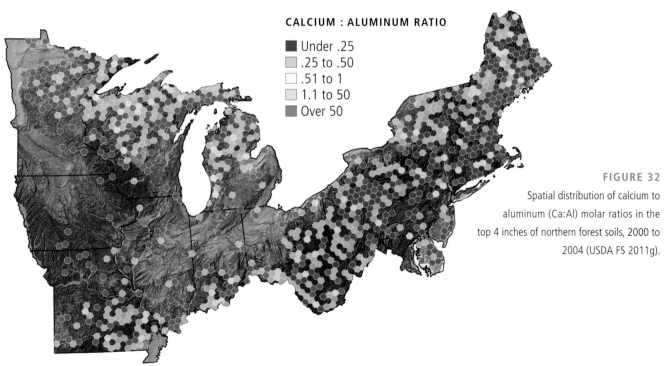

■ Under .25
▨ .25 to .50
□ .51 to 1
▨ 1.1 to 50
▨ Over 50

FIGURE 32

Spatial distribution of calcium to aluminum (Ca:Al) molar ratios in the top 4 inches of northern forest soils, 2000 to 2004 (USDA FS 2011g).

more susceptible to damage from additional stressors such as industrial inputs, drought, insects, and diseases (Cronan and Grigal 1995).

Forests protect the soil both directly and indirectly from wind and water erosion. Sites with exposed soil are at highest risk of accelerated soil erosion, but they represent only a small fraction of all forested lands. Although most forest inventory plots have at least some bare soil, few (0.4 to 5.5 percent) have more than 50-percent bare soil. Estimates of bare soil as a percentage of the forest floor provide an indirect measure of potential soil erosion, which reduces soil fertility, has offsite impacts, and decreases land values. Wind-caused erosion is rare in wooded areas, which are protected by forest canopy, strong soil tree root anchor support, and forest floor mulch (tree litter).

Soil compaction reduces pore space and decreases the volume of air in the soil. Compaction occurs when the mineral portion of the soil becomes compressed by heavy equipment or by repeated passes of light equipment, people, or animals. Only 0.3 to 4.7 percent of observed forest monitoring plots show evidence of compaction on more than half the plot area (Fig. 33). Thus, soil compaction is not so much a widespread problem on forested lands as it is a seemingly localized phenomenon that is largely confined to trails (walking, biking, hiking, equestrian, and motorized) and forest harvest operations (USDA FS 2011g).

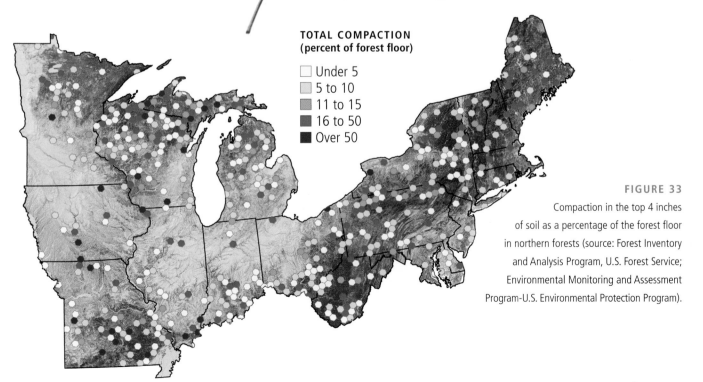

TOTAL COMPACTION
(percent of forest floor)

☐ Under 5
☐ 5 to 10
☐ 11 to 15
■ 16 to 50
■ Over 50

FIGURE 33

Compaction in the top 4 inches of soil as a percentage of the forest floor in northern forests (source: Forest Inventory and Analysis Program, U.S. Forest Service; Environmental Monitoring and Assessment Program-U.S. Environmental Protection Program).

Autumn colors surround
the Glade Creek Grist Mill in West Virginia

Compaction can have a variety of negative effects on soil fertility. Reduction in pore space makes the soil more dense and difficult to penetrate, and can constrain the size, reach, and extent of root systems; this can lead to structural failure of plants and destabilization of entire trees. Reduction in soil aeration and movement of fluids can reduce the ability of roots to absorb water, nutrients, and oxygen, thus resulting in shallow rooting and stunted tree forms. At the landscape scale, destruction of soil structure can limit water infiltration, resulting in increased runoff and of soil loss from erosion. In addition to changes in soil physical properties, compaction can also significantly impact biological and chemical processes occurring in the soil. For example, by reducing the oxygen content below what is required for adequate respiration, severe compaction can disrupt root metabolism and move the soil toward an anaerobic condition (O'Neill et al. 2005).

FIGURE 34

Yearly average water supply (precipitation minus evapotranspiration) by counties in the (A) Northern States and (B) conterminous United States (Brown et al. 2008).

Water supply and quality

Brown et al. (2008) have estimated annual water supply (precipitation minus evapotranspiration) for the conterminous United States (Fig. 34). The areas of largest water supply in the North are associated with dense forest cover (compare Fig. 34 with Figs. 1 and 4), particularly in the highlands and mountains that serve as natural water towers

An estimated 48 percent of the northern water supply originates on forest lands (Table 7), which cover 42 percent of the region's surface area. Approximately 6 percent of the northern water supply originates on Federal forest land, including 5 percent on national forests and national grasslands. The remaining 94 percent of the water supply from northern forests originates on State and private lands (Table 8), compared to 65 percent for western forests. Public forest lands dominate in the West, where 66 percent of forests are in Federal ownership and 51 percent are national forests and national grasslands.

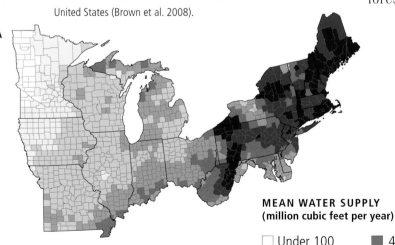

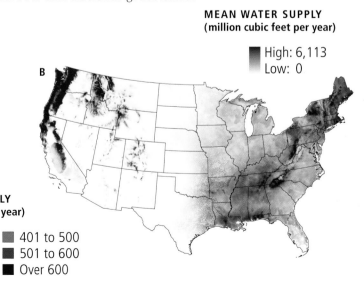

MEAN WATER SUPPLY
(million cubic feet per year)

High: 6,113
Low: 0

MEAN WATER SUPPLY
(million cubic feet per year)

☐ Under 100   401 to 500
☐ 100 to 200   501 to 600
☐ 201 to 300   Over 600
☐ 301 to 400

Table 7—Annual water supply in the conterminous United States by land cover class, region, and State (Brown et al. 2008). Proportions by column are given for regions and U.S. totals. Note that 1 million cubic meters of water is equivalent to approximately 811 acre-feet or 264 million gallons.

State and region	Forest	Rangeland	Agriculture	Water-wetland	Other	Total
			(million cubic meters)			
Connecticut	4,466	0	766	771	1,691	7,694
District of Columbia	18	0	0	0	63	81
Delaware	529	0	976	377	106	1,988
Iowa	2,393	1,772	25,327	863	945	31,300
Illinois	5,691	326	29,864	2,005	2,184	40,070
Indiana	6,442	135	22,887	999	1,273	31,736
Massachusetts	7,375	16	643	1,508	2,546	12,088
Maryland	4,087	0	3,732	971	829	9,619
Maine	40,569	291	2,411	5,318	2,281	50,870
Michigan	19,776	1,004	14,723	9,701	1,681	46,885
Minnesota	6,346	203	12,477	7,995	805	27,826
Missouri	14,842	209	31,852	2,274	1,542	50,719
New Hampshire	12,072	0	768	1,107	735	14,682
New Jersey	4,214	0	1,852	1,383	2,226	9,675
New York	43,133	0	14,240	3,944	3,754	65,071
Ohio	12,748	8	20,691	1,082	2,214	36,743
Pennsylvania	41,310	0	15,707	1,107	3,237	61,361
Rhode Island	1,198	0	53	242	345	1,838
Vermont	10,203	13	1,799	773	374	13,162
Wisconsin	14,760	155	15,944	4,659	889	36,407
West Virginia	26,548	0	3,639	195	700	31,082
North total	278,720	4,132	220,351	47,274	30,420	580,897
Proportion of North (percent)	48	1	38	8	5	100
Alabama	47,321	0	14,545	5,538	3,010	70,414
Arkansas	27,245	69	24,148	6,119	1,303	58,884
Florida	15,094	3,947	7,124	12,822	5,481	44,468
Georgia	35,955	116	13,252	6,133	4,472	59,928
Kentucky	29,720	0	16,728	1,613	1,323	49,384
Louisiana	18,217	278	17,182	17,506	2,434	55,617

Table 7 continued

State and region	Forest	Rangeland	Agriculture	Water-wetland	Other	Total
			(million cubic meters)			
Mississippi	32,512	10	21,885	8,506	2,320	65,233
North Carolina	34,087	0	11,540	6,122	2,580	54,329
Oklahoma	6,388	5,887	9,429	1,361	704	23,769
South Carolina	15,671	0	6,336	4,275	2,041	28,323
Tennessee	38,059	0	18,392	2,663	2,695	61,809
Texas	13,023	8,945	24,202	6,101	3,758	56,029
Virginia	25,743	0	8,817	1,876	1,719	38,155
South total	339,035	19,252	193,580	80,635	33,840	666,342
Proportion of South (percent)	51	3	29	12	5	100
East total (North and South)	617,755	23,384	413,931	127,909	64,260	1,247,239
Proportion of East (percent)	50	2	33	10	5	100
California	53,574	28,587	6,664	784	3,438	93,047
Oregon	78,293	7,899	6,679	977	3,931	97,779
Washington	87,885	7,695	3,032	2,898	11,641	113,151
Pacific Coast total	219,752	44,181	16,375	4,659	19,010	303,977
Proportion of Pacific Coast (percent)	72	15	5	2	6	100
Arizona	1,927	2,734	5	5	37	4,708
Colorado	9,453	11,301	508	224	1,073	22,559
Idaho	38,182	15,756	3,506	863	2,758	61,065
Kansas	378	5,283	9,834	579	390	16,464
Montana	27,805	15,167	2,509	546	2,593	48,620
North Dakota	9	951	2,899	200	30	4,089
Nebraska	16	3,769	7,178	366	171	11,500
New Mexico	2,537	2,826	74	11	38	5,486
Nevada	998	4,582	34	35	149	5,798
South Dakota	51	923	3,736	266	40	5,016
Utah	4,261	5,061	178	111	325	9,936
Wyoming	8,077	10,009	391	730	2,017	21,224
Interior West total	93,694	78,362	30,852	3,936	9,621	216,465
Proportion of Interior West (percent)	43	36	14	2	4	100
West total (Pacific and Interior)	313,446	122,543	47,227	8,595	28,631	520,442
Proportion of West (percent)	60	24	9	2	5	100
Conterminous U.S. total	931,201	145,927	461,158	136,504	92,891	1,767,681
Proportion of Conterminous U.S. (percent)	53	8	26	8	5	100

Table 8—Annual water supply in the conterminous United States by ownership, region, and State (Brown et al 2008). Proportions by column are given for regions and U.S. totals. Note that 1 million cubic meters of water is equivalent to approximately 811 acre feet or 264 million gallons.

State and Region	National Forest System	Bureau of Land Management	National Park Service	Bureau of Indian Affairs	Other Federal	State and Private	Total
			(million cubic meters)				
Connecticut	0	0	0	0	10	7,683	7,694
District of Columbia	0	0	6	0	3	72	81
Delaware	0	0	0	0	39	1,950	1,989
Iowa	0	0	1	4	153	31,141	31,299
Illinois	1,451	0	0	0	272	38,347	40,070
Indiana	1,005	0	9	0	378	30,345	31,737
Massachusetts	2	0	22	0	142	11,922	12,088
Maryland	0	0	80	0	146	9,393	9,619
Maine	199	0	65	79	184	50,343	50,870
Michigan	6,569	0	76	289	392	39,560	46,886
Minnesota	2,505	0	173	1,145	164	23,839	27,826
Missouri	3,490	0	130	0	458	46,642	50,720
New Hampshire	2,715	0	0	0	35	11,932	14,682
New Jersey	0	0	93	0	240	9,343	9,676
New York	30	0	15	164	420	64,441	65,070
Ohio	1,432	0	50	0	132	35,130	36,744
Pennsylvania	1,783	0	84	0	245	59,249	61,361
Rhode Island	0	0	0	0	10	1,828	1,838
Vermont	1,915	0	0	0	97	11,150	13,162
Wisconsin	2,177	0	85	668	220	33,257	36,407
West Virginia	4,990	0	132	0	136	25,824	31,082
North total	30,263	0	1,021	2,349	3,876	543,391	580,900
Proportion of North (percent)	5	0	0	0	1	94	100
Alabama	2,852	0	45	0	902	66,615	70,414
Arkansas	6,170	0	128	0	1,263	51,323	58,884
Florida	2,149	0	303	103	1,982	39,930	44,467
Georgia	5,329	0	53	0	1,676	52,870	59,928
Kentucky	4,183	0	204	0	874	44,123	49,384
Louisiana	1,713	0	38	1	1,379	52,485	55,616
Mississippi	5,303	0	7	35	828	59,060	65,233
North Carolina	8,825	0	1,031	170	1,180	43,123	54,329

Table 8 continued

State and Region	National Forest System	Bureau of Land Management	National Park Service	Bureau of Indian Affairs	Other Federal	State and Private	Total
	---------------------------------------(million cubic meters)---------------------------------------						
Oklahoma	714	0	7	864	866	21,318	23,769
South Carolina	2,034	0	34	0	621	25,634	28,323
Tennessee	2,949	0	1,036	0	1,864	55,960	61,809
Texas	2,373	0	157	3	1,000	52,496	56,029
Virginia	5,398	0	517	0	567	31,673	38,155
South total	49,992	0	3,560	1,176	15,002	596,610	666,340
Proportion of South (percent)	8	0	1	0	2	90	100
East total (North and South)	80,255	0	4,581	3,525	18,878	1,140,001	1,247,240
Proportion of East (percent)	6	0	1	0	2	91	100
California	43,317	5,096	5,878	978	1,568	36,210	93,047
Oregon	43,016	9,212	474	1,049	302	43,727	97,780
Washington	46,950	42	15,963	2,891	2,227	45,080	113,153
Pacific Coast total	133,283	14,350	22,315	4,918	4,097	125,017	303,980
Proportion of Pacific Coast (percent)	44	5	7	2	1	41	1.00
Arizona	2,517	213	93	949	35	902	4,709
Colorado	15,384	1,509	478	107	75	5,006	22,559
Idaho	41,372	3,498	131	1,755	297	14,011	61,064
Kansas	0	0	7	92	218	16,147	16,464
Montana	29,805	1,084	4,057	2,855	234	10,584	48,619
North Dakota	84	1	3	78	51	3,871	4,088
Nebraska	47	0	8	155	51	11,239	11,500
New Mexico	2,468	286	11	365	70	2,287	5,487
Nevada	2,159	2,698	71	46	243	581	5,798
South Dakota	146	2	12	502	26	4,328	5,016
Utah	6,903	801	34	133	27	2,040	9,938
Wyoming	11,270	1,578	4,542	539	127	3,168	21,224
Interior West total	112,155	11,670	9,447	7,576	1,454	74,164	216,466
Proportion of Interior West (percent)	52	5	4	3	2	34	100
West total (Pacific and Interior)	245,438	26,020	31,762	12,494	5,551	199,181	520,446
Proportion of West (percent)	47	5	6	2	1	38	100
Conterminous U.S. total	325,693	26,020	36,343	16,019	24,429	1,339,182	1,767,686
Proportion of conterminous U.S. (percent)	18	1	2	1	1	76	100

More than 52 million people and nearly 1,600 community water systems utilize surface water for municipal drinking water (Barnes et al. 2009). These water supplies are protected largely by private forest lands. Figure 35 illustrates the relative capacity of northern watersheds to produce clean water in juxtaposition to locations of private and public forests.

Many people are unaware of the threats and vulnerabilities to their water, or the connection between clean water and the extent and condition of the forests at the source of their water supplies (Barnes et al. 2009). Figure 36 displays an index of watershed indicators (US EPA 1996b, 2002) that characterizes the condition, vulnerability, and data sufficiency of the aquatic systems in each of 2,111 watersheds in the lower 48 United States. It provides a summary measure of overall watershed health based on 18 indicator variables (US EPA 2010), with three watershed condition scores (better water quality, water quality with less serious problems, and water quality with more serious problems), and two vulnerability scores (high and low).

About 23 percent of the 540 northern watersheds experienced more serious water quality problems with low vulnerability, 35 percent experienced less serious water quality problems with low vulnerability, and

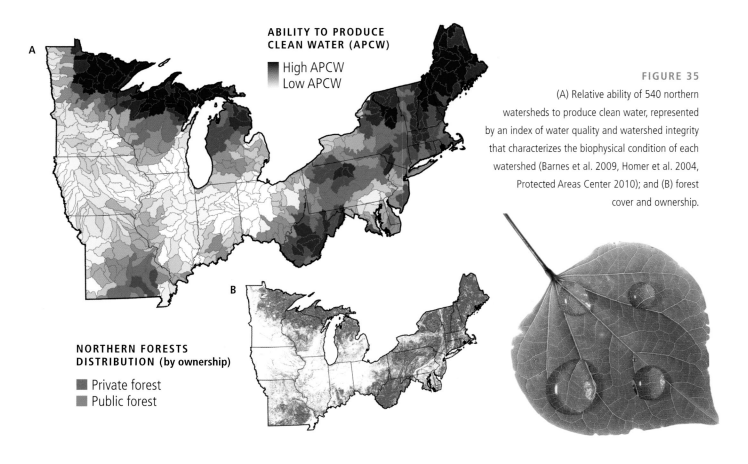

ABILITY TO PRODUCE CLEAN WATER (APCW)

High APCW
Low APCW

NORTHERN FORESTS DISTRIBUTION (by ownership)

Private forest
Public forest

FIGURE 35

(A) Relative ability of 540 northern watersheds to produce clean water, represented by an index of water quality and watershed integrity that characterizes the biophysical condition of each watershed (Barnes et al. 2009, Homer et al. 2004, Protected Areas Center 2010); and (B) forest cover and ownership.

15 percent experienced better water quality with low vulnerability. Only 1.5 percent of the watersheds experienced better water conditions with high vulnerability. About 3 percent experienced less serious water quality problems with high vulnerability, and about 2 percent experienced more serious water quality problems with high vulnerability. Therefore, as the map illustrates, large areas of the northern watersheds may have potential water quality (as well as supply) problems. Some potential problem areas are in southern Illinois, Michigan, Minnesota, Indiana, New Hampshire; and Delaware, New Jersey, and Ohio.

One in 15 U.S. watersheds is highly vulnerable to further degradation (US EPA 2002). The following national indicators are similar to those of northern watersheds:

- Fifteen percent have relatively good water quality
- Thirty-six percent have moderate water quality problems
- Twenty-two percent have more serious water quality problems
- Twenty-seven percent do not have enough information to be characterized

The future abundance and quality of water supplies will not be ensured by a focus on water treatment alone. Protecting and managing forests in source watersheds is essential for providing clean, safe water (Barnes et al. 2009).

FIGURE 36

Watershed characterization—condition, vulnerability, and data sufficiency—in 1999 for (A) Northern States and (B) conterminous United States. Note that the strength of monitoring programs vary—areas with strong monitoring programs may show more problems than those with weaker programs (US EPA 2011).

NATIONAL WATERSHED CHARACTERIZATION - 1999

- More serious water quality problems - high vulnerability
- More serious water quality problems - low vulnerability
- Less serious water quality problems - high vulnerability
- Less serious water quality problems - low vulnerability
- Better water quality problems - high vulnerability
- Better water quality problems - low vulnerability
- Insufficient data

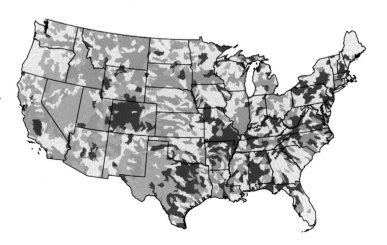

Criterion 5:

MAINTENANCE OF FOREST CONTRIBUTIONS TO GLOBAL CARBON CYCLES

Montréal Process Criterion 5 (Montréal Process Working Group 2010); Northern Area Forest Sustainability Indicators 11.1, 11.2, 11.3, 11.4 (USDA FS 2010d)

The importance of forest contributions to global carbon cycles

Northern forests cover more than 42 percent of the region and are enormous reservoirs of carbon. Through photosynthesis, live trees emit oxygen in exchange for carbon dioxide they pull from the atmosphere. As a tree grows it stores carbon in wood above and below ground, and sequestered carbon comprises about half of its dry weight. Dead trees and down logs are also reservoirs of carbon. Forest soils sequester additional carbon in the form of incorporated organic matter. In temperate northern forest ecosystems, roughly as much carbon is sequestered in forest soils as is sequestered as live biomass. Forests that are converted to other land uses release the carbon stored in the trees. Trees growing in newly established forests (afforestation) can sequester additional carbon.

People and forests are closely linked through the carbon cycle. Human activities emit huge amounts of carbon dioxide during energy production, transportation, and other activities. Increases in atmospheric carbon dioxide have been linked to global warming. Because of their great extent and their capacity to sequester additional carbon or release carbon that is already sequestered, forests have an important role as sinks or sources of carbon in regional and global carbon cycles.

Global climate change associated with changes in atmospheric carbon dioxide levels could significantly impact the future conditions of forests, which would in turn affect the plants, wildlife, and people that depend on them. Maintenance of forest biodiversity and health are associated concerns.

Some forest management activities can increase carbon sequestration or offset human activities that emit carbon. Silvicultural practices that increase forest growth can increase the quantity of carbon sequestered in woody biomass. Wood product utilization can increase the quantity of carbon sequestered in durable wood products. Wood-based energy production can offset carbon that would otherwise be released by burning fossil fuels provided the carbon released during woody bioenergy production is reincorporated into new trees that replace those harvested for bioenergy. In contrast, energy generated from fossil fuels, such as coal and oil, emits carbon that has been sequestered underground for eons.

Key Findings for Criterion 5

- Through photosynthesis, trees pull carbon dioxide, a greenhouse gas, from the atmosphere and sequester it in wood and other tree parts.
- Forests sequester large amounts of carbon in soil organic matter and in the wood of living trees. As forests grow over time the amount of sequestered carbon increases.
- The total amount of sequestered carbon in U.S. forests is equal to approximately 27 years of carbon dioxide emissions for the U.S.
- The annual net increase in carbon sequestered in U.S. forests due to tree growth is equivalent to about 10 percent of the annual emissions of carbon dioxide and associated greenhouse gasses.
- When trees are harvested and converted to wood products, the carbon in those products remains sequestered until they eventually decompose or are burned.
- Using woody biomass to replace fossil fuels for energy production can reduce the release of carbon from the fossil fuels that would be used instead.
- In 2007, the equivalent of 2 percent of the energy consumed in the United States came from wood combustion by industrial (1.3 percent), residential (0.4 percent), utility (0.2 percent), and other (0.1 percent) users.
- Less than 1 percent of U.S. electric power is generated from wood.

Carbon and Wood

A cubic foot of wood in a living oak tree weighs about 60 pounds (green weight)—roughly half composed of water and the other half composed of dry woody biomass, about 15 pounds of which is carbon (half of the dry weight or a quarter of the green weight). Carbon is found in cellulose, hemi-cellulose, lignin, and other compounds that form the wood and other parts of the tree. Woody biomass may be reported in dry tons or in green tons, and carbon is more often reported as equivalent tons of carbon dioxide than as elemental carbon—distinctions that are important when interpreting and comparing biomass and carbon statistics.

When trees grow they absorb carbon from the atmosphere in the form of carbon dioxide. Through photosynthesis trees sequester the carbon in wood, bark, leaves, flowers, roots, and seeds. When a tree or some part of a tree dies, the carbon it contains is released during decomposition. Carbon in decomposing roots may remain in the soil and gradually add to the large store of sequestered carbon in soils. Leaves are short-lived and release carbon back to the atmosphere quickly as they decompose. Carbon may be sequestered for centuries in the wood of living trees. Large dead and down trees may sequester carbon for decades as they decompose slowly and gradually release carbon dioxide back to the atmosphere.

Each year, per capita emissions in the United States—largely due to combustion of fossil fuels—produce 6 tons of carbon or the equivalent of 22 tons of carbon dioxide (USDOE 2009, USDA FS 2011e). That is the amount of carbon in about 800 cubic feet of wood (roughly 10 cords). Stacked as firewood it would equal a wood pile 4 feet high, 4 feet deep, and 80 feet long.

The amount of carbon that U.S. forests sequester each year is about 10 percent of total annual U.S. emissions of carbon dioxide and related greenhouse gasses.

The passages below report on the total quantity of carbon stored in forests, how forest carbon changes over time, the role of forest products in carbon sequestration, and the capacity to avoid carbon emissions from fossil fuels by using woody biomass for energy production. For consistency with other sections of this assessment, we report carbon in U.S. tons (2000 pounds) and acres or provide metric equivalencies to help link reported values to other sources, which—by convention—report carbon in metric units (2204 pounds or 1000 kg) and hectares (2.5 acres).

Indicators of forest contributions to global carbon cycles for northern forests

Carbon sequestered in northern forests
The two largest pools of sequestered carbon in a typical forest are in soil organic matter and in aboveground biomass (Fig. 37). Soil carbon changes slowly compared to aboveground biomass, which increases with forest growth and decreases with mortality or harvesting. Dead wood, litter on the forest floor, and tree roots are other large reservoirs of forest carbon.

The amount of carbon sequestered above ground in a forest is closely associated with wood volume or biomass. In general, more sequestered carbon occurs where more wood volume occurs (Fig. 19). However, inventorying carbon is more complicated than merely measuring aboveground forest volume because of the high proportion of carbon in soils, tree roots, and dead wood and because harvested forest products move sequestered carbon to other locations.

FIGURE 37

When and where carbon occurs in a typical forest—a composite summary for all northern forests showing average carbon by forest age and forest component; note that about 16 percent of live tree carbon is coarse roots (VanDuesen and Heath 2009).

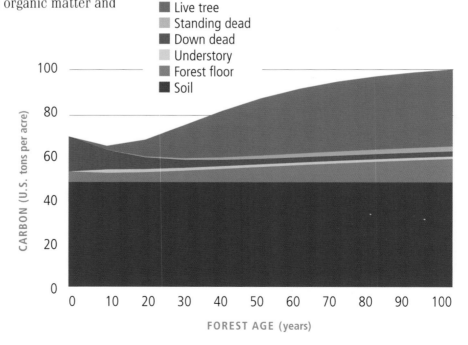

Much of the carbon sequestered in U.S. forests is in Northern States (Fig. 38). This amount can increase over time as trees grow (above and below ground) and hold more carbon, or decrease as trees die or are harvested. As dead trees and down wood slowly decay, they release carbon gradually back into the atmosphere as carbon dioxide; if burned, they release carbon quickly. The total amount of sequestered carbon in U.S. forests is equivalent to about 27 years of carbon dioxide emissions for the United States (USDA FS 2011e). The annual increase in sequestered U.S. carbon from net annual forest growth is about 10 percent of U.S. annual greenhouse-gas emissions. Appendix Table A3 provides additional state-level detail on forest biomass and carbon.

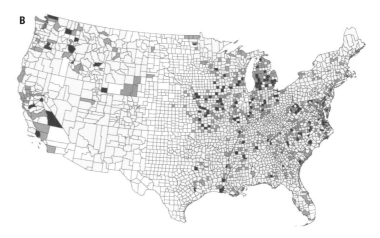

FIGURE 38

In 2006, (A) aboveground live tree biomass for Northern States (Blackard et al. 2008), and (B) estimated change in live tree carbon stock by U.S. county, accounting for harvest, land-use change and changes in live tree biomass of coarse roots, stems, branches, and foliage (Smith et al. 2009). In this case carbon change is reported as the equivalent mass in tons of carbon dioxide (CO_2) rather than carbon per se. One megagram (or metric ton) per hectare is equivalent 0.45 U.S. tons per acre.

CHANGES IN LIVE-TREE CARBON (tons per acre per year)

- ■ More than 4.5   Sequestration
- ▨ 2.2 to 4.5
- ☐ Little to no change
- ▨ 2.2 to 4.5   Emission
- ■ More than 4.5
- ☐ Less than 5 percent forest land or no data

BIOMASS (tons per acre)

- ■ High 527
- Low 0

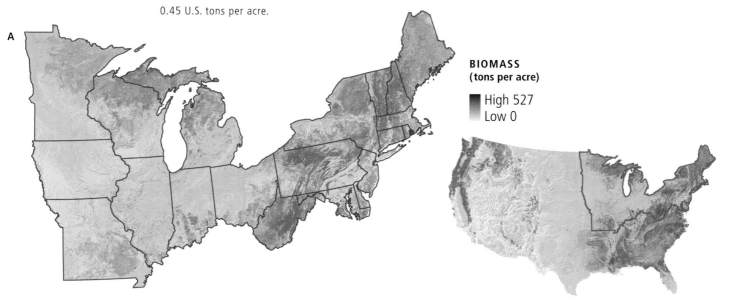

Carbon Sequestered in Forest Products

When trees are harvested and converted to wood products, the carbon in those products remains sequestered until they decompose or are burned. Consequently, paper products typically sequester carbon for shorter periods than wood products such as building materials, flooring, or furniture. Even landfills sequester carbon in the form of discarded wood and paper products that decompose slowly because of compaction and lack of oxygen in the layers of landfill waste material. With the current mix of harvested materials and associate forest products, carbon in wood products from northern forests persists for a relatively long time.

Using Woody Biomass for Energy

The use of fossil fuels to produce energy releases carbon dioxide that was previously sequestered underground as coal, oil, or gas. By using woody biomass instead, society can reduce carbon from fossil fuels. Carbon that is already sequestered in the ground stays there (Malmsheimer et al. 2008) while carbon in woody biomass that is consumed for energy is released to the atmosphere instead. When forests harvested for biomass regenerate and grow, carbon is again sequestered in the wood growing on the regenerated forest. Thus, some carbon from using biomass for energy is cycled from the forest to the atmosphere and gradually back to the forest.

In 2007, about 2 percent of all U.S. energy consumption came from wood combustion by industrial (1.3 percent), residential (0.4 percent), utility (0.2 percent), and other (0.1 percent) users. Electric utilities throughout the North use wood for part of their energy production (Fig. 39), but less than 1 percent of U.S. electric power is generated with wood (USDOE EIA 2010).

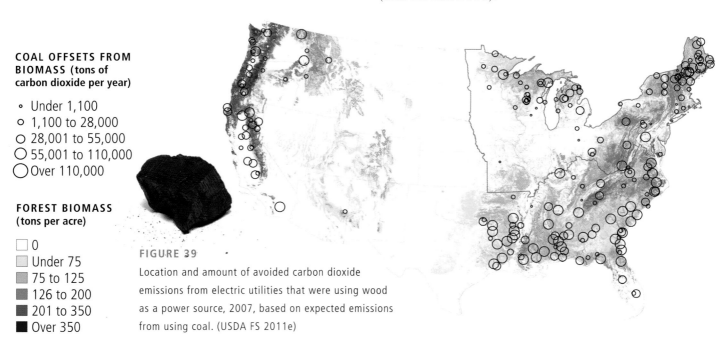

COAL OFFSETS FROM BIOMASS (tons of carbon dioxide per year)

- Under 1,100
- 1,100 to 28,000
- 28,001 to 55,000
- 55,001 to 110,000
- Over 110,000

FOREST BIOMASS (tons per acre)

- 0
- Under 75
- 75 to 125
- 126 to 200
- 201 to 350
- Over 350

FIGURE 39

Location and amount of avoided carbon dioxide emissions from electric utilities that were using wood as a power source, 2007, based on expected emissions from using coal. (USDA FS 2011e)

Criterion 6:

MAINTENANCE AND ENHANCEMENT OF LONG-TERM MULTIPLE SOCIOECONOMIC BENEFITS TO MEET THE NEEDS OF SOCIETIES

Montréal Process Criterion 6 (Montréal Process Working Group 2010); Northern Area Forest Sustainability Indicators 12.1-12.5, 13.1-13.6, 14.1-14.5, 15.1–15.6, 16.1–16.5 (USDA FS 2010d)

The importance of long-term multiple socioeconomic benefits from forests

Forests provide an array of products and services that maintain and enhance benefits to our society and economy. Benefits derived from forests may be categorized into wood products, nontimber products and services, and ecosystem services. The value and volume of these products and services indicate the importance of forests for a wide variety of uses. Tracking

Key Findings for Criterion 6

- Estimated per capita consumption of wood products in the Northern States is 71 cubic feet. A growing population will increase total demand for wood products.
- Northern forests are a major source of wood products, but imports are expected to continue to supply a sizeable amount that is consumed.
- The largest forest products groups are hardwood, saw logs, and pulpwood.
- Most harvested wood is from hardwood species.
- Primary wood products manufacturing in the North had an estimated added value to the economy of $52 billion or 41 percent of the $124 billion value added nationally in this sector.
- From 2002 to 2006 investment in wood products manufacturing increased while investment in pulp and paper production declined.
- In the Northern States 441,000 workers are employed in forest management, logging, forest products, and pulp and paper industries. This is about 40 percent of the 1.1 million employees nationally in these industries.

- Wages for forestry jobs vary with large differences among States, but the average wage for the region is close to the national average.
- The number of injury cases recorded by the forestry and logging, wood product manufacturing, and pulp and paper industries has declined in recent years.
- Logging is the most risky forestry job. The fatality rate in the Northern States is close to the national average.
- Common nontimber forest products in the region include edibles (such as maple sap, nuts, berries, and mushrooms) and decorative materials (such as floral items, boughs, cones, vines, moss, and lichens).
- The North is the source of nearly all U.S. commercial maple syrup production.
- The most common nature-based recreational activities in northern forests are walking for pleasure; family gatherings; viewing/ photographing scenery, wildlife, flowers; picnicking; sightseeing; and driving for pleasure.

values, volumes, and employment through the production process—from the forest to the end of secondary processing or other utilization—explains a key dimension of the socioeconomic contributions that forests make to local, regional, and national economies.

A holistic evaluation of the socioeconomic benefits from forests necessarily includes contributions from ecosystem services as well as market values for wood and nontimber products. In the absence of working markets, the value of ecosystem services can be difficult to quantify. Nevertheless, previous sections present detailed qualitative information about key ecosystem services such as carbon sequestration, watershed protection, and sustaining biological diversity. The following section gives greater—but not exclusive—attention to products and services that can be quantified through actual markets, payments to landowners, or other estimates of value. For example, forest-based and forest-related employment is a tangible and widely understood measure of economic and social well-being. Similarly, declining on-the-job injury rates reflect improved employment quality, which provides personal and community benefits.

The indicators reported here summarize the best available data to report revenues or economic activity associated with producing (or consuming) important commodities and ecosystem services, but may not be full measures of all the values that forests supply to society. Many such values are not reflected in market transactions, and market prices fail to fully capture the total contribution of forests to human well-being. The value of ecosystem services from urban and community forests is addressed in detail in subsequent sections.

Indicators of socioeconomic benefits from northern forests

Consumption of wood and wood products
Consumption of wood and wood products reflects the importance of forests as a source of raw materials. Comparison of consumption and production of wood and wood products illustrates the balance (or lack) between supply and demand. Most timber harvesting in the United States is in response to demand for the wood products that people use in their daily lives.

Total U.S. consumption of timber products including wood products, paper products, and fuelwood was 21 billion cubic feet in 2005 (Fig. 40), equivalent to 71 cubic feet of wood per person (Fig. 41) (also see The Wood You Consume, page 5). Over the past 40 years, per capita annual consumption has ranged from 67 to 83 cubic feet, gradually decreasing since 1987. However, because of population growth, total U.S. consumption of wood products over the past 40 years increased from 13 to 21 billion cubic feet. Consumption statistics are not commonly disaggregated below the national level, so we have assumed that the North consumes about 42 percent of the Nation's timber products because it has about 42 percent of the Nation's population.

Socioeconomic Benefits of Forests

The economic value placed on forests reflects the benefit that society derives from them, as indicated by the prices paid for marketed goods and the values estimated, often by indirect measures, for nonmarketed goods. For example, the value of timber products is partly given by the price of those goods in the market. Conversely, the value of recreation on public forest lands is not easily measured in dollars spent, but surveying recreationists can provide measures of willingness to pay. Observing time and money invested for traveling to and from a recreation site can provide travel-cost estimates. In addition, many people seek the scenic views, privacy, and quiet that come from living near a park or natural area, especially in crowded urban settings; the value of these areas can be estimated by determining the premium paid for adjacent lots. Using such methods can help to account for the many values forests have for society.

Economists often classify the value of forests in the following categories (Pearce 2001):

- **DIRECT USE VALUES**—Values from the consumptive and nonconsumptive uses of products and services such as timber, fuelwood, tree sap, or recreation.
- **INDIRECT USE VALUES**—Values from various forest services, such watershed protection, storage of carbon, and provision of wildlife habitat.
- **OPTION VALUES**—Values from desiring to conserve the option for future use even though not taking advantage of current availability; for example, although many individuals may not visit some forests, they value knowing that they could one day enjoy them.
- **NON-USE VALUES**—Values from individuals supporting forest conservation and sustainability; unrelated to current or planned use of the forest, this is also known as existence or passive value.

FIGURE 40

U.S. timber products consumption by year and product class (Howard 2007).

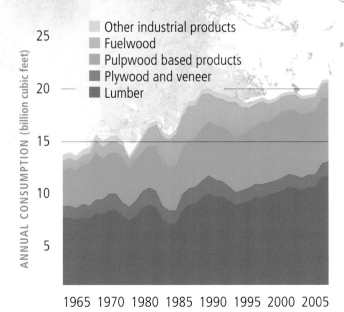

FIGURE 41

U.S. population and per capita consumption of timber products including wood products, paper products, and fuelwood (Howard 2007, U.S. Census Bureau 2009).

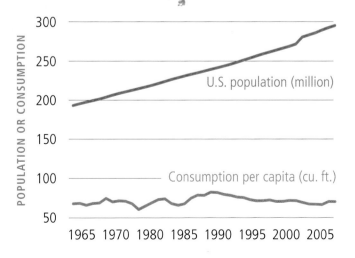

U.S. consumption of timber products is met by a combination of domestic production and net imports (imports in excess of exports). With increased population growth and consumption, imports have increased to supply a greater share of the U.S. wood products market. In 2005, 20 percent of total U.S. wood consumption was from imports (Fig. 42).

FIGURE 42

Total U.S. consumption, imports, and exports of timber products (Howard 2007).

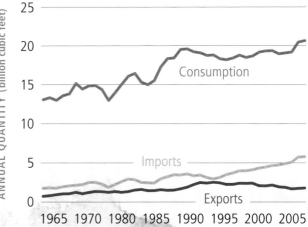

Assessing the Direct Value of Wood Product Manufacturing with the North American Industry Classification System

Information on U.S. product manufacturing is maintained by the U.S. Census Bureau, which classifies wood products under North American Industry Codes (NAICS) 113, 321, 322 and 337.

NAICS 113 industries are involved in growing, cutting, and transporting timber; and in producing wood chips in the field. This includes traditional forestry and logging operations. Because production cycles for NAICS 113 establishments are 10 years or more, Christmas trees and other short-rotation products are classified as crop production, and not included in NAICS 113.

NAICS 321 includes establishments that manufacture wood products such as lumber, plywood, veneers, wood containers, wood flooring, wood trusses, manufactured or mobile homes, and prefabricated wood buildings. NAICS 322 includes industries that make pulp, paper, or converted paper products. Converted paper products include stationary, paperboard, bags, boxes, and other items manufactured from pulp and paper. Together, NAICS 321 and 322 comprise information for the primary wood products manufacturing sector.

NAICS 337 includes manufacturers of furniture and related products such as mattresses, window blinds, cabinets, and fixtures. NAICS 337 captures some of the activity in the secondary wood products manufacturing sector, but does not differentiate wood-based products from other products. Consequently, we exclude information from NCAIS 337.

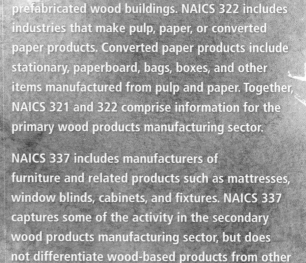

Value and volume of wood
and wood products production

The value of wood products produced by the wood products industry (North American Industry Classification - NAICS 321) and the pulp and paper industry (NAICS 322) was estimated at $281 billion nationally and $112 billion (40 percent) for the Northern States in 2006. Added value of primary wood products manufacturing—calculated by subtracting the cost of manufacturing from the value of shipments—was $124 billion nationally and $52 billion (41 percent) for Northern States.

Table 9 shows the volume of roundwood processed by product categories for Northern States. Roundwood is a term used to represent logs, bolts, or other round sections cut from trees for industrial or consumer use, either in the original round form (such as transmission poles or pilings) or as raw material to be manufactured into sawn wood, panel products, paper, or other industrial products (Stokes et al. 1989, Food and Agriculture Organization 2010).

Northern States produced 3.0 billion cubic feet of roundwood in 2007, 2.3 billion (76 percent) from hardwoods and 0.7 billion from softwoods (Fig. 43). The region's primary roundwood products are hardwood saw logs, pulpwood, and fuelwood. Saw logs are logs whose size and quality meet regional standards to be sawn into boards. Pulpwood is roundwood used as a source of wood fiber in a pulp mill. Fuelwood is

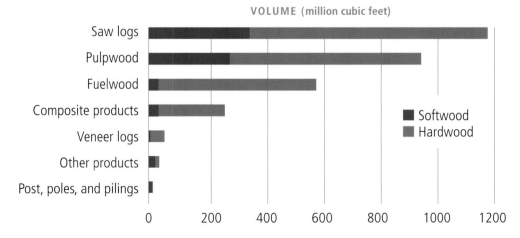

FIGURE 43
Volume of roundwood products by end use in the Northern States, 2007, based on U.S. Forest Service timber product output reports (USDA FS 2011i).

Table 9—Volume of roundwood products by State and type of products, 2006, sorted from most to least total roundwood production (USDA FS 2011i).

State and region	Total roundwood products	Saw logs	Veneer logs	Pulp-wood	Composite products[a]	Posts, poles, and pilings	Fuel-wood	Other products
				(million cubic feet)				
Maine	563	203		239			121	
Wisconsin	414	100	6	219	43	2	38	7
Michigan	373	128	8	135	66	4	30	2
Minnesota	326	48	1	124	113	<1	39	<1
New York	243	82	4	76	3	<1	77	<1
Pennsylvania	223	119	19	64		1	6	13
Missouri	166	113	1	7		1	36	7
West Virginia	164	104	10	6	35	2	5	1
Indiana	108	68	3	2		<1	34	1
Illinois	96	35	1	1		<1	56	3
Ohio	76	48	<1	24			4	1
Vermont	61	33		10			18	
Maryland	60	28		11			20	
Massachusetts	50	7		1			41	<1
New Hampshire	42	25	1	11			5	<1
Iowa	26	15	1			<1	10	<1
New Jersey	26	1		<1		<1	25	
Connecticut	13	5		<1			7	
Delaware	9	4		5			<1	
Rhode Island	5	1					3	
North total	3,045	1,168	56	938	261	12	576	35
U.S. total	14,990	7,179	1,211	4,394	544	100	1,408	155
North as percent of U.S. total	20	16	5	21	48	12	41	23

[a]Many of the products in the composites category are made from logs in the pulpwood size class.

wood mill residues, cull logs, and branches used to fuel fires in a boiler or furnace (Stokes et al. 1989). Other products from Northern States are wood composites including particle board, oriented strand board, and other engineered wood products made using adhesives; logs sliced for veneer; and fence posts, utility poles, and pilings. Only a small portion of roundwood is manufactured into composite products, even though during manufacturing they can deliver greater added value per unit of wood than saw logs, pulpwood, or fuelwood.

Production of wood products in the North has fluctuated over time (Fig. 44). Total roundwood production peaked in the late 1980s, driven primarily by increased harvesting for fuelwood,

saw logs, pulpwood, and composites. Saw log harvesting peaked in 1996, driven by increased standing inventory (especially select oak species and hard maples), demand from the kitchen-cabinet and pallet industries, and exports (Luppold and Bumgardner 2008). Since then, lumber production and harvesting of saw logs have stagnated because of increasing pressure from low-cost imports of finished products. Growth in production in the region appears to be driven by smaller manufacturers producing more customized products (Luppold and Bumgardner 2008). Although northern roundwood production includes 15 major species groups, about two-thirds is from oaks, aspens, maples, spruce, and pines (Fig. 45).

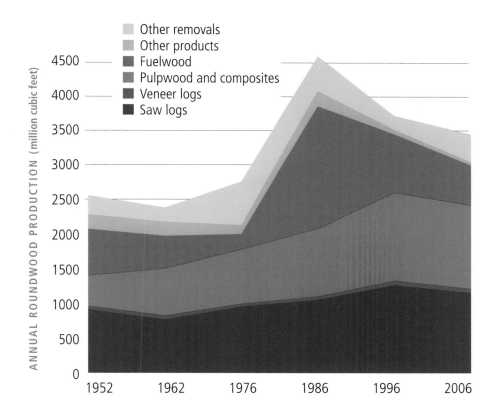

FIGURE 44
Production of roundwood products in the Northern States, 1952 to 2006 (Smith et al. 2009).

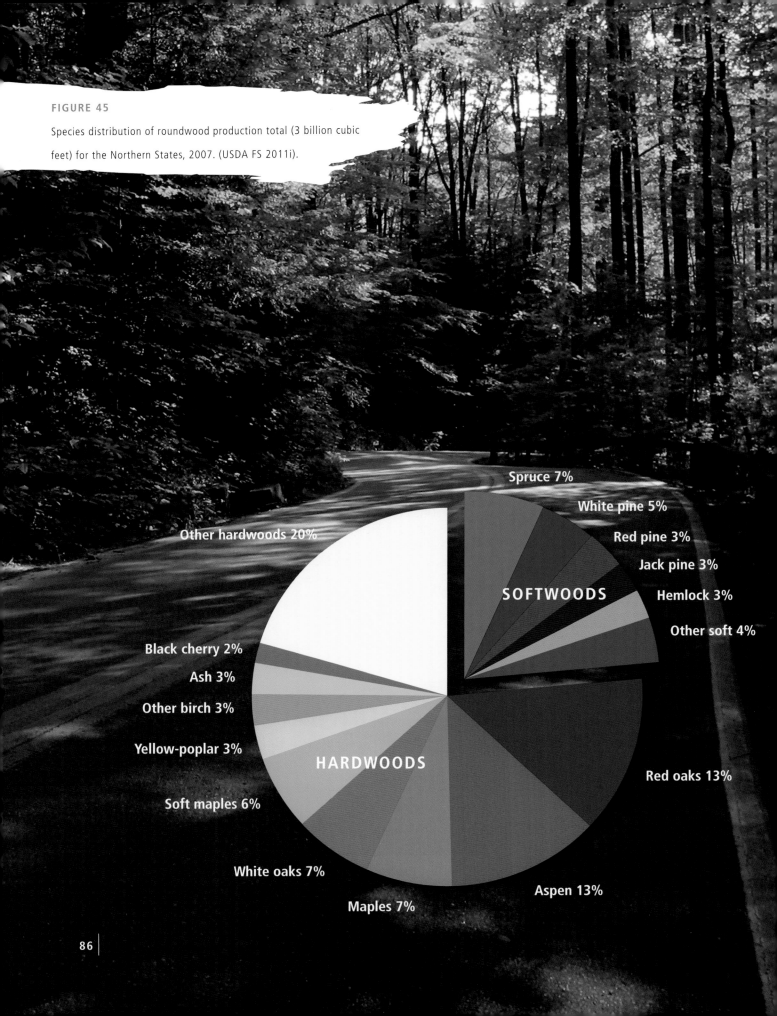

FIGURE 45

Species distribution of roundwood production total (3 billion cubic feet) for the Northern States, 2007. (USDA FS 2011i).

Spruce 7%

White pine 5%

Red pine 3%

Jack pine 3%

Hemlock 3%

Other soft 4%

SOFTWOODS

Other hardwoods 20%

Black cherry 2%

Ash 3%

Other birch 3%

Yellow-poplar 3%

HARDWOODS

Soft maples 6%

Red oaks 13%

White oaks 7%

Aspen 13%

Maples 7%

Recovery or recycling of wood products

Recovery and recycling wood products allows a country or region to maintain or increase consumption without harvesting more trees. Increased recovery and recycling can help reduce environmental impacts associated with harvesting, transporting, and processing trees and can reduce the quantity of materials sent to landfills. The recovery rate is the quantity of material recovered and recycled divided by the amount of sourced product. A high annual recovery rate implies high efficiency in using resources, an important step toward achieving forest sustainability.

Pulp and paper product recovery has become an important activity in Northern States, with both the recovered amount and the recovery rate increasing substantially since the 1970s. From 1976 to 2004, the amount of recovered paper nearly doubled (from 8.7 to 16.4 million tons), mirroring national trends (Fig. 46). Data

from the Paper Industry Association Council (2009) indicate that northern access to curbside recycling was higher than the national average.

Recycling is also common for other wood products. Most residues from the U.S. wood products manufacturing process are converted into fuel or engineered wood products (Ince 1996). Recovery of shipping pallets is a widely adopted and financially sound practice. More than 1,000 U.S. firms are in the business of pallet recycling (Recycler's World 2009). As a result of increased efforts toward recycling, less than 1 percent of pallets are landfilled each year (Bush et al. 2007).

Nontimber forest products

In 2007, nontimber forest product sales in the United States had an estimated retail value of $1.4 billion or about $4.50 per capita. Edibles, decorative materials, medicinal plants, cultural items, and landscaping materials amounted to

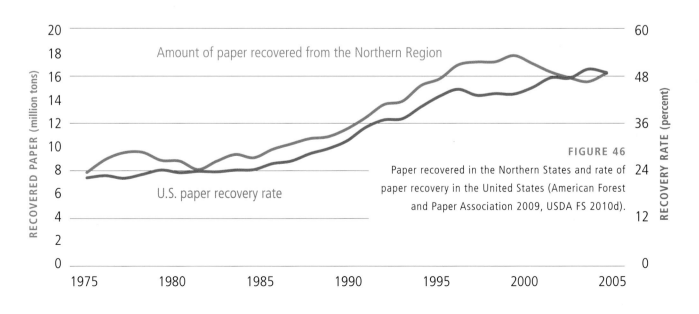

FIGURE 46
Paper recovered in the Northern States and rate of paper recovery in the United States (American Forest and Paper Association 2009, USDA FS 2010d).

roughly $468 million of that total (Alexander et al. 2011, USDA Forest Service 2011e). The remainder was primarily wood products such as firewood or fence posts gathered and sold in small quantities for personal use. National data on nontimber forest products are limited to national forest receipts for permits and small contracts; the dollar estimates presented above are based on collection permits issued for Federal lands that were extrapolated to private forest land lands. Consequently, the estimates are subject to considerable variation and best suited to estimating the relative rankings among product categories rather than the actual dollar value.

Most northern forest land is privately owned. The best available information on collection of nontimber forest products from private forest land comes from voluntary reporting through the National Woodland Owners Survey (USDA FS 2009b). For most States, the most common products collected on private forests are edibles and decorative or medicinal plants (Table 10).

Nontimber Forest Products

Nontimber forest products include edibles (such as nuts, berries, mushrooms, and maple sap), decorative materials (such as floral items, boughs, cones, vines, moss, and lichens), medicinal plants (such as ginseng), cultural items (materials for traditional or ceremonial activities), landscaping materials (such as transplants, rocks, and gravel), and wood products gathered and sold in small quantities (such as wild-grown Christmas trees, residential fuelwood, and fence posts). Gathering nontimber forest products on Federal land is monitored through permits or small contracts, and those can be used to estimate the following national ranking of nontimber forest products which is ordered by greatest to least dollar value of harvested material (USDA FS 2009a).

1. Residential fuelwood
2. Floral/craft items
3. Wild-grown Christmas trees
4. Edibles
5. Landscaping materials
6. Posts and poles
7. Grass/forage
8. Seeds and cones
9. Herbs and medicinal plants

Other rankings of nontimber forest products in the North were compiled from an open-ended survey of National Forest managers who listed the relative importance of each product. Medicinal plants (presumably due to ginseng gathering) rank far higher in this survey than in the national rankings. (McLain and Jones 2005).

1. Residential fuelwood
2. Christmas trees
3. Medicinal plants
4. Mushrooms; tree boughs
5. Sap; Other plants
6. Edible plants; floral greens; moss; rocks, sand, or gravel; posts or poles; transplants
7. Bark
8. Seeds; craft wood; construction wood

Table 10—Collection of nontimber products reported by family forest landowners by State and product category, and forest land acres involved (based on the total area of the forest ownership where the activity occurred). Because products are not mutually exclusive, owners can be tallied in multiple categories and percents cannot be summed across categories (USDA FS 2009b).

State and region	Edibles	Decoratives	Medicinals	Cultural items	Edibles	Decoratives	Medicinals	Cultural items
	----------------------(percent of owners)----------------------				----------------------(percent of acres)----------------------			
Vermont	39	20	3	<1	22	11	4	1
Missouri	20	5	3	<1	21	8	4	<1
Iowa	18	16	1		22	5	4	
Wisconsin	18	8	1	1	20	10	2	1
Illinois	15	3	2		21	7	5	
Ohio	15	14	5	1	17	12	9	<1
Minnesota	13	8	<1	<1	14	9	1	1
Michigan	13	7	1	1	14	7	1	1
Maine	13	5	<1	<1	6	6	1	<1
Indiana	12	9	<1	1	16	9	4	1
New York	12	6	2		13	6	1	
Connecticut	11	12			5	5		
Massachusetts	11	5	2		13	10	2	
Rhode Island	11	5		5	10	10		3
New Hampshire	9	33	1	<1	14	10	1	1
Pennsylvania	7	7	2	<1	10	5	2	<1
Maryland	7	4			10	5		
West Virginia	6	2	3	<1	9	4	3	<1
Delaware[a]	--	--	--	--	--	--	--	--
New Jersey[a]	--	--	--	--	--	--	--	--
Northern total	12	8	2	<1	13	7	2	<1
Total number of owners participating (1,000)	613	386	85	14				
Total acres included (1,000)					17,182	9,020	2,932	428

[a]*Not reported separately by state*

On northern private forest land in aggregate, more than 613,000 owners (one in eight) collect nontimber products.

The value of nontimber forest products sold via permits on northern National Forests was estimated at $175,000 in 2007 (Table 11).

More than half of total revenues were from residential fuelwood, followed by evergreen limbs and boughs for decoration, fence posts, and wild-grown Christmas trees (only 2,000 wild-harvested Christmas trees, in contrast to the annual harvest of 5.7 million Christmas trees from plantations).

Table 11—Estimated proportion and value of nontimber products harvested from National Forests in the Northern United States via permits, 2007. Note that missing entries indicate no reported sales (Personal communication from Susan Alexander, U.S. Forest Service, 13 October 2009).

Product	Proportion of nontimber sales (%)	All National Forests	Wisconsin	Missouri	Michigan	Pennsylvania	West Virginia	Minnesota	New Hampshire	Vermont	Ohio	Illinois	New York	Indiana
							(U.S. dollars)							
Fuelwood	55	97,178	29,207	9,279	18,352	17,075	11,313	1,470	5,250	2,180	1,500	1,020	520	13
Limbs & boughs	17	29,083	15,993		8,850		120	4,020		100				
Posts	17	29,073		29,013				60						
Christmas trees	6	10,270	4,235		1,320		70	2,045	1,540	1,060				
Grass	2	3,296	30	2,646				180			440			
Tree sap	2	2,826			110			1,706	1,010					
Roots	1	1,560					440				1,120			
Mosses	< 1	660	520		140									
Other products	< 1	579	355		70			154						
Transplants	< 1	180	20					160						
Cones	< 1	140	140											
Bark	< 1	123						123						
Needles	< 1	68			68									
Other plants	< 1	60	40		20									
Foliage	< 1	40						40						
Mushrooms	< 1	20								20				
Total	100	175,156	50,540	40,938	28,930	17,075	11,943	9,958	7,800	3,360	3,060	1,020	520	13

Maple sap used in syrup production is an important product collected in northern forests. Commercial maple syrup production in large quantities is limited to 10 States, all of them in the North (Table 12). Total production for 2009 was 2.4 million gallons, with a value exceeding $91 million. In recent years both the value per gallon and the production of maple syrup have risen sharply (Fig. 47).

The total value of nontimber products consumed in the United States exceeds the value of nontimber products produced domestically, because

the United States is a net importer of many nontimber products. For example, annual exports exceed $15 million each for foliage and branches, wild blueberries, mushrooms, and ginseng. However, annual imports exceed $30 million each for foliage and branches, wild blueberries, pine nuts, vanilla beans, and maple syrup (USDA FS 2011e).

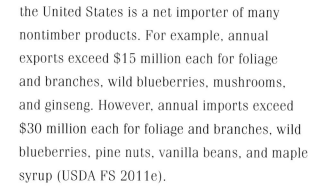

FIGURE 47

Maple syrup production and value, 1992 to 2009; note that virtually all U.S. commercial maple syrup production occurs in the Northern States (USDA NASS 2010).

Table 12—Maple syrup commercial production in the United States, 2009 (USDA NASS 2010). All reported commercial maple syrup production is in these 10 States.

State and region	Production	Value
	(1,000 gallons)	($1,000)
Connecticut	13	800
Massachusetts	46	2,466
Ohio	90	3,627
Pennsylvania	92	3,505
New Hampshire	94	4,756
Michigan	115	5,175
Wisconsin	200	7,340
Maine	395	12,996
New York	439	17,823
Vermont	920	32,292
Northern States and U.S. total	2,404	90,780

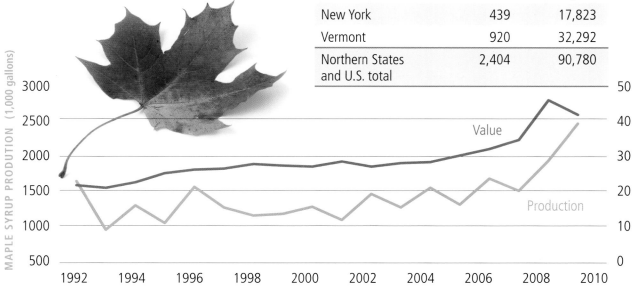

Revenues from forest-based ecosystem services
Private and public markets are evolving
to compensate forest landowners for the
ecosystem services that their forests provide
for the common good. Primarily voluntary
markets have emerged to pay for services such
as carbon sequestration, watershed protection,
and preservation of sensitive forest lands.
Future Federal and international regulations
to facilitate payments for ecosystem services
will be strongly influenced by the adoption or
avoidance of mandatory compensation systems.

From 2003 to 2010, payments for carbon
sequestration contracts were sold through the
Chicago Climate Exchange in these categories:
afforestation/reforestation, sustainably
managed forests, and long-lived wood products.
Landowners entered into contracts for 15 years
or longer to sell future increases in the carbon
stocks that were sequestered in their trees
or wood products (Chicago Climate Exchange

2009). Absent mandatory carbon cap-and-trade
legislation or similar restrictions on carbon
emissions, the value of carbon credits in the
United States has declined to the point where
new U.S. carbon sequestration contracts are no
longer being sold (Gronewold 2011), although
sales continue in some international markets.

Forests can play an instrumental role in
addressing climate change challenges.
Management practices that avoid deforestation,
increase afforestation, or increase net
growth offer the greatest potential for carbon
sequestration (Table 13). Additionally, using
wood for energy—typically considered a
commodity rather than an ecosystem service—
provides an added benefit by reducing emissions
from fossil fuels that would be used instead.

The important role that forests play in
protecting watersheds can also result in
revenues paid to landowners for maintaining

Table 13—Estimated carbon sequestration potential for selected U.S. land-use practices.

Activity	Carbon sequestration	Source
	(tons per acre per year)	
Avoided deforestation	92.3 to 189.7	U.S. Department of State (2000)
Afforestation (previously cropland/pasture)	2.4 to 10.5	Birdsey (1996)
Reforestation	1.2 to 8.5	Birdsey (1996)
Changes in forest management	2.3 to 3.4	Row (1996)
Riparian or conservation buffers (nonforest)	0.4 to 1.1	Lal et al. (1998)
Reduced/conservation tillage	0.7 to 1.1	West and Post (2002)
Grazing management	0.1 to 2.1	Follet et al. (2001)

tree cover. A well publicized example is the New York City Watershed Agreement (US EPA 1996), under which 9 million residents of New York City and surrounding suburbs rely on drinking water from reservoirs located miles away in the Catskill and Delaware watersheds. The Watershed Forestry Program was formally established as a voluntary pollution prevention partnership between New York City and the upstate New York forestry community in September 1997. The program provides cost sharing to landowners for the development of long-term forest management plans written with the help of professional foresters who are specially trained by the partnership. By April 2003, more than 290 management plans were completed covering more than 55,000 acres, of which 45,000 are forested. The project also includes a Best Management Practices component, logger training, and coordination of research, demonstration and education efforts (New York City Department of Environmental Protection 2009).

The Forest Legacy Program, administered by the Forest Service in partnership with individual States, is an example of a voluntary public program aimed at protecting environmentally sensitive forests on private lands (USDA FS 2009a, 2010c). Forest lands supply multiple benefits including timber products, wildlife habitat, soil and watershed protection, aesthetics, and recreational opportunities. When forests become fragmented and disappear, so

do some of the benefits they provide. The Forest Legacy Program encourages and supports acquisition of land-protection agreements (legally binding agreements transferring a negotiated set of property rights from one party to another) without removing the property from private ownership. Most conservation agreements restrict development, require sustainable forestry practices, and protect water quality and other values. In 2009, 1.9 million acres nationally were enrolled in the Forest Legacy Program, of which 1.3 million acres (68 percent) were in Northern States— contributing to the extent of protected areas in the region. Forest Legacy Program goals in most States focus on maintaining water quality, wildlife habitat, and biodiversity (Table 14).

Table 14—Goals commonly identified by State Forest Legacy Programs and their frequency (USDA FS 2011e).

Goal	Number of States
Water quality, wetlands, and riparian buffers	37
Wildlife, habitat, biodiversity	35
Recreation	23
Threatened and endangered species	17

The U.S. Forest Service estimates that government and nongovernment payments for ecosystem services nationwide reached $553 million in 2007 (Table 15). Although this figure is not complete because data are unavailable for several States, the trend in payments from public and private sources (from nongovernmental organizations, for example) is increasing (USDA FS 2009a).

Table 15—Approximate total U.S. payments for environmental services from Federal and State agencies, nongovernment organizations, and individuals in constant 2005 dollars (USDA FS 2011e).

Program	Years		
	2005	2006	2007
	------------($ million)------------		
			Government
Federal programs	248	243	248
State programs	8	9	12
			Nongovernment
Voluntary carbon market	<1	<1	6
Conservation agreements	69	92	111
Fee simple purchases	142	177	177
			Total payments
	468	521	553

Investments and expenditures in forest management, industries, services, and research
Investment in forest management is needed to improve capacity of forests to produce wood and nonwood products and to increase ecosystem services. Research and development investments are required to improve forest management and manufacturing efficiency.

From 1997 to 2006, annual capital expenditures in wood products manufacturing in Northern States increased 46 percent, from $0.8 to $1.2 billion (Fig. 48). However, during that same period, capital expenditures in pulp and paper products manufacturing decreased 18 percent from $3.5 to $2.9 billion (U.S. Census Bureau 2009).

Most Federal investments in forest management in the North were allocated though Forest Service budgets, via Forest Service Region 9 (Eastern Region) for National Forest management or via Northeastern Area State and Private Forestry for forest management, planning, pest management, wildfire management, and other programs with the States. From 2005 to 2010 annual discretionary appropriations increased from $155 million to $160 million for Forest Service Region 9 and from $85 million to $95 million for State and Private Forestry (Fig. 49). In 2010, $42 million of those combined appropriations were allocated to wildfire management and $1 million to land acquisition.

State forestry programs are funded from multiple sources including State government, Federal government, and revenue from services and products. According to the National Association of State Foresters (2011), non-Federal funding for forests in the Northern States (total funding minus Federal funding, excluding missing data for Illinois and Ohio) was $396 million in 2008.

U.S. Forest Service discretionary research appropriations to the Northern Research Station, which serves the 20-State region, increased from $55 million in 2005 to $64 million in 2010 (Fig. 49), some of which went to cooperative research studies with universities. In 2006, forest research funding to universities in the North (all sources) was $95 million compared to $87 million for the South, $67 million for the Pacific Coast, and $40 million for the Interior West. State appropriations funded about half of forest-related research at northern universities, followed by Federal sources for about a third, and industry and other sources for the remainder. (USDA FS 2011e)

FIGURE 48

Capital expenditures in wood products (NAICS 321) and in pulp and paper (NAICS 322) manufacturing in the Northern States, 1997, 2002, and 2006 (U.S. Census Bureau 2009).

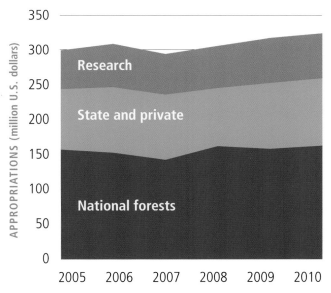

FIGURE 49

U.S. Forest Service discretionary appropriations by fiscal year within the Northern States for national forests in Forest Service Region 9, Northeastern Area State and Private Forestry, and the Northern Research Station.

Employment in the forest products sector
Nationwide, the forestry and logging wood products industries (excluding furniture) and the pulp and paper industries employed 1.1 million people in 2006 (U.S. Bureau of Labor Statistics 2007a). This included more than 72,000 employees in the forestry and logging sector, 556,000 in the wood products manufacturing sector and 468,000 in the paper sector. Forty percent of these employees (441,000) were employed in the Northern States (Table 16). Northern industries supported about 35 percent of the Nation's wood products jobs (194,000 out of 556,000 jobs) and 50 percent of pulp and paper manufacturing jobs (235,000 out of 468,000 jobs).

Quantifying Employment in the Forest Products Manufacturing Sector

The forest products manufacturing sector in the United States is comprised of primary wood products and pulp and paper manufacturers (NAICS 321 and 322). In 2006, the sector employed an estimated 7.3 percent of all manufacturing-related workers and 8.2 percent of all U.S. production workers. The more general category of "manufacturing-related jobs" consists of the average number of production workers plus the number of other employees engaged in factory supervision above the line-supervisor level, sales, sales delivery, advertising, credit, collection, installing and servicing of own products, clerical, executive, purchasing, financing, legal, personnel, professional, and technical activities. The category "production jobs" includes individuals—up through the line-supervisor level—engaged in fabrication, processing, assembly, inspection, receiving, storage, handling, packing, warehousing, shipping but not delivery, maintenance, repair, janitorial services, guard services, product development, auxiliary production of power and other inputs for a plant's own use, recordkeeping, and other services closely associated with these production operations. Neither category includes proprietors and partners of unincorporated businesses (U.S. Census Bureau 2009).

Table 16—Number of jobs in forestry and logging (NAICS113), wood products (NAICS 321), and pulp and paper industries (NAICS 322) of the North in 2006 (U.S. Bureau of Labor Statistics 2007a).

State and region	Forestry and logging	Wood products	Pulp and paper[a]	Total
Connecticut	19	1,745	4,886	6,650
Delaware	--[b]	419	951	1,370
Illinois	171	9,209	24,841	34,221
Indiana	455	19,399	11,488	31,342
Iowa	32	12,549	4,342	16,923
Maine	2,732	6,213	9,040	17,985
Maryland	416	3,568	5,249	9,233
Massachusetts	149	3,378	12,311	15,838
Michigan	1,662	10,737	13,966	26,365
Minnesota	841	16,320	11,866	29,027
Missouri	235	10,437	8,758	19,430
New Hampshire	470	2,758	2,228	5,456
New Jersey	23	4,559	14,070	18,652
New York	934	9,712	20,171	30,817
Ohio	613	16,476	24,726	41,815
Pennsylvania	832	30,291	26,843	57,966
Rhode Island	--	--	1,339	1,339
Vermont	--	2,283	1,291	3,574
West Virginia	1,174	8,252	723	10,149
Wisconsin	970	25,898	36,008	62,876
North total	11,728	194,203	235,097	441,028
U.S. total	72,140	556,110	468,422	1,096,672
North as a percent of U.S. total	16	35	50	40

[a]The paper category includes manufacturers of converted paper products such as packaging and stationery.

[b]Not disclosed.

Fig. 50 shows how national annual average employment fluctuated in forestry and logging, wood products manufacturing, and pulp and paper. From 2003 to 2006, the average number of employees in wood manufacturing increased slightly, but employment declined in 2007, partly as a result of a slowing economy. Declines were more severe in the pulp and paper industry, and the logging industry remained steady.

Wages, income, and injury rates in the forest sector

In 2006, total U.S. wages in the wood products and paper manufacturing industries represented 8 percent of wages paid to production workers across all manufacturing sectors (U.S. Census Bureau 2009). Workers in the North earned 41 percent of U.S. wages paid collectively in the forestry and logging (14 percent of U.S. total), wood products (35 percent), and pulp and paper manufacturing (49 percent) sectors (Table 17).

The wage rates of workers in northern wood products and pulp and paper manufacturing industries were similar to national averages for these industries, but northern wage rates for forestry and logging were only at 85 percent of the national average. Forestry and logging workers in Massachusetts were paid an average of $50,000 per year, the highest of any Northern State and twice as much as their counterparts in Illinois received in average annual wages.

Average annual wages were more than $51,000 in the North paper industry, compared to a little over $34,000 for wood products and $29,000 for forestry and logging.

FIGURE 50

National annual average employment in forestry and logging, wood products manufacturing, and pulp and paper industries (U.S. Bureau of Labor Statistics 2007a).

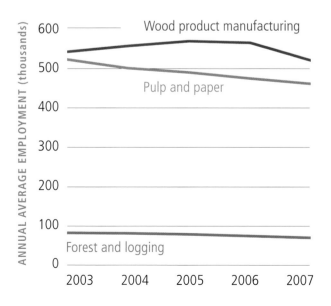

Table 17—Total wages and average wage rates of workers in forestry and logging (NAICS 113), wood products (NAICS 321) and pulp and paper (NAICS 322) industries in the Northern States, 2006. (U.S. Bureau of Labor Statistics 2007a).

State and region	Forestry and logging	Wood products	Pulp and paper[a]	Forestry and logging	Wood products[a]	Pulp and paper
	----------------(thousands of dollars)----------------			-------------(dollars per worker per year)-------------		
Connecticut	572	76,705	309,562	30,131	43,957	63,357
Delaware	-- [b]	15,912	50,801	--	37,975	53,418
Illinois	4,275	324,258	1,242,423	25,000	35,211	50,015
Indiana	11,417	637,781	516,374	25,092	32,877	44,949
Iowa	839	464,564	199,854	26,208	37,020	46,028
Maine	92,552	205,483	543,638	33,877	33,073	60,137
Maryland	11,851	131,445	222,447	28,489	36,840	42,379
Massachusetts	7,468	140,467	635,211	50,121	41,583	51,597
Michigan	50,071	375,366	713,537	30,127	34,960	51,091
Minnesota	25,084	766,616	649,960	29,826	46,974	54,775
Missouri	5,690	280,620	394,241	24,214	26,887	45,015
New Hampshire	17,235	111,285	114,965	36,671	40,350	51,600
New Jersey	1,035	174,792	839,838	45,007	38,340	59,690
New York	28,954	342,066	995,661	31,000	35,221	49,361
Ohio	14,424	531,005	1,167,389	23,530	32,229	47,213
Pennsylvania	20,550	986,426	1,349,183	24,699	32,565	50,262
Rhode Island	--	--	53,259	--	--	39,775
Vermont	--	77,768	65,434	--	34,064	50,685
West Virginia	25,790	245,596	28,123	21,968	29,762	38,897
Wisconsin	26,611	816,305	1,949,581	27,434	31,520	54,143
North total	344,419	6,704,460	12,041,480	29,367	34,523	51,219
U.S. total	2,502,632	19,278,736	24,825,898	34,691	34,667	52,999
North as a percent of U.S. total	14	35	49	85	100	97

[a]The paper category includes manufacturers of converted paper products such as packaging and stationery.

[b]Not disclosed.

Data from 2003 to 2007 show declines in recordable injury rates in the U.S. forestry and logging, wood products, and pulp and paper manufacturing industries (Fig. 51). Nevertheless, the injury rate for wood product manufacturing was higher than the mean rate for other U.S. manufacturing industries. In contrast, injury rates in the forestry and logging and the pulp and paper manufacturing industries tend to be lower than the overall manufacturing averages in the United States.

From 2003 to 2008, 131 job-related fatalities occurred in the North forestry and logging, wood products, and pulp and paper manufacturing industries, or about 14 percent of the national total. Given that 40 percent of the total national workforce for these industries is employed in Northern States, this fatality rate is relatively low, suggesting that working conditions are safer in the North than in other parts of the country. Fatalities were most common in forestry and logging, accounting for 79 percent of total forest industry fatalities and exceeding the national average of 66 percent. The fatality rate for the northern forestry and logging sector was high considering that only 12,000 workers (out of 441,000 total workers in all northern forest industries) were in that sector. However, Tables 16 and 18 show that region's proportion of the nationwide forestry and logging fatalities (17 percent) is consistent with the region's proportion of nationwide forestry and logging jobs (16 percent). The Northern States employed 35 percent of the national wood products workforce with only 10 percent of that industry sector's fatalities reported nationally and 49 percent of the national pulp and paper workforce with only 6 percent of the fatalities reported nationally. These relatively low incidences may suggest safer working conditions for northern workers in these industries compared to the rest of the country (Table 18).

■ Forestry and logging
■ Wood product manufacturing
■ Pulp and paper
■ U.S. manufacturing

FIGURE 51

National total recordable injury cases in the forestry and logging industry, wood products manufacturing, pulp and paper industries; and total U.S. manufacturing (U.S. Bureau of Labor Statistics 2009).

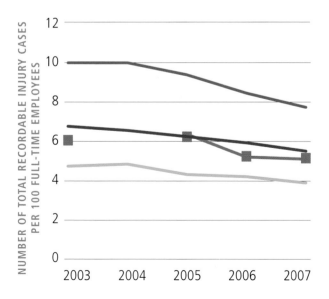

Table 18—Total fatalities reported, 2003 to 2008, in the Northern States by forest products industry (U.S. Bureau of Labor Statistics 2007a).

Industry category	Northern States fatalities	National fatalities	Northern States proportion
	(number)	(number)	(percent)
Forestry and logging (NAICS 113)	103	617	17
Wood products (NAICS 321)	22	229	10
Pulp and paper (NAICS 322)	6	95	6
Total	131	941	14

Recreation and tourism

The forest land that covers 42 percent of the North offers vast opportunities for forest-based recreation. About 85 percent of the total 172 million acres of forest land in the region is available for recreation, but open access to the public varies by ownership group. Nearly all the 44 million acres of public forest land is open to the public for various forms of recreation. In contrast, only about 18 percent of the 100 million acres of nonindustrial private forest land is open for public recreation. Nevertheless, more than 90 percent of that private land is used for recreation by owners, their families, associates, or lessees. The remaining owner group, private corporations, own 28 million acres of forest land, of which roughly 40 percent is available for forest recreation (USDA FS 2011e, Cordell 2004).

Compared to other regions of the United States, the North has a small portion of Federal forest land (6 percent of the U.S. total), and little wilderness (1.5 percent of the U.S. total). However, Northern States have 7,300 miles in the National Recreation Trail System, more than other comparably sized regions of the U.S. Moreover, designated trail mileage in the Northern States increased by 77 percent from 2004 to 2009 (Cordell et al. in press).

In Northern States the most common nature-based recreation activities are walking, participating in family gatherings, gardening or landscaping, and viewing or photographing nature. The fastest growing nature-based recreation activities in the North from 1999 to 2009 were, visiting a farm or agricultural setting, gathering wild-grown edibles, off-road driving, viewing or photographing wildlife or natural environments, warm-water fishing, and day hiking (Table 19). For many forest recreation activities in the United States the majority of participation occurs on public lands and much takes place on urban forest land. Urban and community forests comprise relatively few acres compared to rural forests (see subsequent sections), but are heavily used because of their proximity to people.

Table 19—Participation in nature-based activities from 2005 to 2009 in the North for activities with greater than 10 million participants age 16 and older, and corresponding change in participation 1999 to 2009 (Cordell at al. in press)

Activity	Mean portion of population participating 2005-2009	Participation change 1999-2009
	------------------------------(percent)------------------------------	
Walk for pleasure	85	6
Family gathering	75	7
Gardening or landscaping	67	3
View/photograph natural scenery	64	12
Visit outdoor nature center/zoo	57	5
Picnicking	55	1
View/photograph other wildlife	51	21
View/photograph flowers, etc.	51	23
Sightseeing	51	5
Driving for pleasure	50	4
Visit a beach	45	15
Visit historic sites	44	0
Swimming in lakes, ponds, etc.	44	8
Swimming in an outdoor pool	43	11
Bicycling	37	4
View or photograph birds	38	18
Gather mushrooms, berries, etc.	36	26
Visited farm or agricultural setting	36	28
Day hiking	33	15
Visit a wilderness	31	11
View or photograph fish	25	13
Warmwater fishing	25	17
Motorboating	24	5
Visit waterside besides beach	24	2
Sledding	21	5
Developed camping	21	-10
Mountain biking	20	-6
Boat tours or excursions	19	-2
Visit prehistoric sites	19	3
Drive off-road	18	25
Canoeing	12	8
Primitive camping	12	-3

Walking for pleasure
and viewing or photographing nature
are among the most common
forest recreation activities,
in rural as well as urban forests

103

Ash Cave, Hocking Hills Region, Ohio

The population density is higher in the North than other regions, so the total number of nature-based recreation activity days is greater than elsewhere and concentrated on the relatively few forested acres per capita. However the recent rate of population increase in the Northern States has been slower than for other quadrants of the United States and shows considerable variation among age classes. Population increases in the North have been concentrated in age groups between 45 and 64 years with net population decreases for age cohorts greater than 64 years old, 25 to 34 years old, and less than 6 years old. Thus, recreation choices by members of the current 45-to-64-years-old age cohort will strongly influence nature-based recreation trends in the coming decade (Cordell et al. in press).

The North's large proportion of private forest land, combined with its large population, results in a strong recreation and tourism industry. About half the Nation's 1,600 privately operated campgrounds and recreational vehicle parks are in the North, as are the majority of privately operated downhill skiing facilities and forest-based nature parks. Forest-based sightseeing and transportation businesses are also concentrated in the eastern United States. (Cordell 2004). Seasonal homes are another significant part of the recreation and tourism industry. The States with the highest proportions of seasonal homes nationally were Maine (16 percent seasonal homes), Vermont (15 percent), and New Hampshire (10 percent); Wisconsin ranked eighth with 6 percent (U.S. Census Bureau 2000). These seasonal homes—common across the northern forests in New England, the Adirondacks, the upper Great Lakes, Missouri Ozarks, and other mainly nonmetropolitan places with forests, lakes, rivers, and mountains—function as family housing for vacations, providing ready access to outdoor recreation and informal workplaces for long weekends. Later in life, seasonal homes may become the retirement home (Stewart and Johnson 2006, Stynes et al. 1997).

The importance of forests to people

Many people value and appreciate the forest environment itself; the importance of forests extends beyond what can be extracted from them to what they are, whether they are used or not. The directly experienced features and qualities of the forest environment are one aspect of their importance to society. Aesthetic experiences in outdoor settings are often among the most important experiences in people's lives. Sometimes the experiences that people have in natural environments are strongly felt, but hard to put into words. Emotional experiences of this kind may carry a sense of awe, wonder, joy, and deep meaning; and may directly influence quality of life. Positive experiences in natural environments serve as significant sources of meaning and happiness, often leading people to form strong emotional attachments that can in turn influence second-home development and vacation choices. This can become a source of controversy in natural resource management if management actions threaten to change the character of places where people have formed strong attachments. It is critical for resource managers and planners to recognize the importance of sense of place, to understand why people consider certain places to be special, and to consider how such places may be affected by land management and development policies.

Criterion 7:

LEGAL, INSTITUTIONAL, AND ECONOMIC FRAMEWORK FOR FOREST CONSERVATION AND SUSTAINABLE MANAGEMENT

Montréal Process Criterion 7 (Montréal Process Working Group 2010); Northern Area Forest Sustainability Indicators 15.3–15.5, 17.1, 17.2, 18.1-18.6 (USDA FS 2010d)

The importance of legal, institutional, and economic frameworks for forest conservation and sustainable management

This criterion focuses on the social context of forests—the laws, policies, administrative rules, and social and economic institutions—that governs forest resource management and use. What society permits or restricts, encourages or discourages all influence the sustainability of forest resources. Criterion 7 captures this by turning attention to all the different social institutions that create and enforce rules about resource management and use.

Many of the criteria included in this assessment provide baseline measures, analyzing current conditions and providing a starting point for projecting future conditions (among others, how much land is forested and how many species are at risk). This criterion is different in that it addresses the likely characteristics of change. Forest sustainability is less likely where there are no rules or guidelines protecting resources or where laws and regulations are not enforced; more likely where society has developed social institutions to guide forest management.

Indicators of the legal, institutional, and economic frameworks for forest conservation and sustainable management in northern forests

From the broad range of institutions and practices that can be considered under Criterion 7, we focus on three: (1) forest-related planning and implementation, (2) best practice codes (or best management practices) for forest management, and (3) management of forests to conserve special values.

Forest planning and policy review; and opportunities for public participation in decisionmaking

Planning, assessment, and policy review provide regular opportunities to view forest management from a long-term perspective. Because these activities involve significant efforts to communicate with and involve the public, they also constitute opportunities for public participation in public policy and decisionmaking.

Under the Montréal Process, broad participation in resource management is encouraged, so that people interested in, but without an official role in decisionmaking (often referred to as "stakeholders") have opportunities to voice their opinions about forest policies and management activities. Stakeholders can include local residents, recreational forest users, business people whose livelihood is directly or indirectly tied to forests, technical experts (whether they

Key Findings for Criterion 7

- Each Northern State recently completed a forest resource assessment and strategy.
- State and Federal agencies support forest planning on private forest lands.
- Just over half (11 of 20) of the Northern States require forest-related planning, and nearly all States require periodic planning or assessment for other natural resources or activities.
- Best practice codes, sometimes referred to as best management practices, represent society's collective wisdom about protecting the environment during land management operations like harvesting and road building. These have been adopted across the Northern States, but enforcement and monitoring varies widely.

- Unlike water and soils and wildlife/biodiversity standards, silvicultural best practice codes are seldom mandatory.
- Conserving special forest values in the North, where private and non-Federal ownership account for 92 percent of forested land, requires coordination between many owners. Agreements that transfer, trade or sell some of these property rights (for example, development rights) are key to conservation schemes in landscapes with mixed ownerships.
- Continuing parcelization and turnover in ownership is a concern, because they jeopardize previous arrangements and coordination of resource management.

are affiliated with a management agency or not), or none of the above. What they all have in common is an interest in the fate of a particular forest or forest resource.

Unlike top-down, expert-based management, a participatory process emphasizes joint discovery, where managers learn from, as well as educate, their stakeholders. In many situations, this inclusive style of decisionmaking is more conducive to positive change and innovation than the closed model that was pervasive in the middle of the last century. Collaboration also recognizes the significance of forest management decisions for local communities. Because their economic prospects and quality of life are often directly affected by decisions made in the forest planning process, communities need to be involved in forest planning (Steelman 2001).

Public involvement is a part of virtually all major forest plans, forest plan revisions, and assessments for public lands; and some policy reviews. Public hearings or meetings bring together people who are not regularly involved in forest management, brief them about future issues and options, and hear their views about the strategic direction of forest management. Sustainability efforts can benefit from activities that broaden discussion and debate because sustainability often requires innovation and changes in management practices and priorities. Whether the innovative ideas come from the forestry professionals or the public participants, the process benefits from broad discussion.

Forest-related planning, assessment, and policy review processes take place at all levels of government. Many are required by law and are revisited on a cyclical basis. Others, including the Northern Forest Futures Assessment, are special efforts that are not on a schedule for recurring. Regional assessments often focus on the issues and resources common across ownerships and across States. Variations in resources (human, natural, and fiscal) have less influence at this regional scale, allowing for a more informed perspective on society's progress toward achieving sustainability.

The 2008 Farm Bill modified the Cooperative Forestry Assistance Act requiring that State agencies develop forest resource assessments and strategic plans to be eligible for Federal funding (http://www.northeastern forests.org/FRPC/). In 2010, all State forestry agencies nationwide completed statewide forest resource assessment and strategy documents. Individual State assessments and strategies tier off the national plan and can be accessed through the National Association of State Foresters Web site (http://www.stateforesters.org/issues_and_policy/forest_in_the_farm_bill). Each State assessment includes a description of conditions and trends across all trees and forests; key forest-related threats, benefits, and opportunities; and priority landscape areas. Each State resource strategy addresses the issues and priority landscape areas highlighted in the assessment and identifies the resources needed to address the strategies. State forestry agencies engaged stakeholders and partners in the development of their assessments and strategies.

Table 20—Forest-related planning and assessment laws by Northern State.

State	Forest-related Planning (P) or Assessment (A)	Law	Year enacted
Massachusetts	A	Massachusetts Environmental Policy Act (MEPA) MGL Ch. 30 Sec. 61-62H; Regulations 301 CMR 11.00	1973
Maryland	A	Maryland Forest Conservation Act. Annotated Code of MD Section 5-1601 -- 5-1613	1991
	P	Renewable Forest Resource Plans. Annotated Code of MD Section 5-214	1979
Maine	P	Biennial report on the state of the State's forests 1997 12 MRSA 8879	1997
	A	An Act to Implement the Recommendations of the Majority of the Joint Standing Committee on Agriculture Conservation and Forestry Regarding Enhancing Forest Resource Assessment Public Law 97 Chapter 720	1997
	P, A	Forest Resource Assessment Program 1997 12 MRSA 8876	1997
	P	Forest Sustainability 1997 12 MRSA 8876-A	1997
	A	Determination of supply and demand for timber resources 1997 12 MRSA 8877-A	1997
Michigan	P, A	Part 525 Statewide Forest Resources Plan of the Natural Resources and Environmental Protection Act 1994 Public Act 451	1994
Minnesota	P, A	MN Forest Resource Management Act	1982
	P, A	Sustainable Forest Resources Act	1995
New Hampshire	P, A	RSA 227-I: 8 (originally RSA 220 effective 1981)	1995
New Jersey	P	NJ Stat. Ann 13:1L - 5 (WEST 1983)	1983
New York	P, A	Environmental Conservation Law Section 9 Title 8 Forest Resources Planning (9-0805)	1983
Rhode island	P	Chapter 42-11 of the General Laws of Rhode Island	
Wisconsin	P, A	Wisconsin Statute 28.04 State Forests	1949

State laws that facilitate or require forest-related planning or assessment are shown in Table 20. Planning involves the development of a future-oriented strategic document that outlines what kinds of management activities will be carried out in coming years. Assessment involves research that generates a comprehensive description of the current status of resources, programs, events, and concerns. Ideally, any statewide plan would outline objectives based on information from a statewide assessment and would link to a set of broad goals developed in a previous plan, with new specific objectives arising from current concerns and events. Not surprisingly, planning and assessment activities are required by law in all States that have extensive forest resources.

As Table 21 shows, however, State forestry agencies are not the only organizations engaged in planning, nor are timber resources the only focus of planning; wildlife, recreation, and land use may also be considered part of natural resource planning. Table 21 illustrates the different purposes and targets of planning and assessment activity in the Northern States.

Unlike governments that manage their forests with specialized staffs and resources, private citizens with small parcels may be ill-equipped to develop their own plans for resource management. Forest landowners are offered planning and management assistance through State forestry programs, with funding, technical assistance, and support from U.S. Forest Service State and Private Forestry (Figs. 52 and 53). Forest stewardship plans are of particular value for forest sustainability. Consulting foresters or State forestry staffs work with landowners to determine management goals, assess resources, and develop plans for operations and activities, including harvesting, timber stand improvement work, and wildlife habitat protection and maintenance.

Table 21—Forest planning (2000 to 2005) and advisory (2006) activity for Northern States (National Association of State Foresters 2009).

Type	CT	DE	IA	IL	IN	MA	MD	ME	MI	MN	MO	NH	NJ	NY	OH	PA	RI	VT	WI	WV
Strategic agency/department plan		x	x		x	x	x	x	x	x	x		x	x	x	x	x	x	x	x
Comprehensive statewide forest plan		x	x			x	x	x	x				x	x	x				x	x
State-owned forest land plan		x	x		x	x	x	x	x	x	x	x	x	x	x	x	x	x	x	
Municipal-owned forest land plan		x			x			x	x							x	x			
County-owned forest land plan		x						x											x	
Statewide land-use plan					x	x	x		x	x	x					x	x	x		
Comprehensive wildlife plan		x	x	x	x		x	x	x	x	x							x	x	
Statewide recreation plan		x	x		x	x	x	x	x		x			x		x	x	x	x	
Watershed-based plan		x	x	x	x	x	x	x		x			x	x	x	x	x	x	x	x
Multi-state plan		x	x	x		x	x	x	x				x					x	x	x
Active forest advisory board in 2006	x	x			x	x			x	x	x	x	x	x	x			x	x	x

Ideally, the consulting forester is both a sounding board to help owners clarify their goals and intentions, and a source of expert information and experience about the potential for ensuring sustainability and other likely outcomes.

Variations in the number of plans among States are largely the result of differences in amount of forest acreage and the number of owners, but States also differ in the degree of emphasis they place on stewardship planning in relation to other activities. Because technical assistance from professional foresters is central to plan development, the number of plans and acres covered under stewardship plans is sensitive to changes in the Federal and State funding that support their availability. Approximately 10 percent of the northern nonindustrial private forest land acreage is managed under stewardship plans, but the covered area for individual States ranges from less than 5 percent to more than 30 percent (Table 22).

By 2006, all the National Forests in the 20 Northern States had completed forest plan revisions. National Forest plan revisions are intended to address broad issues that recur often across different forest projects and provide guidance for all major forestwide changes over a 10- to 15-year horizon. For example, because conducting silvicultural treatments and remodeling recreation facilities both can affect the visual character of a National Forest, visual character is an issue that might be addressed in the forest plan. Ongoing litigation since enactment of the National Forest Management Act in 1976 has slowed forest planning and forest plan revision on National Forests, and current efforts focus on issues that are widely acknowledged to need attention.

Across all levels of government, "sunshine" laws that require transparency and access to official government activities have been enacted to support public participation. Laws requiring open meetings, which date back to the 1970s and are present in various forms in all States, ensure that the public and the press have the right to know about upcoming meetings in which government employees will address land management, planning, and other activities that may be of interest to stakeholders. Through these laws, public access to documents and public involvement in decisionmaking have become a more formal and intentional part of government operations in the United States.

Formal advisory boards can also be established to seek outside input (shown in Table 21). Fourteen of the 20 Northern States have active forest advisory boards that regularly meet with the State forester and her/his staff. They are typically made up of key stakeholders, natural resource specialists, government natural resource agencies, nonprofit organizations, and resource interest groups.

FIGURE 52

Number of new or revised stewardship plans by Northern State, 2001 to 2010.

FIGURE 53

Area covered by new or revised stewardship plans by Northern State, 2001 to 2010.

CT	MO
DE	NH
IA	NJ
IL	NY
IN	OH
MA	PA
MD	RI
ME	VT
MI	WI
MN	WV

Table 22—Cumulative area of private, noncorporate forest land covered by active forest stewardship plans, 2010. States are ordered from highest to lowest proportion of stewardship plan coverage.

State	Private noncorporate forest area[a]	Cumulative area under forest stewardship plans[b]	Proportion of area under stewardship plans
	----------------------------------(1,000 acres)----------------------------------		(percent)
Wisconsin	9,674	2,985	31
New Hampshire	2,844	634	22
Maryland	1,462	324	22
Illinois	3,509	628	18
Delaware	244	39	16
Minnesota	5,921	860	15
New Jersey	805	115	14
Massachusetts	1,998	276	14
Indiana	3,588	463	13
Iowa	2,511	295	12
Ohio	6,064	520	9
New York	12,190	975	8
Pennsylvania	9,6030	531	6
West Virginia	7,174	270	4
Vermont	3,109	110	4
Connecticut	1,148	39	3
Maine	6,261	210	3
Missouri	11,755	343	3
Rhode Island	251	7	3
Michigan	9,458	203	2
North total	99,569	9,828	10

[a]From Smith et al. (2009).

[b]From State data in the Performance Measurement Accountability System, via Michael Huneke, U.S. Forest Service. (8 February 2011).

Best practice codes for forest management

Best practice codes (or best management practices) are recommendations for working on the land. They capture and maintain the collective wisdom society has about how to protect the environment during operations such as harvesting and road building. Unlike the strategic plans and assessments discussed above that operate at a large scale and a long time horizon, these standards and guidelines are meant to regulate daily, routine activities undertaken in the course of (often) small projects.

Almost all Northern States have some standards and guidelines across three general areas of management: silviculture, water and soils, and wildlife or biodiversity (Table 23). Best practice codes can be voluntary or mandatory recommendations, guidelines, or standards. Once established, their effectiveness depends on whether they are maintained and whether their use is promoted. The need to monitor the implementation and effectiveness of standards and guidelines is generally recognized, but not always supported. Without monitoring, the potential exists for discrepancies between intentions and actual behavior. The voluntary nature of many guidelines means that implementation is not certain, and effectiveness is largely unknown, although some States have adopted a regional-level protocol for monitoring effectiveness.

Mandatory standards and guidelines are commonly the result of legal requirements, often those associated with environmental regulations such as the National Environmental Policy Act and the Clean Water Act. Monitoring the implementation and effectiveness of standards and guidelines may also be carried out in response to Federal requirements. Federal environmental legislation also accounts for the differences among the three sets of standards

and guidelines: silvicultural guidelines (seldom mandatory), water and soils (often mandatory), and wildlife/biodiversity standards (often mandatory). Federal regulation to implement legislation and the mandatory nature of many State standards and guidelines for water quality and biodiversity also reflect the sensitivity of these systems to poor management.

On private land, few standards and guidelines are mandatory and monitoring is uncommon, primarily because of hesitancy to be perceived as violating private property rights and the practical difficulties of accessing private lands.

Management of forests to conserve special values

The terms of sustainability as set forth in the Montréal Process require that society consider both basic needs, such as fiber and energy production, and conservation. Conserving special forest values—environmental, cultural, social, or scientific—through management is one of the primary motivations for many in the forestry profession, and its significance is reflected here. Forests are not sustainable by the Montréal Process definition unless these special values are preserved.

Table 23—Management standards and guidelines and their monitoring across ownership types, by Northern State, whether mandatory (M) or voluntary (V) and whether measuring compliance (C) or effectiveness (E).

State	Silviculture				Water, soils				Wildlife, biodiversity			
	State forest		Private forest		State forest		Private forest		State forest		Private forest	
	Standard or guide	Monitoring	Standard or guide	Monitoring	Standard or guide	Monitoring	Standard or guide	Monitoring	Standard or guide	Monitoring	Standard or guide	Monitoring
CT												
DE	M	C			M	C	M	C				
IA	M	C,E	V		M	C,E	V		M	C,E	V	
IL		E	V			E	V					
IN	M		V		M	C,E	V		M		V	
MA	M	C,E			M	C,E			M	C,E		
MD	V	C,E			M	C,E	M					
ME	V	C,E	V		V	C,E	V	C,E	V	C,E	V	
MI		C			M	C	V		M	C		
MN	V	C	V	C	V	C	V	C	V	C	V	C
MO	M	C,E	V		M	C,E	V		M	C,E	V	
NH	V		V		M	C	M					
NJ		C,E	V	C	M	C	M	C		C	V	C
NY	M	C	V	C		C	V	C		C	V	C
OH	M	C	M		M	C	M	C	M	C	M	
PA	M	C	V		M	C	M	C	M	C,E	V	
RI	M	C,E	V	C	M	C,E	V	C,E	M	C	V	
VT	V		V		M	C	M	C,E	V	C	V	
WI	V	C	V,M	C	V,M	C,E	V,M	C,E	V,M	C	V,M	C
WV			V		M	C	M	C			V	

In the North, where private and other non-Federal ownerships account for 92 percent of forested land, conservation of habitats must be coordinated among owners, each perhaps controlling only a small portion of a critical landscape. For this reason, clear, enforced property rights are also important, because agreements that transfer, trade, or sell some of these rights (for example, development rights) are key to the success of conservation schemes in mixed landscapes.

The United States has a long history of forest conservation that continues today. Yellowstone, one of the World's first national parks, was established in 1872. Also established in the late 1800s, the forest reserves (now the national forests) protect water and provide timber. The passage of the Wilderness Act in 1964 provides additional protections for millions of acres of forest throughout the Nation.

Protected areas set aside land and water resources (including forests) in perpetuity to preserve natural ecosystems and provide refuges for species of concern. The maps in Figure 54, which distinguish protected forest

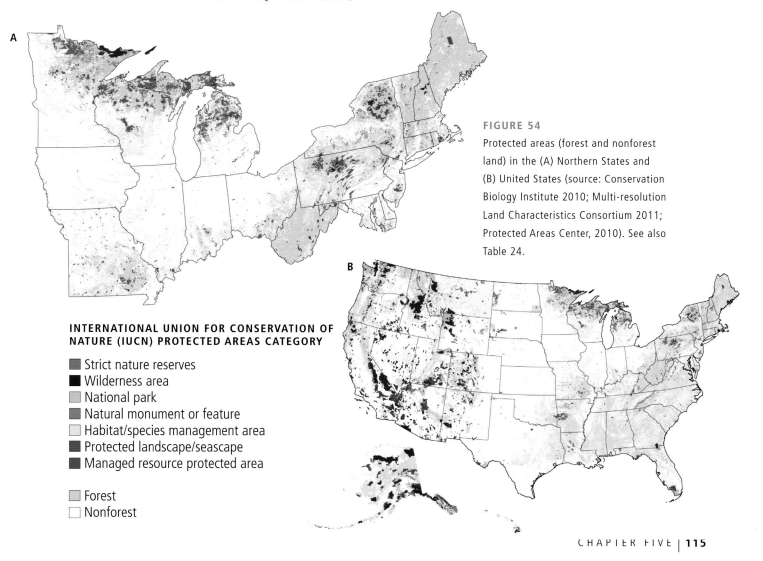

FIGURE 54

Protected areas (forest and nonforest land) in the (A) Northern States and (B) United States (source: Conservation Biology Institute 2010; Multi-resolution Land Characteristics Consortium 2011; Protected Areas Center, 2010). See also Table 24.

INTERNATIONAL UNION FOR CONSERVATION OF NATURE (IUCN) PROTECTED AREAS CATEGORY

- Strict nature reserves
- Wilderness area
- National park
- Natural monument or feature
- Habitat/species management area
- Protected landscape/seascape
- Managed resource protected area

- Forest
- Nonforest

land from other protected land, are based on the latest version of the Conservation Biology Institute Protected Areas Database, a comprehensive geospatial data set (including detailed information on land ownership, management, and conservation status) of all protected areas in the United States. (Conservation Biology Institute 2010, Protected Areas Center 2010).

In addition to major Federal and State-owned protected areas such as national parks, State parks, and wildlife refuges, this database also focuses on lands managed by local governments (such as county forests) and nongovernmental organizations (such as The Nature Conservancy's reserves). Protected areas are classified into six categories ranging from (I) strict nature reserves and wilderness areas to (VI) managed resource protected areas (International Union for Conservation of Nature 1994, 2010; DellaSalla 2001).

Total U.S. protected area acreage, both forested and nonforested, is concentrated in the West and Alaska, predominantly on Federal lands. To determine whether the spatial distribution of protected forest land is more balanced, we estimated the area of forest land by protected category at a 0.22 acre (0.09 ha) spatial scale by intersecting a digital map of forest/nonforest cover with the protected area map boundaries. That analysis showed that 16 percent of northern forest land (27 of 172 million forested acres) falls in a protected category (Table 24), nearly identical to the entire United States, and larger than the conterminous States (13 percent). Compared to the United States as a whole, the North has relatively little forest area in the three most restrictive protected categories and relatively abundant forest area in the least restrictive category.

The protected forest area is concentrated in the Lake States, where the Boundary Waters Canoe Wilderness Area in northern Minnesota encompasses 1.1 million acres of the Superior National Forest; and New York, where the nearly 3-million acre Adirondack and Catskills Reserves were set aside nearly 100 years ago to be managed by the State as "wild forever."

If protected areas are not large enough or widespread enough to support the full range of habitat attributes needed to sustain all ecosystem components, areas outside protected status may be enlisted to contribute to biodiversity goals. The ability to manage both public and private unprotected forest lands for these broader goals depends on the objectives of the owners and their willingness to consider management options that can be integrated with those established for protected areas. One working example is the North Maine Woods, within whose boundaries are over 3.5 million acres of commercial forest land (North Maine Woods 2010), two wild northeastern rivers (the St. John and the Allagash), and the Allagash Wilderness Waterway. This organization of landowners—corporations, individuals, and families—have joined with Maine's natural resource agencies in a partnership to address landscape-scale management issues.

Table 24—Protected forest area and percent by International Union for Conservation of Nature (IUCN) protected status category.

Protected status	Total U.S. protected forest land		Conterminous U.S. protected forest land		Northern States protected forest land	
	Area	Proportion	Area	Proportion	Area	Proportion
	(1,000 acres)	(percent)	(1,000 acres)	(percent)	(1,000 acres)	(percent)
Strict nature reserve[a]	560	0.1	521	0.1	7	<0.01
Wilderness area[a]	30,439	4.1	24,847	4.0	1,796	1.0
National park[b]	8,056	1.1	6,548	1.1	820	0.5
Natural monument or feature[c]	4,195	0.6	1,595	0.3	25	<0.01
Habitat /species management area[d]	33,771	4.5	12,857	2.1	4,355	2.5
Protected landscape[e]	30,046	4.0	19,676	3.2	8,951	5.2
Managed resource protected area[f]	14,416	1.9	12,667	2.0	11,415	6.6
Total protected forest land	121,485	16.2	78,711	12.6	27,370	15.9
Total area of all forest land	751,228	--	622,611	--	172,039	--

[a]*Category I: an area of land and/or sea possessing some outstanding or representative ecosystems, geological or physiological features and/or species, available primarily for scientific research and/or environmental monitoring or a large area of unmodified or slightly modified land, and/or sea, retaining its natural character and influence, without permanent or significant habitation, which is protected and managed so as to preserve its natural condition. Strict nature reserves (Ia) are distinguished from wilderness areas (Ib).*

[b]*Category II: a natural area of land and/or sea, designated to (1) protect the ecological integrity of one or more ecosystems for present and future generations, (2) exclude exploitation or occupation inimical to the purposes of designation of the area, and (3) provide a foundation for spiritual, educational, recreational, and visitor opportunities, all of which must be environmentally and culturally comparable.*

[c]*Category III: an area of land and/or sea containing one or more specific natural or natural/cultural features which are of outstanding or unique value because of their inherent rarity, representative or esthetic qualities, or cultural significance*

[d]*Category IV: an area of land and/or sea subject to active intervention for management purposes so as to ensure the maintenance of habitats and/or to meet the requirements of specific species.*

[e]*Category V: an area of land with coast and sea as appropriate, where the interaction of people and nature over time has produced an area of distinct character with significant esthetic, ecological, and/or cultural value, and often with high biological diversity. Safeguarding the integrity of this traditional interaction is vital to the protection, maintenance, and evolution of such an area.*

[f]*Category VI: an area of land and/or sea containing predominantly unmodified natural systems, managed to ensure long term protection and maintenance of biological diversity, while providing at the same time a sustainable flow of natural products and services to meet community needs protected forest.*

Another example of integrating protected areas with areas managed for multiple and sustainable uses is the Wisconsin County Forests Association—more than 2.3 million acres of county forests established by the Wisconsin legislature for open access to a range of users, from hunters to hikers to birdwatchers. This is the only association of its kind in the United States.

The conservation of special forest values in northern forests depends on programs that enable foresters and other natural resource professionals to work with individual forest landowners as well as governments and nongovernmental organizations. Continuing parcelization and turnover in ownership is a source of concern because these changes can jeopardize previous resource-management arrangements and agreements. Conserving the land and its wide array of values is not simple. For example, setting aside protected areas does not prevent housing growth from fragmenting surrounding landscapes, and protected areas are typically too small to exist as islands cut off from other biological resources (Radeloff et al. 2010). However, forest land preservation agreements and forest stewardship plans that keep land in private ownership and preserve traditional land-use values (such as those that support working family farms and ranches)

can offer viable options for maintaining natural forest areas and preserving water quality in the face of land development pressure. This requires planning and management groups to work across larger landscapes, regardless of ownership patterns, in an effort to understand, manage, and protect their resources in common.

Sustainability relies heavily on the many organizations that teach, communicate, and support resource management. These include professional associations for resource managers (such as regional, State, and local chapters of the Society of American Foresters), student associations (such as Future Farmers of America, 4-H, and the Student Conservation Association), educational institutions at all levels, nongovernmental organizations, and ad-hoc groups that organize around specific issues or events. All contribute significantly to sustainability, and most are locally controlled.

The university-based Cooperative Extension Service is another significant resource for achieving sustainability. Through education, research, and communication, it reaches a wide range of people—professionals and amateurs alike—who support the goals of the Montréal Process.

Criterion 8:

URBAN AND COMMUNITY FORESTS

The importance of urban and community forests

Urban and community forests are the trees and forests found in cities, towns, villages, and communities. This category of forest includes both forested stands and trees along streets, in residential lots, and parks. These trees within cities and communities provide many ecosystem services and values to both urban and rural populations. These benefits include:

- Carbon sequestration and storage
- Removal of air pollution, improving air quality; absorption of ultraviolet radiation; and reduced noise pollution
- Reduced air temperature, improving human comfort and reducing building energy use
- Reduced stormwater runoff, improving water quality
- Improved aesthetics contributing to human physiological and psychological well-being
- Community cohesion and increased property values

Key Findings for Criterion 8

- In the North, 80 percent of the population lives in urban areas which cover 6 percent of the region's land base.
- Urban and community lands together cover 8.5 percent of the North. The State with the highest percent urban or community land is New Jersey at 44.2 percent; the lowest percent is Vermont at 2.9 percent.
- Nationally, States with the greatest increase in percentage of urban land between 1990 and 2000 were in the North: Rhode Island (5.7 percent), New Jersey (5.1 percent), Connecticut (5.0 percent), Massachusetts (5.0 percent), Delaware (4.1 percent), and Maryland (3.0 percent).
- Most of the urbanization in the North in the 1990s occurred in agricultural (42 percent) and forested (37 percent) areas.

- Of the 11 conterminous States that had greater than half of all urban development occur within forests in the 1990s, seven were in the North, including the top two (Rhode Island and Connecticut).
- Overall tree cover in the North is 46.8 percent, with the highest percent tree cover in New Hampshire (88.9 percent) and the lowest in Iowa (10.4 percent).
- Within urban or community lands in the North, tree cover averages 39 percent while impervious cover averages 20 percent. Tree cover in urban or community lands ranged from a high of 67 percent in Connecticut to a low of 19 percent in Iowa.
- Tree cover in urban or community areas provides numerous and valuable ecosystem services.

Urban forest in Central

in New York

Urban and community areas are defined by two U.S. Census Bureau definitions that overlap. Urban land is all the territory, population, and housing units located within urbanized areas or urban clusters, each with a core population density of 1,000 people per square mile and with surrounding areas that have lower population densities (U.S. Census Bureau 2007). Community lands are places that have geopolitical boundaries (such as cities, towns, or unincorporated named places) that may include all, some, or no urban land within their boundaries. As seen in Figure 55, urban land can be found outside community boundaries, and not all areas within communities are urban.

Urban land encompasses the more heavily populated areas (population density-based definition), and community land encompasses both urban and rural (non-urban) communities that are recognized by their geopolitical boundaries (political definition); and both definitions provide information about human settlements and the forest resources within those settlements. As some urban land exists beyond community boundaries and not all community land is urban (communities are often a mix of urban and rural land), the category of "urban or community" was created to understand forest attributes accumulated by the union of these two terms. People in the Northern States depend heavily on both urban and rural forests to sustain quality of life. The majority of people in the Northern States live in urban areas, so healthy urban trees and forests are particularly important for the quality of their environment, their health, and their well-being.

This section describes the extent of urban and community forests and their spatial distribution, and it provides estimates of some of their ecosystem services and values. Though the Montréal Criteria and Indicators could be applied to forests and trees in northern urban areas, much of the data that would be needed are not available, especially data on conservation of soil and water resources (Criterion 4), enhancement of long-term multiple socioeconomic benefits (Criterion 6), and legal, institutional and policy frameworks for sustainable management (Criterion 7).

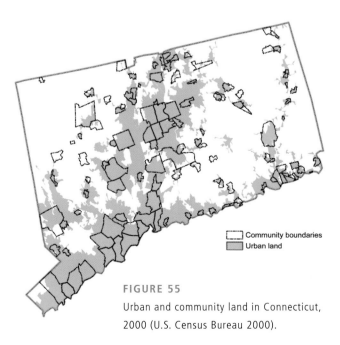

Community boundaries
Urban land

FIGURE 55
Urban and community land in Connecticut, 2000 (U.S. Census Bureau 2000).

However, data on biological diversity (Criterion 1), productive capacity (Criterion 2), ecosystem health (Criterion 3), and contributions to the global carbon cycle (Criterion 5) are partially available for cities that have completed urban forest assessments: New York, Syracuse, Baltimore, Minneapolis, Chicago, Boston, Jersey City, Philadelphia (Nowak et al. 2006a, 2006b, 2007a, 2007b). The focus of these assessments has been on monitoring, quantifying, and comparing the cumulative effects of urban forest ecosystem structure (such as species composition, size distribution, tree health, and leaf area) on ecosystem services and values (such as carbon storage and sequestration, energy use in buildings, air pollution removal, air temperature, stream flows, and water quality). Understanding and quantifying these relationships can lead to improved management plans in urban areas to sustain ecosystem and human health for future generations, but not without detailed data that are currently unavailable and have yet to be added to the U.S. Forest Service inventory and analysis protocols (Cumming et al. 2007, 2008; Nowak et al. 2007c).

Indicators for northern urban and community forests

Urban and community land in the North

In 2000, 95 million people (80 percent) in the North lived in urban areas, and 86 million (71 percent) lived in communities (Table 25, Fig. 56). Six percent of the land was in urban areas, 6.3 percent was in communities, and 8.5 percent was in the combined urban or community category. Proportion of urban land varied from 1.1 percent in Maine to 38 percent in New Jersey (Table 26; Figs. 57 and 58). The U.S. areas with the highest percent urban land were the Northeastern States (10 percent) and the Southern Atlantic States (8 percent for Florida, Georgia, North Carolina, South Carolina, and Virginia combined). Areas with most urban land were the Northeastern (13 million acres) and North Central States (12 million acres), which together comprise the North (Nowak et al. 2005).

Urban growth in the North, 1990 to 2000

Urban land in the conterminous United States increased from 2.5 percent in 1990 to 3.1 percent in 2000, an increase in area about

FIGURE 56
Population density by county, 2000, in the Northern States (U.S. Census Bureau 2000).

FIGURE 57
Urban or community land, 2000, in the Northern States (U.S. Census Bureau 2000).

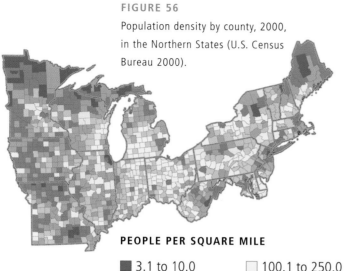

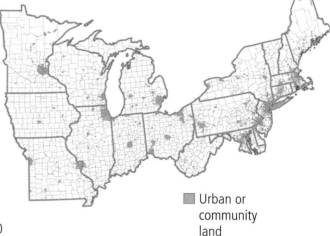

PEOPLE PER SQUARE MILE

- ■ 3.1 to 10.0
- ■ 10.1 to 25.0
- ■ 25.1 to 50.0
- ■ 50.1 to 75.0
- ■ 75.1 to 100.0
- □ 100.1 to 250.0
- □ 250.1 to 500.0
- ■ 500.1 to 1,000.0
- ■ 1,000.1 to 5,000.0
- ■ 5,000.1 to 66,940.1

■ Urban or community land

FIGURE 58
Percent of county area classified as urban or community land, 2000, in the Northern States (U.S. Census Bureau 2000).

PERCENT

- □ 0
- ■ 0.1 to 5
- □ 5.1 to 10
- □ 10.1 to 25
- ■ 25.1 to 75
- ■ 75.1 to 100

Hartford, Connecticut

the size of Vermont and New Hampshire combined. States with the largest percentage increases (Table 27) were Rhode Island (5.7 percent), New Jersey (5.1 percent), and Connecticut and Massachusetts (5.0 percent each). Seven Northeastern States are among the 10 States with the greatest increase in percent urban land. States with the greatest absolute increase in urban land, were Florida (925,000 acres), Texas (871,000 acres), and California (737,000 acres).

Table 25—Population characteristics in the Northern States and urban and community areas ordered from highest to lowest percent urban population.

State	Total for the State			Urban areas[a]				Communities[b]			
	Population, 2000 (1,000)	Percent change from 1990	Density (people per square mile)	Population, 2000 (1,000)	Population percent of State total	Percent change from 1990	Density (people per square mile)	Population, 2000 (1,000)	Population percent of State total	Percent change from 1990	Density (people per square mile)
New Jersey	8,414	8.9	1,136	7,939	94.4	14.9	2,847	6,059	72.0	10.5	3,064
Massachusetts	6,349	5.5	810	5,801	91.4	14.4	2,078	4,512	71.1	6.5	2,561
Rhode Island	1,048	4.5	1,004	953	90.9	10.4	2,477	746	71.1	2.5	3,446
Illinois	12,419	8.6	224	10,910	87.8	12.8	3,072	10,749	86.6	10.5	2,761
Connecticut	3,406	3.6	703	2,988	87.7	14.9	1,697	2,029	59.6	4.6	2,180
New York	18,976	5.5	403	16,603	87.5	9.5	4,241	15,351	80.9	6.1	4,164
Maryland	5,296	10.8	542	4,559	86.1	17.2	2,523	4,246	80.2	12.4	2,319
Delaware	784	17.6	401	628	80.1	29.0	2,084	345	44.0	34.6	2,004
Ohio	11,353	4.7	278	8,782	77.4	9.2	2,214	8,012	70.6	4.1	2,032
Pennsylvania	12,281	3.4	275	9,464	77.1	15.6	2,233	7,167	58.4	0.3	2,247
Michigan	9,938	6.9	175	7,419	74.7	13.2	2,233	6,384	64.2	5.1	2,219.7
Minnesota	4,919	12.4	62	3,490	70.9	14.2	2,331	3,939	80.1	16.3	996
Indiana	6,080	9.7	170	4,304	70.8	19.6	1,967	3,999	65.8	38.4	1,810
Missouri	5,595	9.3	81	3,883	69.4	10.5	2,142	3,862	69.0	8.7	1,344
Wisconsin	5,364	9.6	99	3,664	68.3	14.1	2,261	3,790	70.7	9.3	1,434
Iowa	2,926	5.4	53	1,787	61.1	6.2	2,204	2,272	77.6	6.7	1,178
New Hampshire	1,236	11.4	138	732	59.3	29.5	1,309	586	47.5	7.1	918
West Virginia	1,808	0.8	75	833	46.1	28.5	1,498	760	42.0	-1.2	1,010
Maine	1,275	3.8	41	513	40.2	-6.4	1,459	598	46.9	-2.3	498
Vermont	609	8.2	66	232	38.2	28.3	1,598	213	35.0	2.3	1,032
North total	120,079	6.9	186	95,485	79.5	13.1	2,489	85,617	71.3	8.2	2,094
Conterminous U.S. total	279,585	13.2	95	220,841	79.0	18.9	2,411	204,782	73.2	16.6	1,539

[a] All the territory, population, and housing units located within urbanized areas or urban clusters, each with a core population density of 1,000 people per square mile and with surrounding areas that have lower population densities (U.S. Census Bureau 2007).

[b] Places that have geopolitical boundaries (such as cities, towns, or unincorporated named places) that may include all, some, or no urban land within their boundaries.

Table 26—Urban and community land in Northern States ordered from highest to lowest percent urban or community land.

State and region	State land area	Proportion in urban[a] land	Proportion in community[b] land	Proportion in urban or community land
	(1,000 acres)		(percent)	
New Jersey	4,743	37.6	26.7	44.2
Massachusetts	5,018	35.6	22.5	40.4
Connecticut	3,099	36.4	19.2	39.9
Rhode Island	668	36.8	20.7	39.4
Maryland	6,252	18.5	18.7	23.4
Delaware	1,250	15.4	8.8	17.8
Ohio	26,123	9.7	9.7	12.6
Pennsylvania	28,633	9.5	7.1	12.4
New York	30,120	8.3	7.8	10.8
New Hampshire	5,749	6.2	7.1	10.3
Illinois	35,465	6.4	7.0	8.7
Indiana	22,895	6.1	6.2	8.1
Michigan	36,301	5.9	5.1	7.3
Wisconsin	34,652	3.0	4.9	5.6
Minnesota	50,866	1.9	5.0	5.2
Missouri	43,983	2.6	4.2	4.7
Maine	19,809	1.1	3.9	4.2
West Virginia	15,371	2.3	3.1	4.1
Iowa	35,681	1.5	3.5	3.6
Vermont	5,915	1.6	2.2	2.9
North total	412,594	6.0	6.3	8.5
Conterminous U.S. total	1,891,769	3.1	4.5	5.4

[a]All the territory, population, and housing units located within urbanized areas or urban clusters, each with a core population density of 1,000 people per square mile and with surrounding areas that have lower population densities (U.S. Census Bureau 2007).

[b]Places that have geopolitical boundaries (such as cities, towns, or unincorporated named places) that may include all, some, or no urban land within their boundaries.

Boston, Massachusetts

Autumn 'White Oaks' (Quercus alba) & prairie grasses, Waubonsie State Park, Iowa

Table 27—U.S. urban growth, 1990 to 2000 (Nowak et al. 2005).

State and region	Urban growth	Urban growth	Ranking for urban growth percent
	(acres)	(percent of state)	
Connecticut	159,000	5.0	3
Delaware	53,100	4.1	5
Maine	25,600	0.1	42
Maryland	199,400	3.0	6
Massachusetts	260,600	5.0	4
New Hampshire	103,100	1.7	11
New Jersey	253,100	5.1	2
New York	273,800	0.9	19
Pennsylvania	554,700	1.9	9
Rhode Island	40,500	5.7	1
Vermont	13,900	0.2	34
West Virginia	69,800	0.5	27
Northeast total	2,006,500	1.5	
Illinois	365,500	1.0	18
Indiana	287,200	1.2	15
Iowa	55,300	0.2	41
Michigan	381,900	1.0	17
Minnesota	150,800	0.3	32
Missouri	162,800	0.4	29
Ohio	363,500	1.4	13
Wisconsin	186,300	0.5	25
North Central total	1,953,400	0.7	
North total	3,959,900	1.0	
Florida	924,500	2.5	7
Georgia	694,800	1.8	10
North Carolina	653,600	2.0	8
South Carolina	286,700	1.4	12
Virginia	269,600	1.0	16
Southern Atlantic total	2,829,200	1.8	
Alabama	230,900	0.7	21
Arkansas	113,600	0.3	31

Table 27 continued

State and region	Urban area	Urban area change	Ranking for urban area change in 2000
	(acres)	(percent of state)	
Kentucky	135,200	0.5	24
Louisiana	164,200	0.5	23
Mississippi	108,600	0.4	30
Oklahoma	95,600	0.2	35
Tennessee	359,800	1.3	14
Texas	870,700	0.5	26
Mid-south total	2,078,700	0.5	
Kansas	90,400	0.2	38
Nebraska	41,200	0.1	44
North Dakota	13,000	0.0	45
South Dakota	12,900	0.0	47
Great Plains total	157,500	0.1	
Arizona	308,200	0.4	28
Colorado	165,200	0.2	33
Idaho	58,800	0.1	43
Montana	24,800	0.0	46
Nevada	132,300	0.2	37
New Mexico	129,500	0.2	39
Utah	90,200	0.2	40
Wyoming	12,000	0.0	48
Rocky Mountain total	920,900	0.2	
California	737,300	0.7	20
Oregon	119,100	0.2	36
Washington	275,700	0.6	22
Pacific Coast total	1,132,100	0.5	
Conterminous U.S. total	11,078,300	0.6	

The Motor City: Detroit, Michigan

In aggregate, the Southern Atlantic States had the largest percentage increase in urban land (1.8 percent), followed by the Northeastern States (1.5 percent). For all the Northern States, the increase was 1.0 percent. Regions with largest absolute urban growth were the South (5 million acres) and the North (4 million acres).

Most of the urbanization in Northern States occurred at the expense of agricultural (42.2 percent) and forested (37.0 percent) lands (Table 28, Fig. 59). Eleven of the 48 conterminous States had more than half of the total development occur within forests; of these, seven were Northern States, and two (Rhode Island and Connecticut) were at the top of the national list.

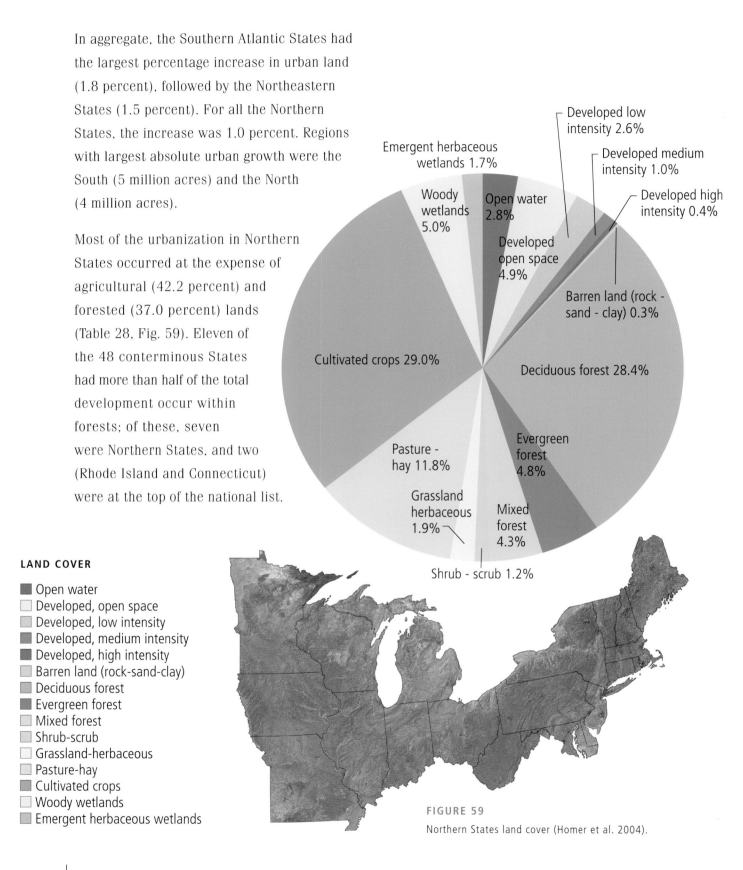

Emergent herbaceous wetlands 1.7%

Woody wetlands 5.0%

Open water 2.8%

Developed open space 4.9%

Developed low intensity 2.6%

Developed medium intensity 1.0%

Developed high intensity 0.4%

Barren land (rock - sand - clay) 0.3%

Deciduous forest 28.4%

Evergreen forest 4.8%

Mixed forest 4.3%

Shrub - scrub 1.2%

Grassland herbaceous 1.9%

Pasture - hay 11.8%

Cultivated crops 29.0%

LAND COVER

- Open water
- Developed, open space
- Developed, low intensity
- Developed, medium intensity
- Developed, high intensity
- Barren land (rock-sand-clay)
- Deciduous forest
- Evergreen forest
- Mixed forest
- Shrub-scrub
- Grassland-herbaceous
- Pasture-hay
- Cultivated crops
- Woody wetlands
- Emergent herbaceous wetlands

FIGURE 59

Northern States land cover (Homer et al. 2004).

Table 28—Distribution of area converted to urban uses from 1990 to 2000, by selected cover types as they existed in 1992 (USGS 2003), for Northern States ordered from greatest to least proportion of forest land subsumed (Nowak et al. 2005).

State and region	Cover type					
	Forest[a]	Agriculture[b]	Other[c]	Developed[d]	Woody wetland[e]	Herbaceous wetland[f]
	------------------------Proportion of the total area subsumed by urbanization (percent)------------------------					
Rhode Island	64.8	5.7	0.8	19.0	7.9	1.9
Connecticut	64.1	11.5	0.9	16.2	5.8	1.7
Massachusetts	62.9	7.6	1.4	17.7	6.1	4.2
West Virginia	62.2	25.4	1.8	10.4	0.2	0.1
New Hampshire	61.3	10.2	1.3	20.7	4.2	2.4
Maine	54.8	7.7	1.3	26.1	3.7	6.3
New York	51.2	28.1	0.5	17.5	1.9	0.7
New Jersey	48.4	28.0	1.0	12.7	8.6	1.3
Maryland	43.5	40.7	2.6	9.5	2.7	0.9
Pennsylvania	42.7	45.5	1.4	9.7	0.4	0.2
Vermont	39.7	28.1	1.7	22.4	5.5	2.6
Ohio	31.6	50.8	0.4	14.3	2.3	0.6
Michigan	31.2	47.5	2.1	12.2	6.1	1.0
Missouri	28.6	44.7	6.5	19.0	0.8	0.3
Delaware	28.4	45.6	1.4	15.3	5.2	4.0
Wisconsin	18.3	62.0	2.2	14.5	2.2	0.6
Minnesota	17.7	52.4	1.1	17.6	3.7	7.4
Indiana	15.2	66.8	0.8	14.9	1.9	0.5
Illinois	15.2	64.8	1.8	15.2	2.4	0.7
Iowa	12.1	52.3	8.0	25.4	1.7	0.6
All North	37.0	42.2	1.6	14.5	3.3	1.3
Conterminous U.S.	33.4	32.7	14.0	15.1	3.5	1.4

[a]*Deciduous, evergreen or mixed forests; tree canopy accounts for 25 to 100 percent of the cover.*

[b]*Pasture/hay, row crops, small grains, or fallow (75 to 100 percent of the cover); or orchards/vineyards/other nonnatural woody (25 to 100 percent of the cover).*

[c]*Bare/rock/sand/clay, quarries/strip mines/gravel pits, transitional, shrubland (25 to 100 percent of the cover), or grasslands/herbaceous (natural/seminatural; 75 to 100 percent of the cover).*

[d]*Areas characterized by a high percentage (30 percent or more) of constructed materials (such as asphalt, concrete, or buildings), or vegetation (primarily grasses) planted in developed settings for recreation, erosion control, or aesthetic purposes (75 to 100 percent of the cover).*

[e]*Areas where forest or shrubland vegetation accounts for 25-100 percent of the cover and the soil or substrate is periodically saturated with or covered with water*

[f]*Areas where perennial herbaceous vegetation accounts for 75-100 percent of the cover and the soil or substrate is periodically saturated with or covered with water*

Preliminary projections of urbanization and forests, 2000 to 2050

Given the growth patterns of the 1990s, urban land is projected to expand substantially in the future—from 3 percent of the conterminous United States in 2000 to 8 percent in 2050, an increase in area greater than the State of Montana (Nowak and Walton 2005). By 2050, four States, all in the North, are projected to have more than half of their States classified as urban land: Rhode Island (71 percent urban), New Jersey (64 percent), Massachusetts (61 percent), and Connecticut (61 percent).

Although Northeastern States tended to have the highest percentage of forest land that is projected to be urbanized by 2050, Southern States are expected to have the highest acreage increases (Fig. 60): 2.2 million for North Carolina and 1.9 million for Georgia,

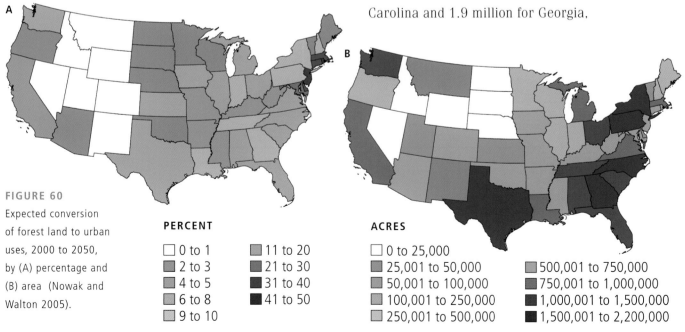

FIGURE 60
Expected conversion of forest land to urban uses, 2000 to 2050, by (A) percentage and (B) area (Nowak and Walton 2005).

PERCENT

- ☐ 0 to 1
- ☐ 2 to 3
- ☐ 4 to 5
- ☐ 6 to 8
- ☐ 9 to 10
- ☐ 11 to 20
- ☐ 21 to 30
- ☐ 31 to 40
- ☐ 41 to 50

ACRES

- ☐ 0 to 25,000
- ☐ 25,001 to 50,000
- ☐ 50,001 to 100,000
- ☐ 100,001 to 250,000
- ☐ 250,001 to 500,000
- ☐ 500,001 to 750,000
- ☐ 750,001 to 1,000,000
- ☐ 1,000,001 to 1,500,000
- ☐ 1,500,001 to 2,200,000

followed by New York (1.7 million), Pennsylvania (1.6 million), and Texas (1.5 million). The projected total U.S. conversion of forest to urban land is about 29 million acres, an area approximately the size of Pennsylvania (Nowak and Walton 2005).

Tree and impervious cover in urban and community areas

Tree and impervious cover data in the conterminous United States are available through the National Land Cover Database using data from circa 2001 (Figs. 61 to 64). However, tree cover is likely underestimated in the database by about 9.7 percent nationally (Greenfield et al. 2009, Nowak and Greenfield 2010). To adjust for this potential underestimation, photo-interpretation of tree cover using GoogleEarth™ imagery (image dates from 2002 to 2009) was conducted for the conterminous United States (n=66,887 points) and for urban and community areas (n = 16,227 points). Based on this image interpretation, total tree cover in the North (Table 29) is 47 percent, ranging from 89 percent in New Hampshire to 10 percent in Iowa. Note that tree canopy cover includes trees on agricultural lands, on wetlands, in urban and community areas, and in other places that would not be classified as forest land. Thus, northern forest land, which has about 87 percent tree cover, is estimated to cover 42 percent of the land area (Fig. 1, Table 1) whereas 47 percent of all land is covered by trees (Figs. 61 and 63, Table 29).

In the North, tree cover averages 38 percent in urban areas, 37 percent in community land, and 39 percent in the combined urban or community category (Table 30). These values are higher than the national average because the Northern States are relatively heavily forested (Fig. 61) and urban tree cover is significantly

Table 29—Percent tree and impervious cover for Northern States based on photo-interpretation of GoogleEarth™ imagery.

State and region	Tree cover	Impervious cover
	-------------------(percent)------------------	
New Hampshire	88.9	5.0
Maine	83.1	3.2
Vermont	81.5	1.9
West Virginia	81.4	2.0
Connecticut	72.6	7.7
Massachusetts	70.8	7.4
Rhode Island	70.3	10.9
Pennsylvania	65.8	4.6
New York	65.0	4.5
Michigan	59.5	4.1
New Jersey	57.0	12.1
Wisconsin	47.7	2.8
Maryland	42.8	6.1
Missouri	40.3	2.4
Ohio	39.9	5.5
Minnesota	34.8	2.2
Delaware	33.3	6.2
Indiana	25.7	3.7
Illinois	15.6	4.8
Iowa	10.4	3.0
All North	46.8	3.8

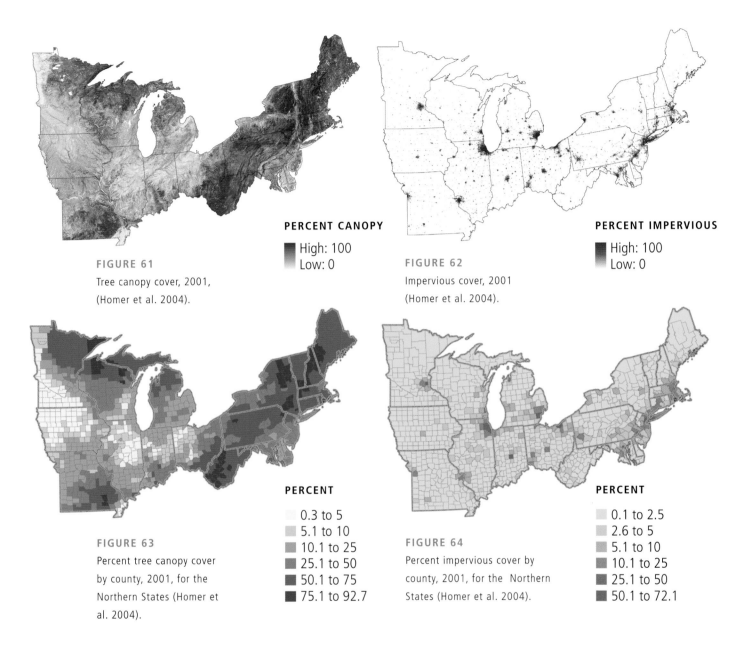

FIGURE 61

Tree canopy cover, 2001,
(Homer et al. 2004).

PERCENT CANOPY

High: 100
Low: 0

FIGURE 62

Impervious cover, 2001
(Homer et al. 2004).

PERCENT IMPERVIOUS

High: 100
Low: 0

FIGURE 63

Percent tree canopy cover
by county, 2001, for the
Northern States (Homer et
al. 2004).

PERCENT

0.3 to 5
5.1 to 10
10.1 to 25
25.1 to 50
50.1 to 75
75.1 to 92.7

FIGURE 64

Percent impervious cover by
county, 2001, for the Northern
States (Homer et al. 2004).

PERCENT

0.1 to 2.5
2.6 to 5
5.1 to 10
10.1 to 25
25.1 to 50
50.1 to 72.1

affected by surrounding vegetation types (Nowak et al. 1996). Within urban areas in the Northern States, tree cover is highest in Connecticut (67 percent) and lowest in Indiana (22 percent). Within community areas, tree cover was highest in New Hampshire (67 percent) and lowest in Iowa (19 percent). Within the combined urban or community category, tree cover was highest in Connecticut (67 percent) and lowest in Iowa

(19 percent). Figures 65 and 66 illustrate the distribution of tree cover and available space within urban or community land, based on NLCD 2001 data.

Impervious cover averages 24 percent in urban areas of the Northern States, 21 percent in communities, and 20 percent in the combined urban or community category (Table 30).

Table 30—Percent tree and impervious cover for urban, community, and urban or community land in the Northern States based on photo-interpretation of GoogleEarth™ imagery.

State and region	Urban land[a]		Community land[b]		Urban or community land	
	Tree cover	Impervious cover	Tree cover	Impervious cover	Tree cover	Impervious cover
			----(percent)----			
Connecticut	66.5	11.6	66.0	12.0	67.4	11.1
Massachusetts	64.5	16.7	60.9	16.1	65.1	14.5
New Hampshire	64.0	18.0	67.0	9.0	66.0	12.0
Maine	54.0	19.0	51.6	13.1	52.3	12.5
Rhode Island	54.0	26.0	40.0	36.0	51.0	24.0
Vermont	53.0	22.0	51.0	20.0	53.0	17.0
New Jersey	50.4	22.5	51.9	21.9	53.3	19.9
West Virginia	47.0	20.0	62.0	14.0	61.0	12.0
New York	41.2	27.4	41.1	24.3	42.6	22.4
Delaware	38.0	19.0	33.0	21.0	35.0	17.0
Michigan	34.6	31.5	34.0	29.0	35.0	26.8
Pennsylvania	34.0	24.6	45.0	18.6	41.0	19.1
Maryland	32.9	21.6	34.7	21.6	34.3	19.0
Missouri	31.1	22.0	29.2	18.3	31.5	18.0
Minnesota	31.0	24.1	33.8	13.2	34.0	13.3
Wisconsin	29.2	22.2	30.9	15.6	31.8	14.8
Ohio	29.0	27.1	31.0	28.1	31.5	24.5
Illinois	26.4	30.7	23.9	30.8	25.4	26.1
Iowa	24.0	27.0	18.8	20.4	19.0	19.5
Indiana	22.3	25.5	23.2	25.6	23.7	22.6
All North	38.2	24.4	36.8	21.4	39.0	19.7

[a]*All the territory, population, and housing units located within urbanized areas or urban clusters, each with a core population density of 1,000 people per square mile and with surrounding areas that have lower population densities (U.S. Census Bureau 2007).*

[b]*Places that have geopolitical boundaries (such as cities, towns, or unincorporated named places) that may include all, some, or no urban land within their boundaries.*

FIGURE 65

Percent tree cover in northern urban or community land by county, 2001 (Homer et al. 2004).

- ☐ < .06
- ☐ .06 to 1
- ☐ 1.1 to 2.5
- ☐ 2.6 to 10
- ☐ 10.1 to 25
- ☐ 25.1 to 50
- ☐ 50.1 to 75
- ☐ 75.1 to 84.9

FIGURE 66

Percent available growing space (areas not occupied by trees, impervious surfaces or water) in urban or community land by county, 2001, in the Northern States (U.S. Census Bureau 2000, Homer et al. 2004).

- ☐ < 8
- ☐ 8 to 36.6
- ☐ 33.7 to 46
- ☐ 46.1 to 56
- ☐ 56.1 to 64
- ☐ 64.1 to 71.3
- ☐ 71.4 to 78.3
- ☐ 78.4 to 91.6

Summary and Synthesis

6

EARLIER CHAPTERS PROVIDED an overview of northern forests—current resource conditions, what makes these forests unique, and the challenges they face. Chapter 2 summarized threats to northern forests expressed by managers and other stakeholders, including concerns about forest area, composition, structure, biodiversity, and fragmentation; wood products production, consumption, and trade; invasive species; insects; disease; water quality; recreation; stewardship; and environmental literacy (Dietzman et al. 2011). One commonality of all these issues is their large spatial scale. Invasive insects, for example, have organismal and stand-scale effects, but the long-term, cumulative effects are observed at the landscape scale. Cumulative effects stemming from changes in forest area, composition, biodiversity, product consumption, and species composition, among others, can limit (or enhance) the capacity of northern forests to provide beneficial products and services to society.

Chapters 3 and 4 introduced the concept of forest sustainability and offered a set of strategies that we believe are essential for sustainable forest management at the spatial scale of ecoregions, States, and the nation. There is no single metric for quantifying forest sustainability; rather we rely on many interrelated indicators.

We used the framework of the Montréal Process Criteria and Indicators for the Conservation and Sustainable Management of Temperate and Boreal Forests (Montréal Process Working Group 2010) to assess current conditions and recent trends in northern forests. The structured format of the Montréal Process provided a convenient way to organize and summarize information related to forest sustainability.

The assessment identified similarities and differences among the 20 Northern States and compared the region with other regions of the United States.

The many indicators of forest conditions are interrelated, and this assessment cannot render a single, definitive judgment about the sustainability of northern forests. As noted earlier, one of the most significant contributions an assessment such as this can make is to provide the context and data needed to facilitate discussions about forest sustainability.

Ultimately it is the work of society to choose among options, make tradeoffs among desirable outcomes, and select the most effective or most equitable solutions. Those choices are implemented through discourse, legislative and rule-making processes, purchases made and forgone, opinions expressed, and investments made.

To foster additional discussion, Table 31 presents 36 indicators of forest sustainability from Chapter 5 and adds condition ratings for each of them, based on analysis of current conditions and recent trends. These ratings subjectively classify the various indicators as highly positive, positive, neutral, negative, or highly negative with respect to forest sustainability. The ratings are based on the assessment for the entire 20-State region. They do not capture local conditions that can be highly variable across the region, nor do they specifically account for the variation observed among individual Northern States. Rather, they help provide a larger spatial context that can be used to evaluate State and local forests. It is important to emphasize that these subjective ratings represent our best judgment. Other people may arrive at different conclusions or even propose alternative rating systems.

No forest resource issue exists in isolation. Forest policies and management practices intended to increase forest sustainability are likely to generate broader support if they simultaneously address multiple issues. For example, a future scenario using more woody biomass for energy might simultaneously decrease net atmospheric carbon emissions, increase renewable energy production, increase early successional habitat for dependent wildlife species, decrease the out-of-pocket costs for woodland habitat restoration, increase forest-based employment, and increase the total area covered by forest management plans. Or landscape-scale planning within priority conservation areas with mixed ownerships might identify opportunities for public-private partnerships to jointly address biodiversity issues and invasive species issues that cross ownership boundaries. Given limited time and money, management practices designed to pursue a single objective are often harder to justify than those designed to provide multiple conservation benefits simultaneously.

The remainder of this chapter discusses some of the interrelationships, interactions, and drivers of change that affect northern forests. The content addresses some of the threats and opportunities identified by Dietzman et al. (2011), and it also addresses findings that emerged from the analysis of conditions and trends. The many issues affecting northern forests are interrelated and so are approaches to achieving desired outcomes.

Table 31—Summary of northern forest sustainability condition ratings for forest sustainability indicators described in Chapter 5. Current conditions and recent trends are rated separately (when possible). Condition ratings represent the best judgment of the authors based on evaluations of each indicator with respect to forest sustainability for the region as a whole. People with different perspectives or people examining different areas within the region are likely to differ in the condition ratings they would assign to a given indicator.

No.	Indicator	Current condition rating[a]	Recent trend condition rating[a]	Rating explanation
1	Forest area	◗	●	Forests cover 42 percent of the land, an increase of 38 million acres over the past 100 years, despite population growth and urban expansion. In recent decades forest area has ceased to increase in many States and has declined in some.
2	Forest ownership	●	●	Public forest lands constitute a small share of the region as whole, but individual States vary greatly in their proportion of public land. A mix of public and private ownerships is usually considered desirable because public and private forest land managers often (but not always) differ in their management objectives and their capacity to provide forest products, amenities, and ecosystem services. (See also Parcelization, item 7.)
3	Protected forest	◗	◗	About 16 percent of forests (27 million acres) are under some category of protection. Compared to the rest of the United States, protected northern forests are concentrated in the least restrictive protected categories. Most protected areas are on public land, but conservation easements and similar instruments are increasingly used to expand the area of protected private forest land. Some habitats of high conservation interest (e.g., floodplains or migration corridors) are underrepresented in current protected areas.
4	Forest cover types	●	●	Forest cover types are the result of past disturbances and management activities. Changing the mix is a long-term endeavor. Loss of pine forest acreage relative to historical levels has reduced forest biodiversity in some areas. The ongoing transition of oak dominated forest to maple-dominated forest continues, at the expense of wildlife habitat quality. As long as native forest cover types are widely distributed across the landscape within their historic ranges there is little basis to judge the condition positive or negative.

[a] ● *Highly positive* ◗ *Positive* ● *Neutral* ◗ *Negative* ● *Highly negative*

Table 31 continued

No.	Indicator	Current condition rating[a]	Recent trend condition rating[a]	Rating explanation
5	Forest age classes	◗	◗	Past patterns of harvesting and wildfire suppression have left the North with relatively little young (early successional) forest or old forest, but with relatively abundant forest in the 40- to 80-year age classes. Lack of age class diversity indicates a lack of forest biodiversity. With current rates of disturbance, the area of old forests is increasing over time, but the area of young forests is not.
6	Fragmentation	◗	●	Northern forests continue a decades-long trend of fragmentation. However, interpretation of this metric differs with timeframe and scale; for example, over the past century unproductive farms abandoned in the first half of the 20th century have reverted back to forest via natural succession—a process that has contributed substantially to maintaining a stable forest area. (See also Forest area, item 1.) In recent decades, however, expansion of urban, suburban, and exurban areas has fragmented millions of acres of forest land.
7	Parcelization	◗	●	The average size of family forest ownerships continues to decrease, reaching a regionwide average of 26 acres in 2006. As forest ownerships become smaller, the economic viability of forest management decreases, and addressing large-scale forest management issues becomes more difficult.
8	Number and status of native forest-associated species	○	◗	Many forest-associated species are at risk or have been previously extirpated. Tools to inventory and monitor forest associated species are improving, but a full inventory of forest associated species is lacking. Ongoing trends in forest fragmentation and conversion of forest to other uses are usually considered detrimental to native forest-associated species. (See also Fragmentation and Urban and community land, items 6 and 34.)
9	Timberland	◖	◖	The region has a high proportion of timberland relative to total forest land, and that has changed little in recent decades.

[a] ● *Highly positive* ◖ *Positive* ○ *Neutral* ◗ *Negative* ● *Highly negative*

Table 31 continued

No.	Indicator	Current condition rating[a]	Recent trend condition rating[a]	Rating explanation
10	Wood volume	●	●	Wood volume is abundant and has increased substantially in the past 50 years. Invasive species have greatly reduced the wood volume of targeted tree species in some locations.
11	Wood growth and removals	●	◠	Wood growth far exceeds removals and has done so for decades. This is locally sustainable but it may represent lost opportunities for forest-associated employment or may result in transfer of harvesting impacts to forests outside the region.
12	Planted forests	●	●	Compared to the rest of the United States, the area of planted forest is low. Planted forests often have greater productivity per acre than native forests, but converting native forests to plantations generally decreases biodiversity.
13	Tree mortality	◠	◡	The current rate of tree mortality across the region is relatively low. However, increasing mortality associated with invasive species is a concern. (See also Insect and disease incidence and risk, item 15.)
14	Indicators of forest damage on standing timber	◠	N/A	Only a small percentage of trees have damage or defects. Temporal trends in damage indicators are not available.
15	Insect and disease incidence and risk	●	●	Old and new invasive species are causing severe localized mortality for some tree species and widespread chronic defoliation or mortality for others. Controlling insects and diseases or managing forests to adapt to them is often a costly, long-term endeavor.
16	Soil quality	●	N/A	Regional inventories show the proportion of bare forest soil and compacted forest soil to be relatively low. Excess aluminum can be toxic to trees and other plants under certain conditions. Many other soil characteristics (such as percent soil organic matter) are now routinely quantified for forest inventory plots, but whether levels are beneficial or detrimental to forest sustainability is debatable. For conserving soil, managing land for forest cover is generally considered preferable to other land uses. Trends in forest soil characteristics are poorly documented.

[a] ● *Highly positive* ◠ *Positive* ● *Neutral* ◡ *Negative* ● *Highly negative*

Table 31 continued

No.	Indicator	Current condition rating[a]	Recent trend condition rating[a]	Rating explanation
17	Water supply and quality	Positive	Neutral	Nearly half of the region's surface water supply originates from forest lands and most drinking water comes from surface water sources. Most rainfall and snowmelt in forests moves into streams through subsurface flows, accelerating nutrient uptake and contaminant absorption processes. Increasing forest area in the last century has benefited water quality, but the more-recent losses of forest land to urban development have not.
18	Carbon sequestered in forests	Highly positive	Highly positive	The quantity of sequestered carbon in forests generally increases as the volume of live trees increases. The volume of timber in the region has increased substantially in the past 50 years. (See also Wood volume, item 10.)
19	Carbon sequestered in forest products	Positive	Negative	Carbon is sequestered in forest products. Regionally about 1.5 billion cubic feet of wood is converted annually to long-lived products. Another 0.9 billion cubic feet is used to produce pulp and paper products. This is a substantial quantity of wood products and associated sequestered carbon, but it is below the region's capacity. Since 1986, the annual volume of roundwood products has decreased. (See also Wood volume and Wood growth and removals, items 10 and 11.)
20	Using woody biomass for energy	Neutral	Positive	Annually about 0.6 billion cubic feet of wood harvested in the region is used for fuelwood (including residential heating). This is a small part of the region's energy needs, but utilization of woody biomass for energy is increasing. Use of fuelwood often offsets consumption of fossil fuels that would be used instead.
21	Consumption of wood and wood products	Neutral	Neutral	Consumption of wood products is about 71 cubic feet per capita. Per capita consumption is expected to remain stable or decrease slightly, but increases in population have and will continue to increase total wood products consumption.

[a]
● *Highly positive* ⌒ *Positive* ● *Neutral* ⌄ *Negative* ● *Highly negative*

Table 31 continued

No.	Indicator	Current condition rating[a]	Recent trend condition rating[a]	Rating explanation
22	Value and volume of wood and wood products	Negative	Neutral	The total value of primary wood product shipments from the region was $112 billion in 2006, and associated wood products manufacturing provided $52 billion of added value. But based on the rate of increase in total forest volume, the value and volume of wood products production appears to be below potential. (See also Wood volume, item 10.) Roundwood harvesting increased from 1952 to 1986, but has remained flat since.
23	Recovery or recycling of wood products	Highly negative	Highly negative	The national paper recovery rate is about 50 percent and has gradually increased in past years. Paper recovery is not tracked separately for the Northern States.
24	Nontimber forest products	Neutral	Positive	Increased attention is being given to quantifying the value of nontimber forest products. Utilization appears to be below potential. Edible and decorative nontimber products are collected by about 10 percent of family forest owners. Sales of maple syrup produced in the region have increased sharply in recent years and now exceed $91 million, annually.
25	Revenues from forest-based environmental services	Neutral	Positive	Values for forest-based environmental services have been difficult to quantify, but are the focus of increased attention as potential sources of income.
26	Investments and expenditures in forest management, industries, services, and research	Negative	Neutral	Investments in forest management are substantial in terms of total dollars, but stewardship plans only cover about 16 percent of private forest area not owned by the forest products industry. The largest industrial investments were in the pulp and paper sector. Active forest industries can increase understanding of and support for forest management. When adjusted for inflation, the combined U.S. Forest Service expenditures on management, State and private programs, and research in the region have declined slightly since 2005. Investments in management and certification by nongovernmental organizations are increasing in impact.

a
● Highly positive ▲ Positive ● Neutral ▾ Negative ● Highly negative

Table 31 continued

No.	Indicator	Current condition rating[a]	Recent trend condition rating[a]	Rating explanation
27	Employment in forest products industries	◗	◗	The region employs 441,000 workers in the forestry and logging, wood products, and pulp and paper industries, a steady decline since 2001. Total employment is probably less than the region's forest resources are capable of supporting. Stable employment opportunities in logging and forest products industries often benefit rural communities economically.
28	Wages, income, and injury rates in forest industries	◗	⬤	Total wages in the forestry and logging, wood products, and pulp and paper industries are about $19 billion annually. Since 2001, average wages have been flat. Injury rates are comparable to the national average and have been decreasing.
29	Recreation and tourism	◗	⬤	Northern forests provide the equivalent of nearly 15 billion activity days of recreation. The number of activity days increases with the increasing population in the region. This creates opportunities for more people to interact with forests, but can result in conflicts over competing uses.
30	The importance of forests to people	◗	N/A	The importance of forests to people extends beyond what can be extracted from forests to what they are. This can become a source of controversy if natural resource management actions threaten to change the character of places where people have formed strong attachments. There is a growing body of knowledge on this topic, but no basis for rating an overall trend.
31	Forest-related planning, assessment, and policy review; and opportunities for public involvement and participation in public policy and decisionmaking	◗	◗	All Northern States recently completed Forest Action Plans. States differ in many forest planning and public involvement policies, but coordination is increasing on regional forest planning and policy issues. (See also Investments and expenditures in forest management, industries, services, and research, item 26.)

a

⬤ *Highly positive*   ◗ *Positive*   ⬤ *Neutral*   ◗ *Negative*   ⬤ *Highly negative*

Table 31 continued

No.	Indicator	Current condition rating[a]	Recent trend condition rating[a]	Rating explanation
32	Best practice codes for forest management	Positive	Positive	Most States have some form of best practice codes or best management practices (BMPs) that address silviculture, water and soils, and wildlife or biodiversity. BMPs are optional in some States, but attention to BMPs and associated forest management issues has increased over the last decade. BMPs require ongoing revision to address emerging issues such as invasive species management or biomass harvesting.
33	Management of forests to conserve environmental, cultural, social, and/or scientific values	Positive	Positive	One forested acre in six is afforded some sort of protected status, a proportion similar to the national average. In addition to widespread conservation of these values on public lands, easements and trusts are increasingly being used on private lands. (See also Protected forest, item 3.)
34	Urban and community land	Negative	Neutral	Eighty percent of the population in the North lives in urban areas, which comprise about 6 percent of the region's land area. The area of urban land increased by nearly 4 million acres or 0.9 percent from 1990 to 2000, and roughly 37 percent of the new urban area came from forests. (See also Population and urbanization, item 35.)
35	Population and urbanization, projected to 2050	Negative	Negative	Losses of forest land to urbanization are expected to continue. By 2050, Rhode Island (71 percent), New Jersey (64 percent), Massachusetts (61 percent), and Connecticut (61 percent) are expected to be more than half urban land.
36	Tree and impervious cover in urban and community areas	Positive	Neutral	Northern urban or community areas have about 20 percent impervious surface and about 39 percent tree cover. By comparison, rural forest cover across the region is about 42 percent. As they expand, urban and community lands reduce the area of rural forest land but retain some tree cover.

[a] ● *Highly positive* ▲ *Positive* ● *Neutral* ▬ *Negative* ● *Highly negative*

FORESTS AND PEOPLE TOGETHER

The 20 Northern States comprise the most heavily forested and most heavily populated quadrant of the United States. Although the forests of the West and especially the South are recognized centers for U.S. wood and paper production, the proportion of the North that is forested (42 percent) is slightly greater than the South (40 percent) and the Pacific Coast (37 percent) and far greater than the Interior West (20 percent) or the overall U.S. average (33 percent).

The abundance of northern forests comes with an abundance of people. A broad based measure of population pressures on forests is forest acreage per capita, which declines if forest area decreases relative to population or population increases relative to forest area. Over the past century, population increased at a faster rate than forest land in the North; this resulted in a gradual decline in forest area per capita from 2.6 to 1.4 acres (Fig. 67). Because the North has 41 percent of the U.S. population (124 million people) but only 23 percent of U.S. forest land, forest area per capita is substantially lower than in other regions (3.3 acres per capita, combined) and well below the U.S. average of 2.5 acres. However, over the last century, changes in forest area per capita have been much greater for the rest of the United States, and this has substantially closed the gap in forest area per capita between the North and the country as a whole.

FIGURE 67

Forest area and population in the Northern States (A),
and forest area per capita in the Northern States and the United States (B)
(Smith et al. 2009, and U.S. Census Bureau 2010).

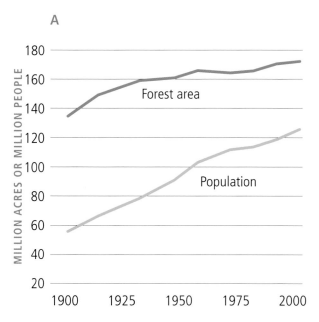

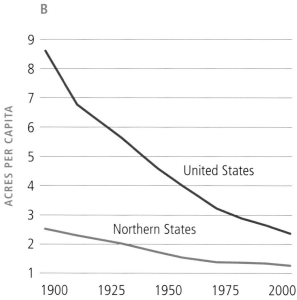

What we find utterly remarkable about northern forests is that their total area has increased over the last century, despite a 56 percent increase in population (Fig. 2). Reversion of abandoned farmland back to tree cover is responsible for much of that increase. However, the area of forest land appears to have peaked, or nearly so.

The location and character of northern forests has also changed over the last century. Conversion of forests to residential and other developed uses has had localized impacts on aesthetics, biodiversity, water quality, carbon sequestration, quality of life, and ability to practice forest management. Pressures to fragment forests, subdivide forest ownerships, and convert forests to developed uses have been substantial and are expected to continue. From 1990 to 2000, expanding urban development in the North subsumed 4 million acres of land, of which 37 percent was forested (Table 28, Fig. 68). From 2000 to 2050 the urban area in the United States is expected to more than double to 8 percent of the total land area, at the cost of about 12 million additional acres of forest land.

Some negative consequences of population pressure on forests notwithstanding, the proximity of people to forests creates some unique opportunities in the North. Urban trees and forests are especially important to quality of life for the 80 percent of residents who live in northern urban areas. The North's rural forests are accessible to and serve many people. And energy or biofuels produced from wood are close to large numbers of energy consumers.

The region's extensive forest cover enables 5 million private woodland owners—almost half of all private woodland owners in the Nation—to have a piece of the region's forest. But 3 million of those northern owners have fewer than 10 acres of forest land. Private forest owner objectives are varied and timber production is often a low priority. A consequence of this ownership pattern is that the majority of forested acres lack forest management plans (Butler 2008).

For Discussion

- Given their changing character, what is the desirable mix of commodities, amenities, and ecosystem services from the 172 million acres of northern forest land?

- To what extent can producing that mix simultaneously help sustain forest health and diversity?

- Given the spatial distribution of forests and people across the region and the importance of forests to human well-being, where are focal points of forest and human interaction, and what, if anything, can be done to improve the frequency and quality of these interactions?

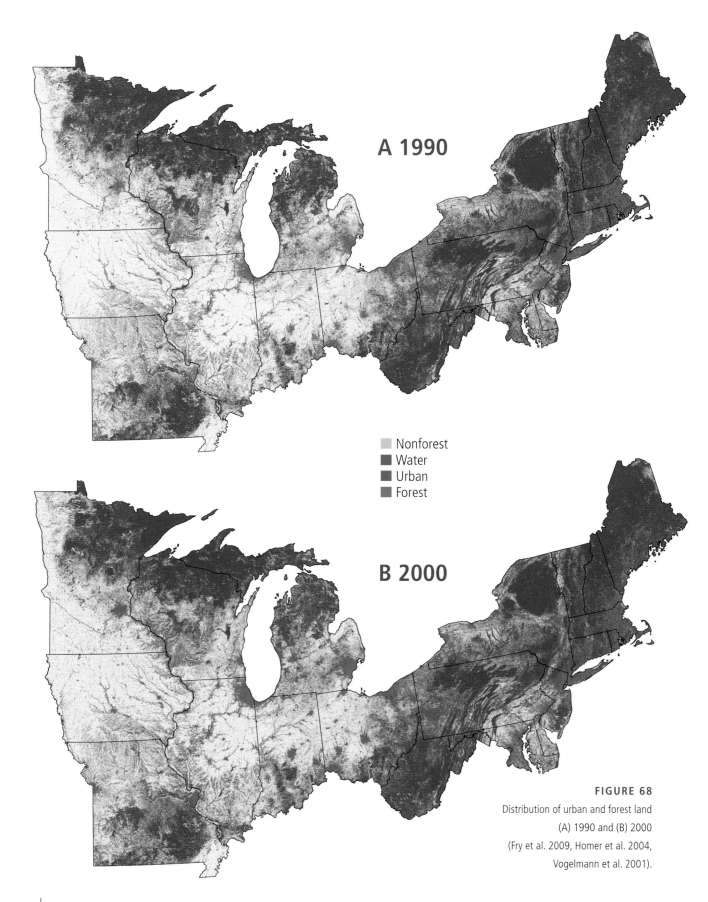

A 1990

B 2000

Nonforest
Water
Urban
Forest

FIGURE 68

Distribution of urban and forest land
(A) 1990 and (B) 2000
(Fry et al. 2009, Homer et al. 2004,
Vogelmann et al. 2001).

INVASIVE SPECIES

Invasive plants and animals are a problem throughout the North. Some invasives drastically reduce the diversity of the forest. They also can have a huge economic impact in terms of lost commodities and ecosystem services. The high costs of invasive species eradication/control and removal/replacement of affected trees saps funds that could be used for other purposes.

For Discussion

- What additional opportunities exist for coordinated approaches to invasive species management?

- How can these approaches converge with other objectives such as maintaining forest health (urban and rural), maintaining native species diversity, managing forests to increase resilience to future forest disturbances, and utilizing wood harvested in the process?

The impacts of invasive species, especially nonnatives, are enduring. More than 140 years after its introduction, the gypsy moth is firmly established in the North; it is being managed—at a cost—along a slowly advancing front. After more than a century since the introduction of chestnut blight, scientists have bred a blight-resistant American chestnut. Since its introduction in the United States 70 years ago, Dutch elm disease is thoroughly established in northern forests. The emerald ash borer, Asian longhorned beetle, hemlock woolly adelgid, and thousand cankers disease of walnut are spreading. Autumn olive, multiflora rose, garlic mustard, and bush honeysuckle are well entrenched. Past experience suggests that (1) despite their best efforts, forest managers will lose battles with some current invasive species and with others yet to arrive, and (2) when a new invasive species gets a foothold, management and mitigation efforts will be long, costly affairs.

Ongoing, active management of urban, community, and rural forests is one method of identifying, resisting, mitigating, and managing invasive species. The fact that a small proportion of rural forest acreage is actively managed limits opportunities to counteract the threat of invasive species through early identification, preemptive actions to reduce risk, or rapid response to treat affected trees and forests.

BIODIVERSITY

Almost 15 percent of forest-associated species in the North are considered at some risk of extinction or extirpation. When a forest-associated species become nationally threatened or endangered, legislative remedies are activated to help its population recover. And some populations do recover. However, such mandated species recovery plans are a remedy of last resort; they are often accompanied by great expense, disruption, and uncertain outcome. Preferably, collective forest management (public and private) across the region would maintain species diversity by supporting a shifting mosaic of diverse forest habitats.

For Discussion

- How would management aimed at increasing forest age-class diversity affect wildlife diversity?

- How would management to increase biodiversity affect recreation, water quality and quantity, commodity production, and bioenergy production?

- How might multiple management objectives converge to sustain or increase forest biodiversity while simultaneously providing other benefits?

One approach to maintaining forest biodiversity is to create diverse, healthy forests that support many species, monitor species of conservation concern, and adapt management practices as necessary to sustain rare habitats and rare or declining species. This is done in a systematic way on many public forests and some private forests. State forest action plans (USDA and NAASF 2011) and wildlife action plans (Association of Fish and Wildlife Agencies 2011) address biodiversity issues in multiple ways, including management emphasis on priority conservation areas. On a regional level, analyses of biodiversity require additional emphasis. For example, as an artifact of past management and disturbance across the region, northern forests are clustered in the 40- to 80-year old age classes (Fig. 10), with relatively few forests younger than 20 years or older than 100 years. Given current rates of forest disturbance and regeneration, old forests will likely increase in abundance as forests across the region increase in age, but the area of young (early successional) forests—and associated habitats—will likely remain small. This has far-reaching implications for the abundance of wildlife species that depend on early- or late-successional forest habitats and, thus, for forest biodiversity in general. Forest age-class diversity is among the simplest measures of forest structural diversity and habitat diversity, and it is a measure for which there are excellent data at local, State, and regional scales. Yet the lack of forest age class diversity has received relatively little attention in discussions of forest sustainability across the North.

CONSUMPTION AND PRODUCTION OF WOOD AND PULP PRODUCTS IN THE NORTH

Consumption of wood and pulp products in the form of lumber, paper, plywood, composite panels, and pallets is about 71 cubic feet of wood per person annually, or roughly 8.8 billion cubic feet for the 124 million people who live in the Northern States. The proportion of U.S. wood products that come from net imports has been steadily increasing (Fig. 42). In 2005, U.S. net imports amounted to 6 billion of 21 billion cubic feet of total U.S. wood and pulp products consumption. The largest component of wood imports is softwood lumber, and most softwood lumber imports come from Canada. The United States is also a net exporter of some types of wood products such as hardwood lumber, but for all wood products in combination, annual imports greatly exceed exports.

In 2006, about 3 billion cubic feet of wood and pulp products were produced in the North (Table 9). This is a relatively small proportion of the total U.S. wood and pulp products production (20 percent) or consumption (15 percent) given that the North includes 32 percent of U.S. timberland (Fig. 1). However, as noted earlier, the North also has a high population and low forest per capita compared to the rest of the United States.

Timber is harvested and processed to meet demand generated by consumers. Where timber harvesting occurs—be it the North, elsewhere in the United States, or elsewhere in the World— it has impacts. It changes forest structure, species composition, habitat characteristics, the quantity of sequestered carbon, water and soil characteristics, recreation opportunities and other conditions. Timber harvesting in conjunction with a management plan can create opportunities to simultaneously address perceived problems with insects, diseases, invasive species, or biodiversity. A viable forest products industry can be an important source of employment and economic support for rural communities. Declines in forest products output can remove those opportunities.

For Discussion

- How does consumption of forest products affect forest sustainability in the North and elsewhere?

- To what extent could the North's forests sustainably meet demand for wood and pulp products by people living in the North and elsewhere?

- To what extent can production of wood and pulp products in the North enhance opportunities to achieve other conservation goals such as improved forest health, increased biodiversity, increased employment, or increased access to renewable energy?

CARBON SEQUESTRATION AND CLIMATE CHANGE

Concerns about climate change focus on the concentration of atmospheric carbon dioxide and other greenhouse gases, which in turn is affected by the amount carbon that is sequestered in forest ecosystems. Northern forests contain vast quantities of sequestered carbon in soils, live trees, dead trees, and down logs. As forests grow, they accumulate woody biomass, about half which is carbon (Fig. 37). The quantity of carbon annually sequestered from the atmosphere by all U.S. forests is only about 10 percent of the quantity of U.S. carbon emissions from burning fossil fuels and other sources. Forest management can increase the quantity of biomass and the amount of carbon sequestered, but carbon accounting is complicated by many variables including the number of years considered in the analysis, what happens to wood that is harvested, and anticipated tree mortality due to fire, insects, and disease. Management practices that enable forests to sequester more carbon annually are likely beneficial, but their impact will be relatively small compared to total carbon emissions from all sources. Some have suggested that a more effective way of reducing atmospheric carbon would be to use wood for energy (heat, electricity, liquid fuels), thereby offsetting carbon released from the fossil fuels and creating opportunities for carbon sequestration in regenerating forests (Malmsheimer et al. 2008).

Other actions that improve the carbon balance by increasing carbon sequestration or decreasing carbon emissions include:

- Keeping forests as forests
- Planting nonforested areas with trees (afforestation)
- Opting for durable wood products that sequester carbon during their useful life, and at the same time regenerating new trees after timber harvesting
- Conserving energy

These and other actions can help reduce new carbon emissions and/or sequester more carbon from the atmosphere. Most can be pursued simultaneously. Such actions are important components of a strategy to reduce net greenhouse gas emissions, but it appears that the annual quantity of carbon sequestered by all forest associated activities in the North will be far less than current annual greenhouse gas emissions.

Climate change has been frequently cited as a management concern for the northern forests, and it has been a high priority for research. Potential effects of climate change on forest ecosystems continue to be studied, including research that forecasts how the spatial distributions of tree species and wildlife are likely to shift under alternative climate change scenarios (Iverson et al. 2008, Matthews et al. 2007), Prasad et al. 2007, Rodenhouse et al. 2008.

For Discussion

- Given the longevity of trees and forest communities compared to the expected rate of climate change, what proactive forest management might be taken in anticipation of altered climate conditions?

- How will forests respond to climate change?

- How and where do management tactics for addressing climate change converge with other complementary management objectives?

BIOENERGY

The motivation to increase utilization of woody biomass for energy is directly related to concerns about greenhouse gas emissions, carbon sequestration, climate change, and our dependence on fossil fuels. Using woody biomass instead of fossil fuels to produce energy has the potential to reduce net carbon emissions. The most efficient strategies for managing carbon may be those that never release it to the atmosphere in the first place—conservation and renewable alternatives to fossil fuels. Knowledge and technologies continue to evolve on efficient ways to convert woody biomass into energy while reducing net greenhouse gas emissions.

The total amount of forest biomass in northern forests is immense, and the annual rate of biomass accumulation is much higher than the current rate of harvesting. However, energy demand is even higher. If the total annual woody biomass growth in northern forests were converted to energy, it could not meet the energy demands of the people who live in the region. Nor could total annual U.S. woody biomass growth meet the Nation's current demand for energy.

- What management interests and objectives align with producing forest-based bioenergy?

- How is bioenergy production in various quantities likely to affect forest employment, the North's renewable energy portfolio, the types and quantities of other forest products produced, revenue to forest owners, and options to simultaneously achieve other compatible conservation goals?

Biomass harvesting for energy production presents opportunities to simultaneously meet (or hinder) other resource objectives. Many convergent interests can affect and be affected by large-scale biomass harvesting. For example, the lack of early successional habitats (Fig. 10) for wildlife in northern forests is a serious concern among wildlife biologists (Askins 2001, Trani et al. 2001). Biomass harvesting has the potential to alter the amount and location of early succession forest habitat. Likewise in the North, oak regeneration failures have been a persistent problem on millions of acres of productive sites that currently have oak overstories. Loss of oaks from the forest reduces tree species diversity and diminishes habitat quality for mast-dependent wildlife species. Biomass harvesting conducted with a joint objective of increasing oak regeneration could be effective on many sites. The high density of people and forests in the North places woody biomass in close proximity to energy users. Under some scenarios this proximity could facilitate bioenergy utilization, but it could also decrease the capacity of forests to provide other commodities or ecosystem services.

CAPACITY FOR FOREST MANAGEMENT

Active forest management with silvicultural treatments is essential to achieve many desired products and services from forests. Outputs of wood products and biomass obviously depend on forest management practices. Less obvious, perhaps, is the importance of active forest management in restoring savanna and woodland habitats, providing habitat for desirable wildlife species, sustaining forest biodiversity, increasing forest carbon sequestration, or sustaining forest health. Northern forests are persistently afflicted by severe weather, invasive species, native insects, diseases, wildfire, and climate change. The undesirable impacts of these disturbance agents can be partially mitigated through proactive management to promote forest health and increase resilience. Reactive management following large-scale disturbance events can speed forest recovery and salvage forest products. Forest management is virtually the only process available for reducing the undesirable impacts of forest disturbances or for increasing the output of desirable forest products, amenities, and ecosystem services.

Active forest management requires motivation and adequate resources on the part of forest owners as well as adequate numbers of skilled and equipped specialists to prescribe and implement treatments—both of which are lacking throughout much of the region. Only 4 percent family forest owners report that they have a written management plan, and they tend to be the owners with larger forest acreages; collectively they manage about 16 percent of the total family forest area in the region (Butler et al. 2010).

For Discussion

- How can State and regional forest assessments be used to monitor the cumulative effects of stand-scale forest management actions?

- How can landscape-scale conservation and management be applied to pursue management objectives that operate at different spatial scales (for example, timber management applied to a 20-acre tract versus migrant songbird habitat management applied across a 1,000-acre landscape)?

- To what extent can forest management be more widely and regularly applied in the North to allow forest owners and managers to pursue multiple conservation objectives?

- To what extent can forest-associated jobs and rural economic stability be supported by forest management activities?

URBAN AND COMMUNITY FORESTS

Most people in the Northern States—80 percent —live within urban areas that cover only 6 percent of the region's land base. However, urban areas in the North are expanding at a rate of nearly 4 million acres per decade, and 1.5 million acres of that expansion spread into land that was formerly classified as forest. This expansion of housing and other development changes the character of forests in important ways. Compared to trees in rural forests, for example, trees in urban or community areas tend to have higher value for aesthetics, cooling, stormwater management, and cleansing the atmosphere; lower value for wood products; and different habitat suitability for wildlife.

Trees cover nearly 40 percent of urban or community lands. Because of their proximity to people, such trees are highly valued and are relatively expensive to treat or replace if attacked by insects or diseases. Parks, preserves, riparian zones, and other forested areas can provide unique habitats and recreation opportunities within urban or community areas. However, expanding urban and community lands along with parcelization, fragmentation, and expansion of impervious surfaces can reduce tree cover, degrade air and water quality, and alter species composition and biodiversity.

For Discussion

• How can forest inventory and monitoring be improved to measure the range of benefits associated along the continuum of urban to rural forests?

• What options are available to manage urban and community expansion so that desirable forest-associated benefits are maintained while sustaining the needs of a growing human population?

• What new forest monitoring and management approaches, if any, are needed for States that are on trajectory to become predominantly urban land?

CONCLUDING REMARKS

This assessment puts information about the forest conditions for individual Northern States in a spatial context and describes trends that have shaped the region's forests. Efforts to address many of the pressing forest resource issues in the North can benefit from this regional perspective. It also complements State Forest Action Plans (USDA FS and NAASF 2011).

Development of policies and practices supportive of forest sustainability requires the capacity to view the consequences of management decisions (including no action) across multiple spatial scales and multiple timeframes. Most forest management is implemented on the ground an acre or a stand at a time. Views of the forest from larger spatial scales and longer temporal scales are necessary to understand the cumulative effects of thousands or millions of individual management actions. Relevant spatial scales include landscapes, ecoregions, watersheds, States, multi-State regions, nations, and the World. Relevant timeframes include a few decades to more than a century.

Other forest assessments at various spatial scales have been conducted using the same Montréal Process format that was followed in this assessment. Such standardization is beneficial because it facilitates comparisons within and across spatial scales (such as within and among States). It also provides opportunities to improve the efficiency of future assessment efforts by standardizing the types of data that are reported for all spatial scales and by coordinating data collection and reporting activities.

Although this assessment provides key information for those interested in forest sustainability, we intentionally avoid stating whether forests and forest management in the North are sustainable, primarily because all definitions of forest sustainability are partially subjective. Nevertheless the assessment identifies some specific conditions and trends that appear consistent with forest sustainability and some that do not. More importantly, it provides necessary facts, figures, and maps for ongoing, detailed discussions about the current and future sustainability of northern forests.

Acknowledgments

This document draws on data and maps from numerous published and unpublished sources including information about the number and status of forest associated species from Curt Flather, forest fragmentation from Kurt Riitters, and carbon sequestration from Christopher Woodall. U.S. Forest Service Forest Inventory and Analysis information spanning 60 years is cited throughout this report. Patrick Miles, John Vissage, and Brad Smith were especially helpful in locating the most current and comprehensive sources of forest resource inventory information.

Reviewers who provided valuable comments include: Mary Beth Adams, Gina Childs, Debra Dietzman, Justine Gartner, Kurt Gottschalk, Eric Gustafson, Katherine LaJeunesse, Kenneth Laustsen, Donald Mansius, Dennis May, Steven Milauskas, Gus Raeker, Phillip Rodbell, Steven Sinclair, Kenneth Skog, and Barbara Tormoehlen. Susan Wright, Carol Whitlock, and Rhonda Cobourn provided editorial guidance and support.

We thank them all

American Forest and Paper Association. 2009. Our industry-paper. Washington, DC: American Forest and Paper Association. http://www.afandpa.org/PaperRecycling.aspx. (20 September 2011).

Alexander, S.J.; Oswalt, S.N.; Emery, M.R. 2011. Nontimber forest products in the United States: Montreal process indicators as measures of current conditions and sustainability. Gen. Tech. Rep. PNW-851. Portland, OR: U.S. Department of Agriculture, Forest Service, Pacific Northwest Research Experiment Station. 37 p.

Askins, R.A. 2001. Sustaining biological diversity in early successional communities: the challenge of managing unpopular habitats. Wildlife Society Bulletin. 29(2): 407-412.

Association of Fish and Wildlife Agencies. 2011. State wildlife action plans. Washington, DC: Association of Fish and Wildlife Agencies. http://www.stateforesters.org/issues_and_policy/forests_in_the_farm_bill. (24 January 2011).

Bailey, R.G. 1977. Ecoregions of North America. [1:15,000,000] scale map. Rev. Washington, DC: U.S. Department of Agriculture, Forest Service.

Baltimore County Maryland Department of Environmental Protection and Resource Management. 2007. The state of our forests – 2007. Baltimore, MD: Baltimore County Department of Environmental Protection and Resource Management. 70 p.

Bancroft, J.S.; Smith, M.T. 2001. Modeling dispersal of the Asian longhorn beetle. In: Fosbroke, S.L.C.; Gottschalk, K.W., eds. Proceedings, U.S. Department of Agriculture interagency research forum on gypsy moth and other invasive species. Gen. Tech. Rep. NE-285. Newtown Square, PA: U.S. Department of Agriculture, Forest Service, Northeastern Research Station: 15-20.

Barnes, M.C.; Todd, A.H.; Lilja, R.W.; Barten, P.K. 2009. Forests, water and people: drinking water supply and forest lands in the Northeast and Midwest United States. NA-FR-01-08. Newtown Square, PA: U.S. Department of Agriculture, Forest Service, Northeastern Area State and Private Forestry. 71 p.

Birch, T.W. 1996. Private forest-land owners of the Northern United States, 1994. Resour. Bull. NE-136. Radnor, PA: U.S. Department of Agriculture, Forest Service, Northeastern Forest Experiment Station. 293 p.

Birdsey, R.A. 1996. Regional estimates of timber volume and forest carbon for fully stocked timberland, average management after final clearcut harvest. In: Sampson, R.N.; Hair, D., eds. Forests and global change. Vol. 2. Forest management opportunities for mitigating carbon emissions. Washington, DC: American Forests: 309-334.

Blackard, J.A.; Finco, M.V.; Helmer, E.H. [et al.]. 2008. Mapping U.S. forest biomass using nationwide forest inventory data and moderate resolution information. Remote Sensing of Environment. 112(4): 1658-1677.

Brown, T.C.; Binkley, D. 1994. Effect of management on water quality in North American forests. Gen. Tech. Rep. RM-248. Fort Collins, CO: U.S. Department of Agriculture, Forest Service, Rocky Mountain Forest and Range Experiment Station. 27 p.

Brown, T.C.; Hobbins, M.T.; Ramirez, J.A. 2008. Spatial distribution of water supply in the coterminous United States. Journal of the American Water Resources Association. 44(6): 1474-1487.

Burger, J.A.; Kelting, D.L. 1999. Using soil quality indicators to assess forest stand management. Forest Ecology and Management. 122: 155-166.

Bush, R.J.; Araman, P.A.; Hager, E.B. 2007. Recovery, reuse and recycling by the United States wood packaging industry: 1993 to 2006. Blacksburg, VA: Virginia Polytechnic Institute and State University. [Poster presentation, Dean's Forum on the Environment.] http://www.srs4702.forprod.vt.edu/pubsubj/pdf/07t5.pdf. (26 October 2009).

Butler, B.J.; Miles, P.D.; Hansen, M.H. 2010. National Woodland Owner Survey table maker [Web application]. Version 1.0. Newtown Square, PA: U.S. Department of Agriculture, Forest Service, Northern Research Station. http://fiatools.fs.fed.us/NWOS/tablemaker.jsp. (27 July 2011).

Butler, B.J. 2008. Family forest owners of the United States, 2006. Gen. Tech. Rep. NRS-27. Newtown Square, PA: U.S. Department of Agriculture, Forest Service, Northern Research Station. 72 p.

Carpenter, C.A. 2007. Forest sustainability assessment for the Northern United States. NA-TP-01-07. Newtown Square, PA: U.S. Department of Agriculture, Forest Service, Northeastern Area State and Private Forestry. 336 p.

Chicago Climate Exchange. 2009. Chicago Climate Exchange®. Forestry carbon sequestration project protocol. http://www.chicagoclimatex.com/docs/offsets/CCX_Forestry_Sequestration_Protocol_Final.pdf. (10 February 2011).

Conservation Biology Institute. 2010. Protected areas database PAD-US 1.1 CBI edition. http://consbio.org/what-we-do/protected-areas-database-pad-version-4. Corvallis, OR: Conservation Biology Institute. (14 November 2010).

Convention on Biological Diversity. 2010. What is forest biological diversity? Montreal, QC: Secretariat of the Convention of Biological Diversity. http://www.cbd.int/forest/what.shtml. (15 November 2011).

Cordell, H.K. 2004. Outdoor recreation for 21st century America. State College, PA: Venture Publishing, Inc. 293 p.

Cordell, H.K.; Betz, C.J.; Mou, S.H.; Gormanson, D. In press. Outdoor recreation in a shifting northern societal landscape. General Technical Report. Newtown Square, PA: U.S. Department of Agriculture, Forest Service, Northern Research Station.

Cronan, C.S.; Grigal, D.F. 1995. Use of calcium/aluminum ratios as indicators of stress in forest ecosystems. Journal of Environmental Quality. 24: 209-226.

Cumming, A.B.; Nowak, D.J.; Twardus, D.B. [et al.]. 2007. Urban forests of Wisconsin 2002: pilot monitoring project 2002. NA-FR-05-07. Newtown Square, PA: U.S. Department of Agriculture, Forest Service, Northeastern Area State and Private Forestry. 33 p.

Cumming, A.B.; Twardus, D.B.; Nowak, D.J. 2008. Urban forest health monitoring: large scale assessments in the United States. Arboriculture and Urban Forestry. 34(6): 341-346.

DellaSalla, D.A.; Staus, N.L.; Strittholt, J.R.; Hackman, A.; Iacobelli, A. 2001. An updated protected areas database for the United States and Canada. Natural Areas Journal. 21: 124-135.

Dietzman, D.; LaJeunesse, K.; Wormstead, S. 2011. Northern forest futures project: Scoping of issues in the forests of the Northeast and Midwest of the United States. Version 3.0. Newtown Square, PA: U.S. Department of Agriculture, Forest Service, Northern Research Station. 42 p.

Doran, J.W.; Parkin, T.B. 1994. Defining and assessing soil quality. In: Doran, J.W.; Coleman, D.C.; Bezdicek, D.F.; Stewart, B.A., eds. Defining soil quality for a sustainable environment. Soil Science Society of America Spec. Publ. 35. Madison, WI: Soil Science Society of America: 3-21.

Drummond, M.A.; Loveland, T.R. 2010. Land-use pressure and a transition to forest-cover loss in the Eastern United States. BioScience. 60(4): 286-298.

Dudley, N., ed. 2008. Guidelines for applying protected area management categories. Gland, Switzerland: International Union for Conservation of Nature. 86 p. http://data.iucn.org/ dbtw-wpd/edocs/PAPS-016.pdf (20 September 2010).

European Commission Joint Research Centre Institute for Environment and Sustainability. 2011. Graphical user interface for the description of image objects and their shapes (GUIDOS). http://forest.jrc.ec.europa.eu/download/software/guidos. (28 January 2011).

Eyre, F.H., ed. 1980. Forest cover types of the United States and Canada. Bethesda, MD: Society of American Foresters. 148 p.

Federal Register. 2009. Executive Order 13514—Federal Leadership in Environmental, Energy, and Economic Performance. Federal Register. 74(194): 52117-52127. http://edocket.access. gpo.gov/2009/pdf/E9-24518.pdf. (26 January 2011). http://www.whitehouse.gov/assets/ documents/2009fedleader_eo_rel.pdf.

Floyd, D.W.; Vonhof, S.L.; Seyfang, H. 2001. Forest sustainability: a discussion guide for professional resource managers. Journal of Forestry. 99(2): 8-28.

Follett, R.F.; Kimble, J.M.; Lal, R., eds. 2001. The potential of U.S. grazing lands to sequester carbon and mitigate the greenhouse effect. Boca Raton, FL: Lewis Publishers. 472 p.

Food and Agriculture Organization of the United Nations. 2010. Global forest resources assessment 2010. FAO For. Pap. 163. Rome, Italy: Food and Agriculture Organization of the United Nations. 342 p.

Fry, J.A.; Coan, M.J.; Homer, C.G.; Meyer, D.K.; Wickham, J.D. 2009. Completion of the national land cover database (NLCD) 1992–2001 land cover change retrofit product. U.S. Geological Survey Open-File Rep. 2008–1379. Reston, VA: U.S. Department of Interior, Geological Survey. 18 p. http://pubs.usgs.gov/of/2008/1379/. (9 January 2011).

Gobster, P.H.; Rickenbach, M.G. 2004. Private forestland parcelization and development in Wisconsin's Northwoods: perceptions of resource-oriented stakeholders. Landscape and Urban Planning. 69: 165-182.

Godman, R.M.; Lancaster, K. 1990. Eastern hemlock (*Tsuga canadensis* (L.) Carr. In: Burns, R.M.; Honkala, B.H., tech. coords. Silvics of North America. 1: Conifers. Agric. Handb. 654. Washington, DC: U.S. Department of Agriculture, Forest Service: 604-612.

Gorte, R.S. 2009. U.S. tree planting for carbon sequestration. R40562. Washington, DC: Congressional Research Service. http://www.fas.org/sgp/crs/misc/R40562.pdf. (11 February 2011).

Greenfield, E.J.; Nowak, D.J.; Walton, J.T. 2009. Assessment of NLCD tree and impervious surface cover estimates. Photogrammetric Engineering and Remote Sensing. 75(11): 1279-1286.

Gronewold, N. 2011. Chicago Climate Exchange closes Nation's first cap-and-trade system but keeps eye to the future. New York Times. January 3. http://www.nytimes.com/cwire/2011/01/03/03 climatewire-chicago-climate-exchange-closes-but-keeps-ey-78598.html. (11 March 2011).

Haack, R.A. 2001. Intercepted *Scolytidae* at U.S. ports of entry: 1985-2000. Integrated Pest Management Reviews. 6(3): 253-282.

Haugen, D.A.; Hoebeke, E.R. 2005. Pest alert: sirex woodwasp—*Sirex noctilio* F. (Hymenoptera: Siricidae). NA-PR-07-05. Newtown Square, PA: U.S. Department of Agriculture, Forest Service, Northeastern Area State and Private Forestry. 2 p.

Helms, J.A. 1998. The dictionary of forestry. Bethesda, MD: Society of American Foresters. 210 p.

Homer, C.; Huang, C.; Yang, L.; Wylie, B.; Coan, M. 2004. Development of a 2001 national land-cover database for the United States. Photogrammetric Engineering and Remote Sensing. 70(7): 829-840. Data from Multi-resolution Land Characteristics Consortium. www.mrlc.gov. (14 August 2008).

Howard, J.L. 2007. U.S. timber production, trade, consumption, and price statistics 1965 to 2005. Res. Pap. FPL-RP-637. Madison, WI: U.S. Department of Agriculture, Forest Service, Forest Products Laboratory. 91 p.

Ince, P. 1996. Recycling of wood and paper products in the United States. Gen. Tech. Rep. FPL-GTR-89. Madison, WI: U.S. Department of Agriculture, Forest Service, Forest Products Laboratory. 10 p.

International Union for Conservation of Nature. 1994. Guidelines for protected areas management categories. Gland, Switzerland and Cambridge, UK: International Union for Conservation of Nature: 15-23. http://app.iucn.org/dbtw-wpd/edocs/1994-007-En.pdf. (16 November 2011).

International Union for Conservation of Nature. 2010. The International Union for Conservation of Nature. http://www.iucn.org/. (8 July).

Iverson, L.R.; Prasad, A.M.; Matthews, S.N.; Peters, M. 2008. Estimating potential habitat for 134 Eastern U.S. tree species under six climate scenarios. Forest Ecology and Management. 254: 390-406.

Kennedy, A.C.; Papendick, R.I. 1995. Microbial characteristics of soil quality. Journal of Soil and Water Conservation. 50(3): 243-248.

Kurtz, J.C.; Jackson, L.E.; Fisher, W.S. 2001. Strategies for evaluating indicators based on guidelines from the Environmental Protection Agency's Office of Research and Development. Ecological Indicators. 1: 49-60.

Kuykendall, H. 2008. Soil quality physical indicators: selecting dynamic soil properties to assess soil function. Soil Quality Tech. Note 10. Washington, DC: U.S. Department of Agriculture, Natural Resources Conservation Service, Soil Quality National Technology Development Team. 5 p.

Lal, R.; Kimble, J.M.; Follett, R.F.; Cole, C.V. 1998. The potential of U.S. cropland to sequester carbon and mitigate the greenhouse effect. Boca Raton, FL: Lewis Publishers. 144 p.

Luppold, W.; Bumgardner, M. 2008. Regional analysis of hardwood lumber production: 1963–2005. Northern Journal of Applied Forestry. 25(3): 146-150.

Malmsheimer, R.W.; Heffernan, P.; Brink, S. [et al.]. 2008. Forest management solutions for mitigating climate change in the United States. Journal of Forestry. 106(3):119-171.

Matthews, S.N.; Iverson, L.R.; Prasad, A.M.; Peters, M.P. 2007. A climate change atlas for 147 bird species of the Eastern United States [Database]. Newtown Square, PA: U.S. Department of Agriculture, Forest Service, Northern Research Station. http://www.nrs.fs.fed.us/atlas/bird. (24 January 2011).

McClure, M.S. 1990. Role of wind, birds, deer, and humans in the dispersal of hemlock woolly adelgid (Homoptera: Adelgidae). Environmental Entomology. 19(1): 36-43.

McLain, R.J.; Jones, E.T. 2005. Nontimber forest products management on national forests in the United States. Gen. Tech. Rep. PNW-GTR-655. Portland, OR: U.S. Department of Agriculture, Forest Service, Pacific Northwest Research Station. 85 p.

McManus, M.; Schneeberger, N.; Reardon, R.; Mason, G. 1989. Gypsy moth. For. Insect and Dis. Leafl. 162. Washington, DC: U.S. Department of Agriculture, Forest Service. 14 p.

McNab, W.H.; Avers, P.E. 1994. Ecological subregions of the United States: section descriptions. Admin. Publ. WO-WSA-5. Washington, DC: U.S. Department of Agriculture, Forest Service. 284 p.

Miles, P.D. 2010. Forest inventory EVALIDator [Web application]. Version 4.01 beta. Newtown Square, PA: U.S. Department of Agriculture, Forest Service, Northern Research Station. http://fiatools.fs.fed.us/Evalidator401/tmattribute.jsp. (14 November 2010).

Montréal Process Working Group. 2010. The Montréal Process. http://www.rinya.maff.go.jp/mpci/criteria_e.html. (5 July 2011).

Morin, R.S.; Liebhold, A.M.; Luzader, E.R. [et al.]. 2005. Mapping host-species abundance of three major exotic forest pests. Res. Pap. NE-726. Newtown Square, PA: U.S. Department of Agriculture, Forest Service, Northeastern Research Station. 11 p.

Multi-Resolution Land Characteristics Consortium (MRLC). 2011. National land cover database. Sioux Falls, SD: U.S. Department of Interior, Geologic Survey, Earth Resources Observation and Science Center. www.mrlc.gov. (14 August 2008).

National Association of State Foresters. 2011. State forestry statistics. Washington, DC: National Association of State Foresters. http://www.stateforesters.org/publication-type/stats. (30 July 2011).

National Association of State Foresters. 2010. State forest action plans. Washington, DC: National Association of State Foresters. http://www.forestactionplans.org/. (11 June 2011).

NatureServe. 2010. NatureServe explorer. Arlington, VA: NatureServe. http://www.natureserve.org/ explorer/. (28 March 2011).

North Maine Woods. 2010. North Maine Woods, Inc. Ashland, ME: North Maine Woods. http://www.northmainewoods.org/. (8 July 2011).

Nowak, D.J.; Greenfield, E. 2010. Evaluating the National Land Cover Database tree canopy and impervious cover estimates across the conterminous United States: a comparison with photo-interpreted estimates. Environmental Management. 46: 378-390.

Nowak, D.J.; Hoehn, R.; Crane, D.E.; Stevens, J.C.; Walton, J.T. 2006a. Assessing urban forest effects and values: Minneapolis' urban forest. Resour. Bull. NE-166. Newtown Square, PA: U.S. Department of Agriculture, Forest Service, Northeastern Research Station. 20 p.

Nowak, D.J.; Hoehn, R.; Crane, D.E.; Stevens, J.C.; Walton, J.T. 2006b. Assessing urban forest effects and values: Washington D.C.'s urban forest. Resour. Bull. NRS-1. Newtown Square, PA: U.S. Department of Agriculture, Forest Service, Northern Research Station. 24 p.

Nowak, D.J.; Hoehn, R.; Crane, D.E.; Stevens, J.C.; Walton, J.T. 2007a. Assessing urban forest effects and values: New York's urban forest. Resour. Bull. NRS-9. Newtown Square, PA: U.S. Department of Agriculture, Forest Service, Northern Research Station. 22 p.

Nowak, D.J.; Hoehn, R.; Crane, D.E.; Stevens, J.C.; Walton, J.T. 2007b. Assessing urban forest effects and values: Philadelphia's urban forest. Resour. Bull. NRS-7. Newtown Square, PA: U.S. Department of Agriculture, Forest Service, Northern Research Station. 22 p.

Nowak, D.J.; Rowntree, R.A.; McPherson, E.G. [et al.]. 1996. Measuring and analyzing urban tree cover. Landscape and Urban Planning. 36: 49-57.

Nowak, D.J.; Twardus, D.; Hoehn, R. [et al.]. 2007c. National Forest Health Monitoring program, monitoring urban forests in Indiana: pilot study 2002. Part 2: Statewide estimates using the UFORE model. NA-FR-01-07. Newtown Square, PA: U.S. Department of Agriculture, Forest Service, Northeastern Area State and Private Forestry. 13 p.

Nowak, D.J.; Walton, J.T. 2005. Projected urban growth (2000-2050) and its estimated impact on the U.S. forest resource. Journal of Forestry. 103(08): 383-389.

Nowak, D.J.; Walton, J.T.; Dwyer, J.F.; Kaya, L.G.; Myeong, S. 2005. The increasing influence of urban environments on U.S. forest management. Journal of Forestry. 103(8): 377-382.

O'Neill, K.P.; Amacher, M.C.; Perry, C.H. 2005. Soils as an indicator of forest health: a guide to the collection, analysis, and interpretation of soil indicator data in the Forest Inventory and Analysis program. Gen. Tech. Rep. NC-258. St. Paul, MN: U.S. Department of Agriculture, Forest Service, North Central Research Station. 53 p.

Ottinger, R.L.; Wooley, D.R.; Robinson, N.A. [et al.]. 1990. Environmental costs of electricity. White Plains, NY: Oceana Publications. 769 p.

Paper Industry Association Council. 2009. National paper recycling access/paper/paperboard collection by state. Washington, DC: American Forest and Paper Association. http://www.paperrecycles.org/community_recycling/index.html. (20 November 2010).

Pearce, D.W. 2001. The economic value of forest ecosystems. Ecosystem Health. 7(4): 285-296.

Pearce, D.W.; Atkinson, G.D.; Dubourg, W.R. 1994. The economics of sustainable development. Annual Review Energy and the Environment. 19: 457-474.

Pinchot, G. 1947. Breaking new ground. Washington, DC: Island Press. 522 p.

Prasad, A.M.; Iverson, L.R.; Matthews, S.; Peters, M. 2007. A climate change atlas for 134 forest tree species of the Eastern United States [Database]. Newtown Square, PA: U.S. Department of Agriculture, Forest Service, Northern Research Station. http://www.nrs.fs.fed.us/atlas/tree. (24 January 2011).

Protected Areas Center. 2010. Data basin: PAD-US 1.1 (CBI edition). http://www.databasin.org/protected-center/features/PAD-US-CBI. Corvallis, OR: Conservation Biology Institute. (12 November 2010).

Radeloff, V.C.; Hammer, R.B.; Stewart, S.I. [et al.]. 2005. The Wildland urban interface in the United States. Ecological Applications. 15: 799-805.

Radeloff, V.C.; Stewart, S.I.; Hawbaker, T.J. [et al.]. 2010. Housing growth in and near United States protected areas limits their conservation value. Proceedings of the National Academy of Sciences. 107(2): 940-945.

Recycler's World. 2009. Wooden pallet recycling category. Salt Lake City, UT: RecyclersNet Corp. http://www.recycle.net/Wood/pallet/index.html. (9 November 2010).

Riitters, K.H.; Wickham, J.D.; Wade, T.G. 2008. An indicator of forest dynamics using a shifting landscape mosaic. Ecological Indicators. 9(1): 107-117.

Rodenhouse, N.L.; Matthews, S.N.; McFarland, K.P. [et al.]. 2008. Potential effects of climate change on birds of the Northeast. Mitigation and Adaptation Strategies for Global Change. 13: 517-540.

Row, C. 1996. Effects of selected forest management options on carbon storage. In: Sampson, R.N.; Hair, D., eds. Forests and global change: Vol. 2. Forest management opportunities for mitigating carbon emissions. Washington, DC: American Forests: 59-90.

Ruefenacht, B.; Finco, M.V.; Nelson, M.D. [et al.]. 2008. Conterminous U.S. and Alaska forest type mapping using Forest Inventory and Analysis data. Photogrammetric Engineering and Remote Sensing. 74(11): 1379-1388.

Smith, W.B.; Miles, P.D.; Perry, C.H.; Pugh, S.A. 2009. Forest resources of the United States, 2007. Gen. Tech. Rep. WO-78. Washington, DC: U.S. Department of Agriculture, Forest Service. 336 p.

Steelman, T.A. 2001. Elite and participatory policy making: finding a balance in a case of national forest planning. Policy Studies Journal. 29(1): 71-89.

Stewart, S.I.; Johnson, K.M. 2006. Balancing leisure and work: evidence from the seasonal home. In: Peden, J.; Schuster, R., eds. Proceedings, 2005 northeast recreation research conference. Gen. Tech. Rep. NE-341. Newtown Square, PA: U.S. Department of Agriculture, Forest Service, Northeastern Research Station: 144-150.

Stokes, B.J.; Ashmore, C.; Rawlins, C.L.; Sirois, D.L. 1989. Glossary of trees used in timber harvesting and forest engineering. Gen. Tech. Rep. SO-73. New Orleans: U.S. Department of Agriculture, Forest Service, Southern Forest Experiment Station. 33 p.

Stynes, D.J.; Zheng, J.J.; Stewart, S.I. 1997. Seasonal homes and natural resources: patterns of use and impact in Michigan. Gen. Tech. Rep. NC-194. St. Paul, MN: U.S. Department of Agriculture, Forest Service, North Central Forest Experiment Station. 39 p.

Trani, M.K.; Brooks, R.T.; Schmidt, T.L.; Rudis, V.A.; Gabbard, C.M. 2001. Patterns and trends of early successional forests in the Eastern United States. Wildlife Society Bulletin. 29(2): 413-424.

Treiman, T.; Gartner, J.; Tuttle, J. 2008. Emerald ash borer: How much will it hurt Missouri's pocketbook? Notes for For. Managers 15. Jefferson City, MO: Missouri Department of Conservation. 3 p.

U.S. Census Bureau. 2000. Census of population and housing; census geography. Washington, DC: U.S. Department of Commerce. www.census.gov. (10 February 2011).

U.S. Census Bureau. 2007. 2007 economic census. Washington, DC: U.S. Department of Commerce. www.census.gov. (10 January 2011).

U.S. Census Bureau. 2009. Annual survey of manufactures. Washington, DC: U.S. Department of Commerce. http://www.census.gov/manufacturing/asm/index.html. (10 January 2011).

U.S. Census Bureau. 2010. Population estimates. Washington, DC: U.S. Department of Commerce. http://www.census.gov/popest/estimates.html. (26 March 2011).

U.S. Department of Agriculture, Forest Service. 1958. Timber resource for America's future. Forest Resource Rpt. No. 14. Washington, DC: U.S. Department of Agriculture, Forest Service. 713 p.

U.S. Department of Agriculture, Forest Service. 2004. National report on sustainable forests--2003. FS-766. Washington, DC: U.S. Department of Agriculture, Forest Service. 139 p.

U.S. Department of Agriculture, Forest Service. 2005. Pest alert: hemlock wooly adelgid. NA-PR-09-05. Newtown Square, PA: U.S. Department of Agriculture, Forest Service, Northeastern Area State and Private Forestry. 2 p.

U.S. Department of Agriculture, Forest Service. 2009a. Forest legacy program. Protecting private forest lands from conversion to non-forest uses. Washington, DC: U.S. Department of Agriculture, Forest Service. http://www.fs.fed.us/spf/coop/programs/loa/aboutflp.shtml. (10 February 2011).

U.S. Department of Agriculture, Forest Service. 2009b. National woodland owner survey. Washington, DC: U.S. Department of Agriculture, Forest Service. http://www.fia.fs.fed.us/nwos/. (18 November 2010).

U.S. Department of Agriculture, Forest Service. 2009c. Timber output mapmaker. Version 1.0. Washington, DC: U.S. Department of Agriculture, Forest Service. http://fia.fs.fed.us/tools-data/other/default.asp. (18 September 2011).

U.S. Department of Agriculture, Forest Service. 2010a. Forest Inventory and Analysis national program. Washington, DC: U.S. Department of Agriculture, Forest Service. http://fia.fs.fed.us/library/field-guides-methods-proc/. (7 July 2011).

U.S. Department of Agriculture, Forest Service. 2010b. Forest inventory data online (FIDO). Washington, DC: U.S. Department of Agriculture, Forest Service. http://fiatools.fs.fed.us/fido/index.html. (10 February 2011).

U.S. Department of Agriculture, Forest Service. 2010c. Forest legacy program: funded and completed projects. Washington, DC: U.S. Department of Agriculture, Forest Service. http://www.fs.fed.us/spf/coop/programs/loa/flp_projects.shtml. (15 November 2010).

U.S. Department of Agriculture, Forest Service. 2010d. Forest sustainability indicators information system. Washington, DC: U.S. Department of Agriculture, Forest Service. http://apps.fs.fed.us/fsiis/index.jsp. (13 February 2012).

U.S. Department of Agriculture, Forest Service. 2010e. Forest sustainability indicators information system: indicator 15 metrics. Forest ownership, land use, and specially designated areas. Washington, DC: U.S. Department of Agriculture, Forest Service. http://apps.fs.fed.us/fsiis/indicatorhome.do?IndicatorId=15. (13 February 2012).

U.S. Department of Agriculture, Forest Service. 2010f. Forest sustainability indicators information system: indicator 4 metrics. Status of forest/woodland communities and associated species of concern. Washington, DC: U.S. Department of Agriculture, Forest Service. http://apps.fs.fed.us/fsiis/indicatorhome.do?cId=6&menuId=2&IndicatorId=4. (13 February 2012).

U.S. Department of Agriculture, Forest Service. 2011a. Alien pest explorer: alien forest pest explorer maps. Washington, DC: U.S. Department of Agriculture, Forest Service. http://www.fs.fed.us/foresthealth/technology/invasive_species.shtml. (28 January 2011).

U.S. Department of Agriculture, Forest Service. 2011b. Forest health technology enterprise team: invasive species information. Washington, DC: U.S. Department of Agriculture, Forest Service. http://nrs.fs.fed.us/tools/afpe/maps/. (28 January 2011).

U.S. Department of Agriculture, Forest Service. 2011c. Forest health technology enterprise team: national insect and disease risk map/data. Washington, DC: U.S. Department of Agriculture, Forest Service. http://www.fs.fed.us/foresthealth/technology/nidrm.shtml. (28 January 2011).

U.S. Department of Agriculture, Forest Service. 2011d. Gypsy moth in North America: an atlas of historical gypsy moth defoliation and quarantined areas in the U.S. Washington, DC: U.S. Department of Agriculture, Forest Service. http://www.fs.fed.us/ne/morgantown/4557/gmoth/atlas/#spread. (28 January 2011).

U.S. Department of Agriculture, Forest Service. 2011e. National report on sustainable forests – 2010. FS-979. Washington, DC: U.S. Department of Agriculture, Forest Service. 212 p. http://www.fs.fed.us/research/sustain/2010SustainabilityReport/. (11 June 2011).

U.S. Department of Agriculture, Forest Service. 2011f. Northeastern Area State and Private Forestry Forest Health Protection aerial survey results viewer. Washington, DC: U.S. Department of Agriculture, Forest Service. http://www.na.fs.fed.us/ims/aerial/viewer.htm. (28 January 2011).

U.S. Department of Agriculture, Forest Service. 2011g. Soil quality: soil as an indicator of forest health. Washington, DC: U.S. Department of Agriculture, Forest Service. http://nrs.fs.fed.us/fia/topics/soils/. (28 January 2011).

U.S. Department of Agriculture, Forest Service. 2011h. Stewardship of the New York City watersheds. Washington, DC: U.S. Department of Agriculture, Forest Service. http://www.na.fs.fed.us/ra/specialinitiatives/nycwatershed/2010/ny_city_watersheds.pdf. (14 February 2011).

U.S. Department of Agriculture, Forest Service. 2011i. Timber product output (TPO) reports. Washington, DC: U.S. Department of Agriculture, Forest Service. http://srsfia2.fs.fed.us/php/tpo_2009/tpo_rpa_int1.php. (14 January 2011).

U.S. Department of Agriculture, Forest Service; Northeastern Area Association of State Foresters. 2011. 2010 Statewide forest resource assessments and strategies in the Northeast and Midwest: A regional summary. Newtown Square, PA: U.S. Department of Agriculture, Forest Service, Northeastern Area State and Private Forestry. 51 p. http://www.forestactionplans.org/regions/northeastern-region (12 August 2011).

U.S. Department of Agriculture, National Agricultural Statistics Service. 2009. Data and statistics. Washington, DC: U.S. Department of Agriculture, National Agricultural Statistics Service. http://www.nass.usda.gov/Data_and_Statistics/index.asp. (18 November 2010).

U.S. Department of Agriculture, National Agricultural Statistics Service. 2010. Crops and plant statistics. Washington, DC: U.S. Department of Agriculture, National Agricultural Statistics Service. http://www.nass.usda.gov/. (12 December 2010).

U.S. Department of Agriculture, Natural Resources Conservation Service. 2006. Land resource regions and major land resource areas of the United States, the Caribbean, and the Pacific basin. Agric. Handb. 296. Washington, DC: U.S. Department of Agriculture, Natural Resources Conservation Service. 669 p.

U.S. Department of Agriculture, Natural Resources Conservation Service. 2011. U.S. general soil map (STATSGO2). Washington, DC: U.S. Department of Agriculture, Natural Resources Conservation Service. http://www.soils.usda.gov/survey/geography/statsgo/. (2 February 2011).

U.S. Department of Agriculture, Natural Resources Conservation Service, Soil Survey Staff. 2010. Keys to soil taxonomy. 11th ed. Washington, DC: U.S. Department of Agriculture, Natural Resources Conservation Service. 338 p.

U.S. Department of Energy. 2010. Carbon dioxide information analysis center. Oak Ridge, TN: Oak Ridge National Laboratory. http://cdiac.ornl.gov/. (28 March 2011).

U.S. Department of Energy, Energy Information Administration. 2010. Renewable energy consumption by energy use sector and energy source. Washington, DC: U.S. Department of Energy, Energy Information Administration. http://www.eia.doe.gov/cneaf/solar.renewables/page/trends/table2.html. (12 December 2010).

U.S. Department of Labor, Bureau of Labor Statistics. 2007a. Databases, tables and calculators by subject. Washington, DC: U.S. Department of Labor, Bureau of Labor Statistics. http://www.bls.gov/data/. (28 August 2009).

U.S. Department of Labor, Bureau of Labor Statistics. 2007b. Injuries, illnesses, and fatalities. Washington, DC: U.S. Department of Labor, Bureau of Labor Statistics. http://www.bls.gov/iif/oshsum.htm#07Summary%20Tables. (28 August 2009).

U.S. Department of State. 2000. United States submission on land-use, land-use change, and forestry. Washington, DC: U.S. Department of State. 65 p. http://www.state.gov/www/global/global_issues/climate/000801_unfccc1_subm.pdf. (7 February 2011).

U.S. Environmental Protection Agency. 1996a. Environmental indicators of water quality in the United States. EPA 841-R-96-2002. Washington, DC: U.S. Environmental Protection Agency.

U.S. Environmental Protection Agency. 1996b. Watershed progress: New York City watershed agreement. EPA840-F-96-005. Washington, DC: U.S. Environmental Protection Agency. http://www.epa.gov/owow/watershed/ny/nycityfi.html. (10 February 2011).

U.S. Environmental Protection Agency. 2010. Surf your watershed. Washington, DC: U.S. Environmental Protection Agency. http://cfpub.epa.gov/surf/locate/index.cfm. (8 July 2011).

U.S. Environmental Protection Agency. 2011. National watershed characterization-1999. Washington, DC: U.S. Environmental Protection Agency. http://www.unl.edu/nac/atlas/Map_Html/Clean_Water/National/EPA_IWI-1999/National_water_quality.htm. (14 January 2011).

U.S. Environmental Protection Agency, Office of Wetlands, Oceans, and Watersheds. 2002. Environmental indicators of water quality in the United States. Washington, DC: U.S. Environmental Protection Agency. http://www.sarasota.wateratlas.usf.edu/upload/ documents/EPA%20Indicators%202002.pdf. (8 June 2010).

U.S. Geological Survey. 2010. Land cover institute. Washington, DC: U.S. Department of Interior, Geological Survey. http://landcover.usgs.gov/. (8 October 2010).

U.S. Geological Survey. 2011. Water resources of the United States: hydrologic unit maps. Washington, DC: U.S. Department of Interior, Geological Survey. http://water.usgs.gov/GIS/ huc.html. (11 January 2011).

Van Deusen, P.; L.S. Heath, L.S. 2009. COLE web applications suite. NCASI and USDA Forest Service, Northern Research Station. http://www.ncasi2.org/COLE/ Research Triangle Park, NC: National Council for Air and Stream Improvement; and Newtown Square, PA: U.S. Department of Agriculture, Forest Service, Northern Research Station. (28 March 2010).

Vogelmann, J.E.; Howard, S.M.; Yang, L. [et al.]. 2001. Completion of the 1990's national land cover data set for the conterminous United States. Photogrammetric Engineering and Remote Sensing. 67: 650-662.

West, T.O.; Post, W.M. 2002. Soil organic carbon sequestration rates by tillage and crop rotation: a global data analysis. Soil Science Society of America Journal. 66: 1930-1946.

Wickham, J.D.; Norton, D.J. 1994. Mapping and analyzing landscape patterns. Landscape Ecology. 9: 7-23.

World Commission on Environment and Development. 1987. Our common future. Oxford, UK: Oxford University Press. 400 p.

Hiking trail in the Cumberland Mountains

Glossary

activity day—The number of days per year that an individual (or a collective group of individuals) participates for any period of time in a particular activity. This metric is commonly used to measure recreational activities. Multiple recreation activities (such as hiking, photographing nature, and fishing) could be recorded for one person on the same day.

afforestation—Planting trees to establish a forest in an area where the prior land use was not forest (as in planting trees on former agricultural land).

annual growth—The average annual net increase in the volume of trees during the period between inventories. Components include the increment in net volume of trees at the beginning of the specific year surviving to its end, plus the net volume of trees reaching the minimum size class during the year, minus the volume of trees that died during the year, and minus the net volume of trees that became cull trees during the year.

anaerobic—Occurring in the absence of free oxygen.

biomass—The living or dead weight of organic matter in a tree, stand, or forest measured in units such as weight of live and dead material, green or dry weight, or weight of components such as boles, bark, tops, and roots (Helms 1998).

carbon emissions—Quantity (typically tons or metric tons) of carbon emitted to the atmosphere from combustion of fuels, decomposition of organic matter, and other activities. Often expressed as quantity of carbon dioxide (CO_2) with the mass of oxygen molecules included. Sometimes expressed as carbon dioxide equivalent (CO_{2e}) where the quantity of greenhouse gasses other than carbon dioxide (for example methane) are included in the total by converting those gasses to the amount of carbon dioxide expected to have a comparable greenhouse effect.

carbon sequestration (in forests)—The quantity of carbon (or CO_2 equivalent) held in plant tissues and soils in a forest ecosystem. The amount of sequestered carbon is often estimated by components (including live trees, dead trees, above ground tree parts, below ground tree parts, soil, or forest floor).

climate change—Long term trends or fluctuations in temperature, precipitation, wind, and other climate variables. In contemporary usage the term climate change often is used to indicate changes and fluctuations associated with increased atmospheric carbon dioxide and other greenhouse gasses (Helms 1998).

community land—Places that have geopolitical boundaries (such as cities, towns, or unincorporated named places) that may include all, some, or no urban land within their boundaries.

composite products—Wood products comprised of a resin matrix in combination with a wood fiber reinforcement. Composite wood pertains to, but is not limited to, particleboard, plywood, medium density fiberboard, composite veneer, and oriented strandboard.

cull tree—A tree at least 5 inches in diameter at breast height (d.b.h.) that is unmerchantable because it is rotten, poorly formed, or of an undesirable species.

d.b.h.—Tree diameter at breast height measured as inches of tree diameter at a height of 4.5 feet above ground level (diameter at breast height).

early successional forest habitat—Young forest (typically no more than 10 years old) that has regenerated on forest land following a large disturbance such as a timber harvest or via planting or natural succession on other open land.

ecological region—See ecoregion.

ecoregion—A contiguous geographic area with relatively uniform macroclimate, altitude, predominant natural vegetation, and/or other features that influence ecosystem function. Ecoregions can be split into finer divisions or aggregated into coarser categories based on macroclimate, landform, geology, hydrology, native vegetation, or other factors that affect plants and animals.

ecosystem services—The benefits people obtain from ecosystems. These include provisioning services such as food and water; regulating services such as flood and disease control; cultural services such as spiritual, recreational, and cultural benefits; and supporting services such as nutrient cycling that maintain the conditions for life on Earth. Ecosystems provide food, clothes, fuels and many of the commodities used to manufacture the products used in daily life. Ecosystems also purify and store water, help clean air, regulate climate, provide protection from natural hazards such as hurricanes, pollinate crops, and regulate pests. They have the ability to process and detoxify wastes. Ecosystems also provide places to play and reflect, and they contribute to our cultural, inspirational, and intellectual well-being by providing a sense of place.

edge—The transition between forest and nonforest land, between mature forest and young forest, or between two other contrasting forest conditions.

employees (number of)—All full-time and part-time employees who are on the payrolls of establishments who worked or received pay for any part of the pay period including the 12th of March, June, September, and December. Included are employees on paid sick leave, paid holidays, and paid vacations; not included are proprietors and partners of unincorporated businesses. Employment data for earlier years represent the average number of production workers for the payroll periods that include the 12th of March, May, August, and November. The "all employees" number is the average number of production workers plus the number of other employees in mid-March.

family forest owners—Families, individuals, trusts, estates, family partnerships, and other unincorporated groups of individuals that own forest land. This group is a subset of nonindustrial private forest owners.

FIA—See Forest Inventory and Analysis.

forest associated birds, mammals, and vascular plants—Birds, mammals, and vascular plants that normally spend part of their lives in a forest habitat.

Forest Inventory and Analysis (FIA)—The U.S. Forest Service research and development group charged with conducting and reporting inventories of forest vegetation, soils, health, and product outputs.

forest land—Land at least 120 feet wide and 1 acre in size with at least 10 percent cover (or equivalent stocking) by live trees of any size, including land that formerly had such tree cover and that will be naturally or artificially regenerated. Forest land includes transition zones, such as areas between forest and nonforest lands that have at least 10 percent cover (or equivalent stocking) with live trees and forest areas adjacent to urban and built-up lands. Roadside, streamside, and shelterbelt strips of trees must have a crown width of at least 120 feet and continuous length of at least 363 feet to qualify as forest land. Unimproved roads and trails, streams, and clearings in forest areas are classified as forest if they are less than 120 feet wide or an acre in size. Tree-covered areas in agricultural production settings, such as fruit orchards, or tree-covered areas in urban settings, such as city parks, are not considered forest land.

forest stand—A contiguous group of trees of similar age structure and size structure. In the North, stands are typically 5 to 40 acres in extent.

forest stewardship plan—A forest management plan that addresses the management objectives of the forest owner while maintaining the forest in a healthy condition for future generations.

forest type—A classification of forest land based on the tree species that presently form the plurality of live tree stocking (for example oak-hickory forest type or red pine forest type).

forest-type group—A group of forest types with similar tree species and/or habitat requirements.

fragmentation (forest)—The process of breaking up contiguous forest cover with various nonforest land uses.

fuelwood—Wood used for conversion to some form of energy.

growing stock—A classification of timber inventory that includes live trees of commercial species meeting specified standards of quality or vigor. Cull trees are excluded. When measured as cubic foot volume, it includes only trees 5.0 inches d.b.h. and larger.

habitat restoration—Returning forest species composition, size structure and/or ecosystem processes to a range of conditions representative of a former period of time (for example prior to European settlement).

hardwood—Trees belonging to the botanical group Angiospermae. These broad-leaved trees typically drop their leaves in autumn. Examples include oaks, maples, elms, cottonwood, aspen, and birch. The wood of hardwoods may be physically hard or soft relative to softwoods.

indicator—Qualitative or quantitative variable that functions as a signal to relay complex ecological information in a simple and useful manner. Effective indicator variables must be indicative of a larger ecological process, easily measured, cost-effective, and repeatable.

interior—Locations within mature forest cover that are removed by some minimum distance (e.g., 50 yards) from a forest edge.

invasive plants and animals—See invasive species.

invasive species—A species whose introduction does, or is likely to cause economic or environmental harm or harm to human health. Only a small proportion of nonnative species are invasive.

IUCN protected status—See protected area.

national forest—An ownership class of Federal lands, designated by Executive Order or statute as National Forests or purchase units, and other lands under the administration of the U.S. Forest Service.

net annual forest growth—See annual growth.

nonindustrial private forest—See private noncorporate owners.

nontimber forest products—These products are not commonly listed as outputs of the forest products industry, but are important in the herbal medicine, culinary, crafts, and floral industries. They include edible products such as fruits, nuts, mushrooms, ramps, and maple syrup; medicinal type products such as ginseng and bloodroot; ornamental products such as pine cones, boughs, and grapevines; landscape products such as native plants; specialty woods such as burl and crotch wood for fine crafts; and wild-grown Christmas trees. As used here they also include post, poles, or residential fuelwood sold in small quantities.

old-growth forest—A subjective term describing forests that are relatively old for their forest cover type and relatively undisturbed by humans. Old-growth forests are characterized by the presence of large trees of late-successional (climax) species, multiple age cohorts, decadent trees, large snags, down wood in multiple stages of decay, and down trees of large diameter.

other Federal—An ownership class of Federal lands other than those administered by the Forest Service or the Bureau of Land Management. This category includes the National Park Service, Fish and Wildlife Service, Department of Defense, Department of Energy, and other miscellaneous Federal ownerships.

parcelization—The division of parcels (individual ownerships) of land into smaller parcels split among multiple owners.

primary forest—See old-growth forest.

private forest—Forest owned by private individuals, corporations, or other nongovernmental entities.

private forest owners—Owners other than federal, State, county, or municipal government. This category includes private corporate (wood using industry and other incorporated) and private noncorporate.

private noncorporate owners—An ownership class of private lands that are not owned by corporate interests. This category includes land owned by individuals, Native American lands, unincorporated partnerships, clubs, and lands leased by corporate interests.

protected area—An area of land and/or sea especially dedicated to the protection and maintenance of biological diversity, and of natural and associated cultural resources, and managed through legal or other effective means (see also reserved forest). Although all protected areas meet the general purposes contained in this definition, in practice the precise purposes for which protected areas are managed differ greatly. The International Union for Conservation of Nature (IUCN) has defined a series of six protected area management categories, based on primary management objective (DellaSalla et al. 2001; Dudley 2008; International Union for Conservation of Nature 1994, 2004):

Category I: An area of land and/or sea possessing some outstanding or representative ecosystems, geological or physiological features and/or species, available primarily for scientific research and/or environmental monitoring or a large area of unmodified or slightly modified land, and/or sea, retaining its natural character and influence, without permanent or significant habitation, which is protected and managed so as to preserve its natural condition. Strict nature reserves (Ia) are distinguished from wilderness areas (Ib).

Category II: A natural area of land and/or sea, designated to (1) protect the ecological integrity of one or more ecosystems for present and future generations, (2) exclude exploitation or occupation inimical to the purposes of designation of the area, and (3) provide a foundation for spiritual, educational, recreational, and visitor opportunities, all of which must be environmentally and culturally comparable.

Category III: An area of land and/or sea containing one or more specific natural or natural/cultural features which are of outstanding or unique value because of their inherent rarity, representative or esthetic qualities, or cultural significance.

Category IV: An area of land and/or sea subject to active intervention for management purposes so as to ensure the maintenance of habitats and/or to meet the requirements of specific species.

Category V: An area of land with coast and sea as appropriate, where the interaction of people and nature over time has produced an area of distinct character with significant esthetic, ecological, and/or cultural value, and often with high biological diversity. Safeguarding the integrity of this traditional interaction is vital to the protection, maintenance, and evolution of such an area.

Category VI: An area of land and/or sea containing predominantly unmodified natural systems, managed to ensure long term protection and maintenance of biological diversity, while providing at the same time a sustainable flow of natural products and services to meet community needs.

protected forest—See protected area.

public forest land—Forest owned by federal, State, county, municipal, or other governmental entities.

pulpwood—Roundwood, whole-tree chips, or wood residues that are used for the production of wood pulp. Composite products are often made from similar material.

removals—The net volume of growing-stock trees removed from the inventory by harvesting, cultural operations such as timber stand improvement, or land clearing during a specified period of time (usually expressed as an annual average for a specified period of time).

reserved forest land—Forest land withdrawn from timber utilization through statute, administrative regulation, or designation without regard to productive status. This is usually public forest land. See also protected area.

roundwood products—Logs, bolts, and other round timber generated from harvesting trees for industrial or consumer use.

softwood—Trees belonging to the botanical group Gymnospermae. These needle-bearing trees typically produce seeds in cones. Examples include pines, spruces, firs, hemlocks, and cedars. The wood of softwoods may be physically soft or hard relative to hardwoods.

soil horizon—A specific layer in the land area that is parallel to the soil surface and possesses different physical characteristics from the layers above and beneath.

spatial scale—The degree of aggregation or disaggregation that one chooses to examine an issue. Spatial scales are hierarchical, and each scale can be split into finer units or combined into coarser units. Examples of spatial scale include national > State > county > township > section > woodlot (about 20 acres) < all woodlots along same south-facing ridge (about 100 to 500 acres) < small landscape (about 1,000 acres) < cluster of landscapes (up to 10,000 acres). Other relevant spatial scales might include the area around an individual tree, a forest stand, a group of forest stands, the typical home range of a wildlife species, an ecoregion, a watershed, a community, or an urban area.

stand—See forest stand.

stewardship—The administration of land and associated resources in a manner that enables their passing on to future generations in a healthy condition.

stewardship plan—See forest stewardship plan.

susceptibility—The potential for introduction and establishment, over a 15 year period, of a forest pest within a tree species or tree species group.

timberland—Forest land that is producing or is capable of producing crops of industrial wood and not withdrawn from timber utilization by statute or administrative regulation. Areas qualifying as timberland are capable of producing in excess of 20 cubic feet per acre per year of industrial wood in natural stands. Currently inaccessible and inoperable areas are included.

total wages—The annual payroll or gross earnings paid in each calendar year to employees at the establishment. It includes all forms of compensation, such as salaries, wages, commissions, dismissal pay, bonuses, vacation and sick leave pay, and compensation in kind, prior to such deductions as employees' Social Security contributions, withholding taxes, group insurance, union dues, and savings bonds. The total includes salaries of officers of corporations; it excludes payments to proprietors or partners of unincorporated concerns. Also excluded are payments to members of Armed Forces and pensioners carried on the active payrolls of manufacturing establishments. This term also includes fringe benefits for employees, including the employer's costs for social security taxes, unemployment taxes, workmen's compensation insurance, State disability insurance pension plans, stock purchase plans, union-negotiated benefits, life insurance premiums, and insurance premiums on hospital and medical plans for employees. Also included are the employer's costs for benefits to individual employees such as stock purchase plans, deferred profit-sharing plans, and defined benefit and defined contribution retirement plans. They exclude such items as company-operated cafeterias, in-plant medical services, free parking lots, discounts on employee purchases, and uniforms and work clothing for employees.

urban or community land—Urban land is all territory, population, and housing units located within urbanized areas or urban clusters, which are based on population density (areas with core population density of 1,000 people per square mile, but includes surrounding areas with lesser population density). Community lands are places that have geo-political boundaries (for example, cities, towns, or unincorporated named places) that may include all, some, or no urban land within their boundaries. As urban land reveals the more heavily populated areas (population density-based definition) and community land indicates both urban and rural (i.e., nonurban) communities that are recognized by their geopolitical boundaries (political definition), both definitions provide information related to human settlements and the forest resources within those settlements. As some urban land exists beyond community boundaries and not all community land is urban (communities are often a mix of urban and rural land), the category of "urban or community" was created to understand forest attributes accumulated by the union of these two definitions (U.S. Census Bureau 2007).

urban or community population—Total population within a region that resides within urban or community land.

urban land—All the territory, population, and housing units located within urbanized areas or urban clusters, each with a core population density of 1,000 people per square mile and with surrounding areas that have lower population densities (U.S. Census Bureau 2007).

vulnerability—The potential for experiencing mortality of a tree species, over a 15 year period, if a forest pest were to become established.

volume of timber—The gross volume in cubic feet of wood for standing trees or for cut trees less deductions for rot, roughness, and poor form. Volume is computed for the central stem from a 1-foot stump to a minimum 4.0-inch top diameter outside bark, or to the point where the central stem breaks into limbs.

watershed—Defined in nature by topography, a watershed is the land area that drains to a waterbody and affects its flow, water level, loadings of pollutants, and other processes. In both a real and figurative sense, a lake or river is a reflection of its watershed. The U.S. Geological Survey has developed a Hydrologic Unit Classification (HUC) System of watersheds at various scales and mapped these watersheds. The HUC's depicted in the figures are at the "eight-digit scale" (USGS 2011).

wildland-urban interface—Where houses meet or intermingle with wildland vegetation. The wildland-urban interface is composed of both interface and intermix communities. In both interface and intermix communities, housing must meet or exceed a minimum density of one structure per 40 acres. Intermix communities are places where housing and vegetation intermingle. In intermix, wildland vegetation is continuous, more than 50 percent vegetation, in areas with more than 1 house per 16 ha (39.54 acres). Interface communities are areas with housing in the vicinity of contiguous vegetation. Interface areas have more than 1 house per 40 acres, have less than 50 percent vegetation, and are within 1.5 mi of an area (made up of one or more contiguous Census blocks) over 1,325 acres (500 ha) that is more than 75 percent vegetated. The minimum size limit ensures that areas surrounding small urban parks are not classified as interface.

Appendix

Table A1—Population and forest land area by State, 2007 (Smith et al. 2009, U.S. Census Bureau 2010). Note that data have been standardized to an inventory year of 2007 and that newer State-specific data for some attributes are available from online sources (Miles 2010).

State and region	Population	Total area	Forest land area	Forest land area per person	Forest land proportion of all land	Public forest land	Public proportion of all forest land	Federal proportion of all forest land
		-------(million acres)-------		(acres)	(percent)	(million acres)	----------------(percent)----------------	
Connecticut	3,488,633	3.10	1.8	0.51	58	0.41	23	0.0
Delaware	864,896	1.25	0.4	0.44	31	0.03	8	0.0
Illinois	12,779,417	35.61	4.5	0.35	13	0.79	18	8.1
Indiana	6,346,113	22.98	4.7	0.73	20	0.77	16	8.6
Iowa	2,978,719	35.84	2.9	0.97	8	0.33	11	3.6
Maine	1,317,308	19.75	17.7	13.42	89	1.10	6	0.9
Maryland	5,634,242	6.26	2.6	0.46	41	0.61	24	2.8
Massachusetts	6,499,275	5.02	3.2	0.49	63	0.99	31	3.3
Michigan	10,050,847	36.27	19.5	1.94	54	7.43	38	15.1
Minnesota	5,191,206	51.02	16.4	3.16	32	9.28	57	17.0
Missouri	5,909,824	44.09	15.1	2.55	34	2.69	18	12.2
New Hampshire	1,317,343	5.74	4.9	3.68	85	1.20	25	15.9
New Jersey	8,636,043	4.75	2.1	0.25	45	0.81	38	5.0
New York	19,422,777	30.22	18.7	0.96	62	4.23	23	0.8
Ohio	11,520,815	26.21	7.9	0.69	30	0.92	12	3.5
Pennsylvania	12,522,531	28.68	16.6	1.32	58	4.84	29	3.6
Rhode Island	1,055,009	0.67	0.4	0.34	53	0.05	15	0.0
Vermont	620,460	5.92	4.6	7.44	78	0.75	16	8.0
West Virginia	1,811,198	15.42	12.0	6.63	78	1.59	13	10.3
Wisconsin	5,601,571	34.79	16.3	2.91	47	5.16	32	9.7
Washington DC	586,409							
Northern States	123,568,227	413.59	172.0	1.39	42	43.98	26	8.1
United States	301,579,895	2,263.87	751.2	2.49	33	328.20	44	33.1

Table A1 continued

State and region	National Forest proportion of all forest land	State proportion of all forest land	Private forest land area	Private proportion of all forest land	Private corporate proportion of all forest land	Private noncorporate proportion of all forest land	Reserved forest land	Reserved proportion of all forest land
	--------------(percent)--------------		(million acres)	--------------------------------(percent)--------------------------------			(million acres)	(percent)
Connecticut	0.0	14.3	1.38	77	13.1	64.0	0.03	1.7
Delaware	0.0	8.4	0.35	92	27.9	63.7	0.00	0.0
Illinois	6.4	4.5	3.73	82	4.9	77.5	0.16	3.6
Indiana	4.1	7.2	3.89	84	6.5	77.1	0.12	2.6
Iowa	0.0	5.7	2.55	89	1.4	87.2	0.01	0.5
Maine	0.3	4.4	16.57	94	58.4	35.4	0.32	1.8
Maryland	0.0	16.5	1.96	76	19.3	57.0	0.18	7.0
Massachusetts	0.0	19.0	2.18	69	5.7	63.0	0.13	4.1
Michigan	13.5	21.1	12.12	62	13.6	48.4	0.33	1.7
Minnesota	15.0	26.8	7.11	43	7.3	36.1	0.82	5.0
Missouri	9.9	5.2	12.39	82	4.2	78.0	0.24	1.6
New Hampshire	14.8	5.5	3.65	75	16.5	58.6	0.13	2.6
New Jersey	0.0	24.9	1.32	62	24.3	37.7	0.16	7.5
New York	0.1	19.4	14.44	77	12.0	65.3	2.50	13.4
Ohio	2.9	5.4	6.97	88	11.5	76.8	0.23	2.9
Pennsylvania	3.0	23.0	11.74	71	12.9	57.9	0.46	2.8
Rhode Island	0.0	11.9	0.30	85	14.6	70.6	0.00	0.0
Vermont	7.3	6.8	3.86	84	16.4	67.3	0.11	2.5
West Virginia	8.9	2.3	10.42	87	27.0	59.8	0.17	1.4
Wisconsin	8.6	6.6	11.12	68	8.9	59.4	0.11	0.7
Washington DC								
Northern States	6.6	13.1	128.06	74	16.6	57.9	6.22	3.6
United States	19.6	9.2	423.03	56	18.4	37.9	74.64	9.9

Table A2—Timberland area and volume by State, 2007 (Miles 2010, Smith et al. 2009). Newer State-specific data for some attributes are available from online sources (Miles 2010).

State and region	Timberland	Timberland proportion of all land	Timberland proportion of all forest land	Planted timberland	Planted proportion of timberland	Net volume of timber on timberland	Net volume of growing stock on timberland	Growing stock proportion of all timber
	(million acres)	----------------(percent)----------------		(1,000 acres)	(percent)	(million cubic feet)	(million cubic feet)	(percent)
CT	1.7	56	97	27	1.6	3,501	3,314	94.6
DE	0.4	30	98	16	4.4	737	695	94.3
IL	4.4	12	96	96	2.2	7,642	6,875	90.0
IN	4.5	20	97	171	3.8	9,098	8,281	91.0
IA	2.8	8	98	23	0.8	4,046	3,114	77.0
ME	17.2	87	97	381	2.2	23,935	22,402	93.6
MD	2.4	38	92	162	6.8	5,254	5,092	96.9
MA	2.9	59	93	36	1.2	6,978	6,530	93.6
MI	19.0	52	97	1,143	6.0	30,418	28,029	92.1
MN	15.1	30	92	615	4.1	16,657	14,931	89.6
MO	14.7	33	97	84	0.6	18,886	16,596	87.9
NH	4.7	81	96	25	0.5	9,880	9,156	92.7
NJ	1.9	40	88	6	0.3	2,968	2,819	95.0
NY	16.0	53	86	811	5.1	27,761	25,862	93.2
OH	7.6	29	97	387	5.1	13,311	12,324	92.6
PA	16.0	56	97	766	4.8	31,265	29,859	95.5
RI	0.4	52	99	0	0.1	663	637	95.8
VT	4.5	76	97	34	0.8	9,493	8,696	91.6
WV	11.8	77	98	108	0.9	23,539	22,524	95.7
WI	16.0	46	99	929	5.8	22,268	20,271	91.0
Northern States	164.0	40	95	5,820	3.5	268,303	248,005	92.4
United States	514.2	23	68	62,672	12.2	1,013,407	932,089	92.0

State and region	Net growth of growing stock on timberland	Net growth of growing stock as a proportion of growing stock	Removals of growing stock on timberland	Removals of growing stock as a proportion of growing stock	Mortality of growing stock on timberland	Mortality of growing stock as a proportion of growing stock	Ratio of growing stock growth to removals	Years included for growth, removals and mortality estimates
	(million cubic feet/year)	(percent)	(million cubic feet/year)	(percent)	(million cubic feet/year)	(percent)		
CT	89	2.7	41	1.2	19	0.6	2.2	2003-2007
DE	31	4.5	7	1.0	5	0.7	4.5	2004-2008
IL	231	3.4	58	0.8	88	1.3	4.0	2004-2008
IN	318	3.8	80	1.0	75	0.9	4.0	2004-2008
IA	105	3.4	46	1.5	36	1.2	2.3	2004-2008
ME	573	2.6	562	2.5	269	1.2	1.0	2008
MD	178	3.5	67	1.3	44	0.9	2.6	2004-2008
MA	144	2.2	62	1.0	36	0.6	2.3	2003-2007
MI	703	2.5	339	1.2	272	1.0	2.1	2004-2008
MN	417	2.8	294	2.0	241	1.6	1.4	2004-2008
MO	518	3.1	175	1.1	127	0.8	3.0	2004-2008
NH	164	1.8	150	1.6	98	1.1	1.1	2002-2007
NJ	95	3.4	29	1.0	23	0.8	3.3	2004-2008
NY	600	2.3	288	1.1	269	1.0	2.1	2008
OH	410	3.3	189	1.5	124	1.0	2.2	2008
PA	743	2.5	414	1.4	237	0.8	1.8	2008
RI	19	3.0	4	0.7	2	0.3	4.4	2003-2007
VT	180	2.1	109	1.3	85	1.0	1.7	2003-2007
WV	611	2.7	323	1.4	169	0.7	1.9	2004-2008
WI	598	3.0	327	1.6	203	1.0	1.8	2004-2008
Northern States	6,726	2.5	3,564	1.4	2,420	1.0	1.9	Various
United States	26,744	2.9	15,533	1.7	7,826	0.8	1.7	Various

Table A3—Biomass, carbon, and number of trees by State (Smith 2009, Miles et al. 2010, U.S. Census Bureau 2010). Newer State-specific data for some attributes are available from online sources (Miles 2010).

State and region	Total aboveground biomass on timberland 2007	Total aboveground biomass on timberland 1997	Change in total aboveground biomass on timberland 1997-2007	Total carbon on forest land including soil organic carbon, 2009	Total carbon on forest land excluding soil organic carbon, 2009
	--(million dry tons)--				
Connecticut	98	71	27	137	90
Delaware	22	17	5	28	18
Illinois	210	146	64	309	187
Indiana	243	188	54	310	200
Iowa	112	68	43	172	95
Maine	654	690	(36)	1,343	695
Maryland	151	129	23	204	135
Massachusetts	174	112	62	257	165
Michigan	799	719	80	2,081	755
Minnesota	450	421	29	1,761	484
Missouri	592	432	160	853	520
New Hampshire	253	259	(5)	405	248
New Jersey	90	70	20	148	88
New York	755	647	108	1,557	949
Ohio	365	426	(61)	594	366
Pennsylvania	862	748	115	1,287	826
Rhode Island	19	11	8	27	17
Vermont	314	249	65	400	249
West Virginia	688	635	53	923	610
Wisconsin	606	510	96	1,617	567
Northern States	7,457	6,548	909	14,413	7,262
United States	24,421	22,036	2,385	45,152	

Table A3 continued

State and region	Per capita carbon on forest land including soil organic carbon, 2009	Per capita carbon on forest land excluding soil organic carbon, 2009	Number of trees on forest land, 2007	Forest land trees per capita, 2007
	----------------------(dry tons)----------------------		(millions)	(trees)
Connecticut	39	26	857	246
Delaware	33	21	235	271
Illinois	24	15	2,096	164
Indiana	49	31	2,242	353
Iowa	58	32	1,152	387
Maine	1,020	527	22,034	16,726
Maryland	36	24	1,365	242
Massachusetts	39	25	1,510	232
Michigan	207	75	13,716	1,365
Minnesota	339	93	11,964	2,305
Missouri	144	88	8,205	1,388
New Hampshire	308	188	3,750	2,846
New Jersey	17	10	1,010	117
New York	80	49	9,967	513
Ohio	52	32	3,971	345
Pennsylvania	103	66	8,244	658
Rhode Island	26	16	180	171
Vermont	644	401	3,417	5,507
West Virginia	510	337	5,998	3,312
Wisconsin	289	101	10,640	1,899
Northern States	117	59	112,554	911
United States	150		296,634	984

Table A4—Volume of roundwood products, 2006, and wood products consumption, 2005 (Howard 2007, USDA FS 2011i).

State and region	Total products	Saw logs	Pulpwood	Fuelwood	Composite products
			(million cubic feet)		
Connecticut	13	5	<1	7	
Delaware	9	4	5	<1	
Illinois	96	35	1	56	
Indiana	108	68	2	34	
Iowa	26	15		10	
Maine	563	203	239	121	
Maryland	60	28	11	20	
Massachusetts	50	7	1	41	
Michigan	373	128	135	30	66
Minnesota	326	48	124	39	113
Missouri	166	113	7	36	
New Hampshire	42	25	11	5	
New Jersey	26	1	<1	25	
New York	243	82	76	77	3
Ohio	76	48	24	4	
Pennsylvania	223	119	64	6	
Rhode Island	5	1		3	
Vermont	61	33	10	18	
West Virginia	164	104	6	5	35
Wisconsin	414	100	219	38	43
Northern States	3,045	1,168	938	576	261
United States	14,990	7,179	1,211	4,394	543

Table A4 continued

State and region	Veneer logs	Other products	Post, poles, and pilings	Annual wood consumption per state	Wood consumption per person
	------------------------(million cubic feet)------------------------				(cubic feet)
Connecticut				248	71
Delaware				61	71
Illinois	1	3	<1	907	71
Indiana	3	1	<1	451	71
Iowa	1	<1	<1	211	71
Maine				94	71
Maryland				400	71
Massachusetts		<1		461	71
Michigan	8	2	4	714	71
Minnesota	1	<1	<1	369	71
Missouri	1	7	1	420	71
New Hampshire	1	<1		94	71
New Jersey			<1	613	71
New York	4	<1	<1	1,379	71
Ohio	<1	1		818	71
Pennsylvania	19	13	1	889	71
Rhode Island				75	71
Vermont				44	71
West Virginia	10	1	2	129	71
Wisconsin	6	7	2	398	71
Northern States	56	35	12	8,773	71
United States	1,408	100	155	21,412	71

Table A5—Private forest owners and utilization or production of nonwood forest products (Smith et al. 2009, USDS FS 2009b, USDA NASS 2010).

State and region	Number of private forest land owners	Mean acres per private forest land owner	Mean age of family forest owners	Family forest owners who utilize edibles	Family forest owners who utilize decoratives	Family forest owners who utilize medicinals
	(thousand)	(acres)	(years)	----------------------------(percent owners)----------------------------		
Connecticut	108	13	56	11	12	
Delaware	55	6	55	na	na	na
Illinois	184	20	61	15	3	2
Indiana	225	18	58	12	9	<1
Iowa	150	17	58	18	16	1
Maine	252	66	59	13	5	<1
Maryland	157	12	60	7	4	
Massachusetts	293	7	58	11	5	2
Michigan	498	24	58	13	7	1
Minnesota	202	35	59	13	8	<1
Missouri	359	34	59	20	5	3
New Hampshire	128	28	62	9	33	1
New Jersey	122	11	65	na	na	na
New York	687	21	62	12	6	2
Ohio	345	20	59	15	14	5
Pennsylvania	497	24	58	7	7	2
Rhode Island	38	8	57	11	5	
Vermont	88	42	58	39	20	3
West Virginia	251	41	59	6	2	3
Wisconsin	362	30	58	18	8	1
Northern States	5,002	25	59	12	8	2
United States	11,322	37	59	NA	NA	NA

Table A5 continued

State and region	Family forest owners who utilize cultural items	Family forest area utilized for edibles	Family forest area utilized for decoratives	Family forest area utilized for medicinals	Family forest area utilized for cultural items	Maple syrup production	Maple syrup value
	(percent owners)	-----------------------------------(percent acres)-------------------------------------				(1,000 gallons)	($1,000)
Connecticut		5	5			13	800
Delaware	na	na	na	na	na		
Illinois		21	7	5			
Indiana	1	16	9	4	1		
Iowa		22	5	4			
Maine		6	6	1	<1	395	12,996
Maryland		10	5				
Massachusetts		13	10	2		46	2,466
Michigan	1	14	7	1	1	115	5,175
Minnesota	<1	14	9	1	1		
Missouri		21	8	4	<1		
New Hampshire		14	10	1	1	94	4,756
New Jersey	na	na	na	na	na		
New York		13	6	1		439	17,823
Ohio	1	17	12	9	<1	90	3,627
Pennsylvania	<1	10	5	2	<1	92	3,503
Rhode Island	5	10	10		3		
Vermont		22	11	4	1	920	32,292
West Virginia		9	4	3	<1		
Wisconsin	1	20	10	2	1	200	7,340
Northern States	<1	13	7	2	<1	2,404	90,780
United States	NA	NA	NA	NA	NA	2,404	90,780

Table A6—Employment and wages in forest industries, 2006 (U.S. Bureau of Labor Statistics 2007a). Values reported for the pulp and paper industries include manufacturers of converted products such as packaging and stationery.

State and region	Forestry and logging employment (NAICS 113)	Wood products employment (NAICS 321)	Pulp and paper employment (NAICS 322)	Total forest sector employment	Forestry and logging total wages (NAICS 113)
	------------------------------------(jobs)------------------------------------				$1,000
Connecticut	19	1,745	4,886	6,650	572
Delaware		419	951	1,370	
Illinois	171	9,209	24,841	34,221	4,275
Indiana	455	19,399	11,488	31,342	11,417
Iowa	32	12,549	4,342	16,923	839
Maine	2,732	6,213	9,040	17,985	92,552
Maryland	416	3,568	5,249	9,233	11,851
Massachusetts	149	3,378	12,311	15,838	7,468
Michigan	1,662	10,737	13,966	26,365	50,071
Minnesota	841	16,320	11,866	29,027	25,084
Missouri	235	10,437	8,758	19,430	5,690
New Hampshire	470	2,758	2,228	5,456	17,235
New Jersey	23	4,559	14,070	18,652	1,035
New York	934	9,712	20,171	30,817	28,954
Ohio	613	16,476	24,726	41,815	14,424
Pennsylvania	832	30,291	26,843	57,966	20,550
Rhode Island			1,339	1,339	
Vermont		2,283	1,291	3,574	
West Virginia	1,174	8,252	723	10,149	25,790
Wisconsin	970	25,898	36,008	62,876	26,611
Northern States	11,728	194,203	235,097	441,028	344,419
United States	72,140	556,110	468,422	1,096,672	2,502,632

Table A6 continued

State and region	Wood products total wages (NAICS 321)	Pulp and paper total wages (NAICS 322)	Forestry and logging average wage rate (NAICS 113)	Wood products average wage rate (NAICS 321)	Pulp and paper average wage rate (NAICS 322)
	----------------($1,000)----------------		-------------------------------($/year)-------------------------------		
Connecticut	76,705	309,562	30,131	43,957	63,357
Delaware	15,912	50,801		37,975	53,418
Illinois	324,258	1,242,423	25,000	35,211	50,015
Indiana	637,781	516,374	25,092	32,877	44,949
Iowa	464,564	199,854	26,208	37,020	46,028
Maine	205,483	543,638	33,877	33,073	60,137
Maryland	131,445	222,447	28,489	36,840	42,379
Massachusetts	140,467	635,211	50,121	41,583	51,597
Michigan	375,366	713,537	30,127	34,960	51,091
Minnesota	766,616	649,960	29,826	46,974	54,775
Missouri	280,620	394,241	24,214	26,887	45,015
New Hampshire	111,285	114,965	36,671	40,350	51,600
New Jersey	174,792	839,838	45,007	38,340	59,690
New York	342,066	995,661	31,000	35,221	49,361
Ohio	531,005	1,167,389	23,530	32,229	47,213
Pennsylvania	986,426	1,349,183	24,699	32,565	50,262
Rhode Island		53,259			39,775
Vermont	77,768	65,434		34,064	50,685
West Virginia	245,596	28,123	21,968	29,762	38,897
Wisconsin	816,305	1,949,581	27,434	31,520	54,143
Northern States	6,704,460	12,041,480	29,367	34,523	51,219
United States	19,278,736	24,825,898	34,691	34,667	52,999

Table A7—Urban and community population, area, and forest characteristics by State, 2000.

State and region	Proportion urban population	Proportion community population	Urban land proportion of all land	Community land proportion of all land	Urban or community land proportion of all land	Urban growth 1990-2000 (percent of state)	Urban growth 1990-2000 (acres)
	--(percent)--						
Connecticut	88	60	36.4	19.2	39.9	5.0	159,000
Delaware	80	44	15.4	8.8	17.8	4.1	53,100
Illinois	88	87	6.4	7.0	8.7	1.0	365,500
Indiana	71	66	6.1	6.2	8.1	1.2	287,200
Iowa	61	78	1.5	3.5	3.6	0.2	55,300
Maine	40	47	1.1	3.9	4.2	0.1	25,600
Maryland	86	80	18.5	18.7	23.4	3.0	199,400
Massachusetts	91	71	35.6	22.5	40.4	5.0	260,600
Michigan	75	64	5.9	5.1	7.3	1.0	381,900
Minnesota	71	80	1.9	5.0	5.2	0.3	150,800
Missouri	69	69	2.6	4.2	4.7	0.4	162,800
New Hampshire	59	48	6.2	7.1	10.3	1.7	103,100
New Jersey	94	72	37.6	26.7	44.2	5.1	253,100
New York	88	81	8.3	7.8	10.8	0.9	273,800
Ohio	77	71	9.7	9.7	12.6	1.4	363,500
Pennsylvania	77	58	9.5	7.1	12.4	1.9	554,700
Rhode Island	91	71	36.8	20.7	39.4	5.7	40,500
Vermont	38	35	1.6	2.2	2.9	0.2	13,900
West Virginia	46	42	2.3	3.1	4.1	0.5	69,800
Wisconsin	68	71	3.0	4.9	5.6	0.5	186,300
Northern States	80	71	6.0	6.3	8.5	1.1	3,959,900
Conterminous United States	79	73	3.1	4.5	5.4	0.6	11,078,300

Table A7 continued

State and region	Proportion of urban growth that subsumed forest land 1990-2000	Proportion of tree cover on urban or community land	Proportion of impervious cover on urban or community land	Proportion of tree cover on all land	Proportion of impervious cover on all land
			(percent)		
Connecticut	64	67	11	73	7.7
Delaware	28	35	17	33	6.2
Illinois	15	25	26	16	4.0
Indiana	15	24	23	26	3.7
Iowa	12	19	20	10	3.0
Maine	55	52	13	83	3.2
Maryland	44	34	19	43	6.1
Massachusetts	63	65	15	71	7.4
Michigan	31	35	27	60	4.1
Minnesota	18	34	13	35	2.2
Missouri	29	32	18	40	2.4
New Hampshire	61	66	12	89	5.0
New Jersey	48	53	20	57	12.1
New York	51	43	22	65	4.5
Ohio	32	32	25	40	5.5
Pennsylvania	43	41	19	66	4.6
Rhode Island	65	51	24	70	10.9
Vermont	40	53	17	82	1.9
West Virginia	62	61	12	81	2.0
Wisconsin	18	32	15	48	2.8
Northern States	37	39	20	47	3.8
Conterminous United States	33	35	18	34	2.4

Table A8—Timberland area and volume time series, 1953-2007 (Smith et al. 2009, USDA FS 1958). For 1953, two sources that report different area and volume estimates for some States are included; all estimates after 1953 are based on Smith et al. (2009). To facilitate regional and national summaries over time, the State data in this table were standardized to common years using various methods described in the source publications. State forest inventory reports published periodically in the past may provide more accurate trend information for a given state.

State and region	Timberland area by year						Net volume of growing-stock on timberland by year		
	2007	1997	1987	1977	1953[a]	1953[b]	2007	1997	1987
	(1000 acres)						(million cubic feet)		
Connecticut	1,732	1,815	1,776	1,805	1,973	1,973	3,314	2,755	2,707
Delaware	376	376	388	384	392	448	695	639	642
Illinois	4,363	4,058	4,030	4,033	3,830	3,938	6,875	4,835	4,835
Indiana	4,533	4,342	4,296	3,815	4,015	4,045	8,281	6,900	5,216
Iowa	2,824	1,944	1,460	1,461	2,595	2,505	3,114	1,669	1,251
Maine	17,163	16,952	17,174	16,864	16,609	16,601	22,402	20,892	22,448
Maryland	2,372	2,423	2,462	2,523	2,855	2,897	5,092	4,511	4,490
Massachusetts	2,946	2,965	3,010	2,798	3,259	3,259	6,530	4,862	4,729
Michigan	19,023	18,667	17,364	18,200	19,121	18,849	28,029	26,734	20,972
Minnesota	15,112	14,819	13,572	13,697	16,580	18,098	14,931	15,266	13,731
Missouri	14,674	13,411	11,995	12,289	14,300	15,064	16,596	8,997	7,935
New Hampshire	4,674	4,551	4,803	4,692	4,819	4,682	9,156	9,039	7,879
New Jersey	1,877	1,864	1,914	1,857	2,050	1,910	2,819	2,378	1,895
New York	16,015	15,406	15,798	15,405	11,952	12,002	25,862	21,826	20,089
Ohio	7,645	7,568	7,141	6,917	5,450	5,396	12,324	10,158	7,553
Pennsylvania	16,019	15,853	15,918	15,925	14,574	15,108	29,859	24,903	24,746
Rhode Island	351	356	368	395	430	430	637	395	428
Vermont	4,482	4,461	4,424	4,430	3,846	3,713	8,696	8,675	6,243
West Virginia	11,797	11,900	11,799	11,484	10,276	9,860	22,524	20,304	15,837
Wisconsin	16,042	15,701	14,726	14,478	15,349	16,325	20,271	18,509	16,412
Northern Region	164,018	159,433	154,419	153,447	154,275	157,103	248,005	214,246	190,038
United States	514,213	503,664	486,318	492,355	508,855	488,609	932,089	835,669	781,656

[a]based on Smith et al. 2009

[b]based on USDA FS 1958; U.S. total excludes interior Alaska

Table A8 continued

State and region	Net volume of growing stock on timberland by year			Net volume of growing stock per acre of timberland by year					
	1977	1953a	1953b	2007	1997	1987	1977	1953a	1953b
	----------------(million cubic feet)----------------			---(cubic feet/acre)---					
Connecticut	2,662	1,304	1,304	1,912	1,518	1,524	1,475	661	661
Delaware	625	455	464	1,851	1,697	1,655	1,628	1,161	1,036
Illinois	4,266	2,404	3,050	1,576	1,191	1,200	1,058	628	775
Indiana	3,759	2,903	3,041	1,827	1,589	1,214	985	723	752
Iowa	1,038	1,361	1,183	1,103	859	857	710	524	472
Maine	22,603	15,471	12,601	1,305	1,232	1,307	1,340	931	759
Maryland	3,492	2,770	2,899	2,147	1,862	1,824	1,384	970	1,001
Massachusetts	3,893	1,871	1,871	2,216	1,640	1,571	1,391	574	574
Michigan	18,304	9,980	9,912	1,473	1,432	1,208	1,006	522	526
Minnesota	11,455	6,951	7,235	988	1,030	1,012	836	419	400
Missouri	6,023	5,714	5,503	1,131	671	662	490	400	365
New Hampshire	7,286	3,965	4,452	1,959	1,986	1,640	1,553	823	951
New Jersey	1,534	1,167	952	1,503	1,276	990	826	569	498
New York	13,256	10,523	11,675	1,615	1,417	1,272	860	880	973
Ohio	6,395	3,249	4,013	1,612	1,342	1,058	925	596	744
Pennsylvania	23,403	12,945	10,629	1,864	1,571	1,555	1,470	888	704
Rhode Island	413	161	161	1,817	1,108	1,163	1,046	374	374
Vermont	4,990	3,479	3,956	1,940	1,945	1,411	1,126	905	1,065
West Virginia	14,154	9,114	7,864	1,909	1,706	1,342	1,232	887	798
Wisconsin	13,457	7,961	8,071	1,264	1,179	1,114	929	519	494
Northern Region	163,008	103,748	100,836	1,512	1,344	1,231	1,062	672	642
United States	733,056	615,884	516,935	1,813	1,659	1,607	1,489	1,210	1,058

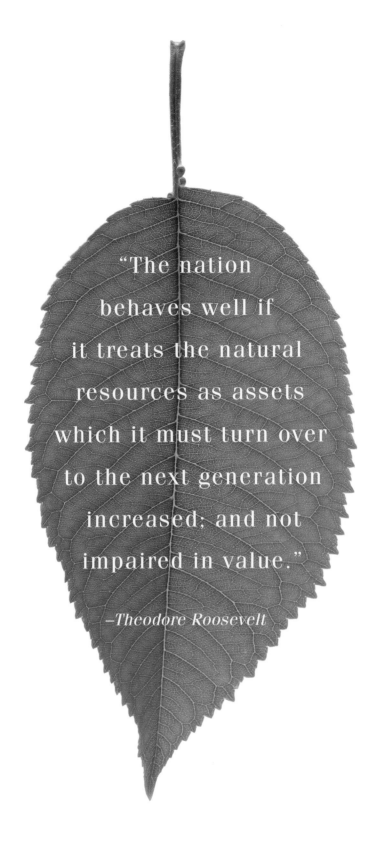

"The nation
behaves well if
it treats the natural
resources as assets
which it must turn over
to the next generation
increased; and not
impaired in value."

—*Theodore Roosevelt*